Feminists and Bureaucrats

To Ralph, who was both

Feminists and Bureaucrats

A study in the development of girls' education
in the nineteenth century

SHEILA FLETCHER

CAMBRIDGE UNIVERSITY PRESS

CAMBRIDGE

LONDON   NEW YORK   NEW ROCHELLE

MELBOURNE   SYDNEY

Published by the Press Syndicate of the University of Cambridge
The Pitt Building, Trumpington Street, Cambridge CB2 1RP
32 East 57th Street, New York, NY 10022, USA
296 Beaconsfield Parade, Middle Park, Melbourne 3206, Australia

First published 1980

Printed in Great Britain by The Anchor Press Ltd
Tiptree, Essex

Library of Congress Cataloguing in Publication Data
Fletcher, Sheila.
Feminists and bureaucrats.
Bibliography: p.
Includes index.
1. Education of women – England – History. 2. Public schools,
Endowed (Great Britain) 3. Education and state – England –
History. I. Title.
LC2052.F56   376'.942   79–20630
ISBN 0 521 22880 8

Contents

Preface

This is a study of the relative commitment of two groups of Victorian administrators, the Endowed Schools Commissioners and the Charity Commissioners, to promoting the education of girls under the Endowed Schools Act, 1869. It is based on a thesis which was supervised by Professor O. R. McGregor of London University (now Lord McGregor) and the sources used come largely from the Public Record Office.

The selection of data needs a word of explanation. The Record Office holds, in its Ed. 27 class, several thousand files which record the work of both sets of Commissioners in making Schemes under the Endowed Schools Acts to reorganise the grammar schools. Only some of these Schemes include provision for girls and it is this group which has been scrutinised, leaving unmapped a very large hinterland which must contain a number of cases where the Commissioners did their best to provide for girls but were unsuccessful. Ideally, of course, the whole field of their endeavour should be surveyed as the essential context of what they achieved in this particular area, but an enquiry of such magnitude lies beyond the individual researcher. It seems, in any case, unlikely that the whole corpus of material would reveal attitudes quite at variance with those which emerge from the 'successful' sample; and this view is confirmed by the pilot study of the West Riding of Yorkshire which forms the basis of chapter 2 and rests on a scrutiny of every Scheme establishing a secondary school in that area, whether it provided for girls or not.

I am obliged to the Comptroller of Her Majesty's Stationery Office for permission to make use of Crown Copyright material. I would also like to express my thanks to Jeffrey Ede, who was Keeper of the Public Record Office, and to Tom Donovan and Derek Steer, who were in charge of the Ashridge Repository at the time my research was undertaken. I am indebted to the Trustees of the British Library, to the Mistress and Fellows of Girton College,

Cambridge, the Governors of the North London Collegiate School, the Yorkshire Ladies' Council of Education, the Trustees of the Chatsworth Settlement, the Goodwood Estate Company Ltd, the National Trust, the Girls' Public Day School Trust, the Governors of Berkhamsted School, the Governors of Nottingham High School and the Secondary Heads Association for permission to make use of archive material.

Over a period of several years, during the preparation of the thesis and of the book, I have had encouragement and critical advice from Dr Gillian Sutherland of Newnham College, Cambridge. To her more than anyone my thanks are due; it would indeed be hard to assess what I owe to her scholarship and generosity.

Many friends have put themselves out to discuss this work or help in other ways and I am most grateful to Barney Blackley, Cecily Blackley, Margaret Bottomley, Margaret Gardner, Pamela Hawker, Dick and Sylvia Wheeler, Emily White and Eric Wightman. Particular thanks are due to my friend and colleague Trevor May for his meticulous scrutiny of the final text. I am also indebted to Pat Bromley, Pauline Hughes and Doreen Jones for their co-operative and expert typing.

Finally, I must say I owe a great deal to the interest and judgement of my son-in-law, Robert Green, over a long period, and (over an even longer period) to the forbearance of my daughters.

January 1979   S.F.

Introduction: The Endowed Schools Act

> The result of all this movement . . . was one of the best measures in the history of this government of good measures.
>
> John Morley, *Life of William Ewart Gladstone*, 1903

It is not fashionable these days, either for historians of education or for those interested in women's history, to dwell on the importance of Acts of Parliament. For one thing, we have learnt that there is more to life than ever appears in the statute book; that it will not do to pursue Education Acts 'like mountain goats, jumping from peak to peak'[1] nor to subsume the complex progress of women towards emancipation into little more than the campaign for the vote. To devote much time, then, to a minor statute largely concerned with the formal schooling of the Victorian middle classes calls for some sort of justification. And broadly this must rest upon the interest which should attach to the Endowed Schools Act, 1869, as an early essay in social engineering and one which unusually, if not uniquely, singled out girls as beneficiaries.

It is important to understand the bureaucratic pretensions of this measure. If, in the nineties, our education system could be likened by Morant to a house built by someone 'working spasmodically on odd portions of the structure on quite isolated plans . . . his very best efforts . . . rendered abortive by the fact that . . . he possesses no clearly thought-out plan of the structure as a whole',[2] it can only be said that this Act was not to blame. Its purpose was to provide machinery to operate a very well-thought-out plan: namely, the methodical reorganisation of the old grammar schools so as to ensure that everywhere in England middle-class parents, from clerks to country gentlemen, would find their wants supplied. It is actually the case that, in point of time, power was taken here to give them secondary schools before it was taken to give them elementary schools, or even drains. When the work was attempted the man put in charge of it, Lord Lyttelton, averred that he and his colleagues 'never meant to introduce that phalansterian system, as it may be called, that has been imputed to us . . . to cut up the country into so many squares, and have so many schools in each square'.[3] They may not have meant to; but if they had, they would have done no more than work to the drawings prepared for them by the Taunton Commission, that great inquiry into secondary education whose very drastic recommendations they had been appointed to carry out.

Had all gone as planned, then, Robert Morant would have inherited an education building with a well-ordered secondary wing where the superstructure really matched the foundations. The fact that the plan failed should not distract us either from the boldness of the conception or from the importance of what was possibly its most original component: that endowment should be taken from the old foundations to establish grammar schools for girls. At a time when, to all intents and purposes, secondary schools for girls did not exist, when hardly anyone wished them to exist, this Act created them.

It has not been much praised for it. Admiration attaches more readily to individuals than to Acts of Parliament. Although the climate of apathy and prejudice in which this pioneering measure was administered was precisely that in which those pioneering women – Frances Buss, Maria Grey and Emily Davies – also laboured for girls' education, they are more acclaimed in the standard histories. There, legislation is essentially bloodless and we read of what *was done* under an Act as if it was done by no human agency.

The Endowed Schools Act of 1869 is well fitted to dispel this illusion. A good deal of blood was spilt over it at one time; and even with the passage of years, in the last decades of the nineteenth century when it no longer attracted headlines, its operation was fiercely opposed. This is not surprising since it authorised Commissioners more or less completely to overturn the past in an endeavour to adapt the endowed schools to the needs of contemporary society. They could combine or divide endowments, alter governing bodies and curricula, impose fees and abolish those restrictions which so often had had the effect of making the grammar schools an Anglican preserve. In the same innovatory spirit they could take money away from boys' schools to benefit girls; an extraordinary provision, but of a piece with the rest of the Act which in its every clause seemed meddling, destructive, even sacrilegious to many people. For it broke with the practice of administering charities in conformity with the wishes of the founder; or, as some would have preferred to put it, released them from the grasp of 'the dead hand'.

In practice, however, the exceptional powers bestowed on Lyttelton and his colleagues were modified by the hoops they had to go through before their Schemes could have the force of law. A Scheme was a trust deed, the school's constitution, and laid down for ever – unless it was amended – what was to be taught there, to whom, at what fee. The composition of the governing body as well as its powers and those of the headmaster were all defined and the Act provided elaborately for objections to be heard, both in and out of Parliament, before any Scheme attained the Royal Assent. As to girls, the position was clouded by the fact that, far from issuing a directive that they should share in every endowment, the Act left it open: in the words of Section 12, they should share 'so far as conveniently may be'. The question comes to mind, how could it be convenient? When is it convenient to part with money – and for the education of girls? In 1869 the prospect was such as to daunt any modern appeals consultant.

Public sympathy was almost non-existent. The Act began to be applied at a time when Miss Buss's schools, for all their success, could scarcely raise £50 on appeal, though £60,000 was quickly contributed to endow a new boys' school in the City. It was still being applied nearly thirty years later at a time when the claims for women at Cambridge made by Emily Davies and others were hailed by the display of an effigy in bloomers while the debate went on in the Senate. Between these two points, though, some ninety girls' schools were established under the Endowed Schools Act. This means that something approaching that number of governing bodies parted with endowment. When we look at how they were persuaded to do so we are led directly into the area where the Victorians fought to resolve their conflicting views of the position of women.

We are also led to observe at close quarters the working of a group of Victorian administrators at a time when bureaucratic orthodoxy in its modern sense was just taking root. The 'heroic' generation of civil servants – Edwin Chadwick, Kay-Shuttleworth and others – had receded long before 1869. Those master-builders of Victorian social policy, tireless in inquiry, openly partisan, had mainly given way to men who did not see their function as creative. When Kay-Shuttleworth's successor, Lingen, told a committee in 1865 that he had never thought it part of his duty to extend the country's educational system, this was the voice of the new bureaucracy. Relics of the old one might continue. Patronage survived for nearly half a century after open competition came in and the individuality of government departments was noticeable up to 1914. But the individuality of government servants was not a marked influence in policy-making in the last decades of the nineteenth century. The new profession shaped by Northcote and Trevelyan was essentially unassertive. Much was done, for instance, over these years, in the field of elementary education but very little of it derived from the initiative of civil servants.[4] In this context, against the background of 'a bureaucracy gently ossifying, concerning itself primarily with pushing out again the paper that came in',[5] it is startling to discover a group of civil servants who were as conspicuous as others were discreet: these were the three Commissioners appointed to administer the Endowed Schools Act.

Between them they demonstrate the hybrid nature of the public service in the 1860s. Lord Lyttelton, who was in charge of the Commission, a man connected by marriage to Gladstone, had never worked for a salary before but was exceedingly glad to have one. Apart from that, he took on the Commission rather as Lord Shaftesbury took on the Board of Health: out of an overriding sense of duty. Arthur Hobhouse had made his mark as a lawyer and Charity Commissioner and Canon Hugh Robinson came to the work from being Principal of St John's College, York. They were united by a common zeal, not for the drudgery which lay before them – which Lyttelton was certainly disposed to dread – but for the principles behind it. 'I always looked upon ourselves', wrote Hobhouse, 'as missionaries sent to lighten the heathen, and to be persecuted and perish at their hands; as a forlorn hope told off to die in the ditch, and who are successful if those who come after can mount the wall.'[6] Such words alone are enough to distinguish him from the new style of professional civil servant which was beginning to emerge at this period. They might have come, though, from Edwin Chadwick if he had been given to flights of fancy; and Hobhouse, looking back, compared the new Commission with the Poor Law Commissioners appointed in the thirties. Both made 'a brave and sincere attempt to put in action a law sound in principle but new and distasteful in character'. Both, he might have added, were applying legislation which gave them enough rope to hang themselves. And both did hang themselves; that is to say, both were disbanded after public outcry.

The missionary spirit of Hobhouse and his colleagues and their

Secretary, Henry Roby, sprang from involvement with the problems the Endowed Schools Act was intended to solve and a firm faith in the solutions it offered. These were men of a reforming temper. To fellow-reformers in that lively body, the Social Science Association, Hobhouse and Lyttelton had spoken frankly against the dead hand which lay upon endowments and Robinson had urged the drastic remodelling of endowed schools in the national interest. Further, there existed an umbilical cord between the Commission now appointed to administer the Endowed Schools Act and the Royal Commission which had given rise to it. The great inquisition into secondary schooling chaired by Lord Taunton had led to revelations of the sad state of so many grammar schools that there was considerable support for an Act which promised to restore the nation's heritage. And now the restorers were strongly recruited from those who had made the investigation. Lyttelton had served upon the Taunton Commission. Henry Roby had been its Secretary. The famous Report included chapters they had drafted and its recommendations for grading schools owed much to the evidence of Canon Robinson. There was another link of great importance. The uniquely experienced Assistant Commissioners who had tramped round the grammar schools of England for Taunton now supplied the Assistant Commissioners and Assistant Secretary of the new body.

Here, then, in the 1870s were public servants with a stake in their work; men who cared for, indeed had helped to formulate, the principles they were called on to apply. At a time when Education Department officials spent their days poring over grant agenda and John Simon wrestled with the sterile paperwork that occupied the Local Government Board the Endowed Schools Commissioners made themselves notorious by their wholehearted commitment to reform and in the end were sacked for it. This small red splash in the bureaucratic greyness may intrigue the student of administrative history. Somewhere the Commissioners must have a place in the nineteenth-century revolution in government. Were they a throwback to the 1830s? What is the importance of their curious status as an administrative Board without a minister?

However, what we are concerned with here is the effect they had on people at the time and, in particular, with their importance to girls' education and the women's movement. The omens for women were very good in the missionary appointments of 1869. Here were men wholly sympathetic to the view that modernisation of the grammar schools should entail some provision for girls; who, as we shall see, were already involved in the movement to advance girls' education and now, for the five years while they held office, did their utmost against great odds to apply the girls' clause of the Endowed Schools Act. The claims of women, the feminists conceded, as that period approached its end, had been considered by the Commissioners 'in a way they have never been considered before'.[7]

Then came a change. The Endowed Schools Commission, so very much a creation of the Liberals, almost from the first had managed to upset powerful Anglican and Tory interests. Disraeli could not wait to get rid of it and in 1874 when the Conservatives came in the Commission was disbanded. As for the Act, that was handed over lock, stock and barrel to be administered by the Charity Commissioners in what was hoped would be a more temperate vein, and they applied it until 1903.

Whoever gained from this change girls were losers. The *rapport* which had hitherto existed between feminists and bureaucrats melted away. The law was unaltered and Schemes for girls' schools continued to be made; but their share in the reorganised endowments fell and in this respect, relative to boys, they were worse off at the end of the century than they had been in 1875. Section 12 of the Endowed Schools Act may have been, as a Victorian writer put it, 'the Magna Carta of girls' education'[8] but only in the hands of those determined that it should be. This determination was greatly reduced by the changeover of 1874.

The women's movement had foreseen what would happen but, in the event, did nothing much about it. Perhaps there was nothing much it could do. In this area bureaucrats were pacemakers. Yet the tailing off is all the more striking because, to begin with, it was the women who had set the pace. Here indeed is the essential starting point: in the 1860s, when bridges were built between the women and the administrators. Before we turn to that, though, we must look more closely at the Act itself, for the seeds of the débâcle of 1874 and, as a result, of the loss to girls, were sown already in the passage of this exceedingly forceful measure.

It was a first-fruit of Liberal government in that era which Gladstone looked back on as one of liberation and advance. With the Endowed Schools Act, it might be said, the Liberals had begun as they meant to go on. Here, before they created School Boards or ended religious

Tests at Oxford and Cambridge, they breached the Anglican hold on education.[9] Here, too, before the idea of merit was thrust upon the Army and the Civil Service, it was thrust upon the grammar schools.[10] And here the Liberals made a break with the past as bold in its way as Irish Disestablishment, rejecting the legal dogma of *cy près* which for generations had tied charitable funds ball-and-chain to the wishes of the founder.[11] The Act's preamble looks ahead: the endowed schools are to be reformed with the object of 'putting a liberal education within the reach of children of all classes'. W. E. Forster, presenting the Bill as minister responsible for education, acknowledged that those who had endowed the grammar schools were guided by the new ideas of their own age: 'they were fighting for industry against feudalism . . . And now, again, new ideas have power – this new central idea, bringing with it many others, that no special class is to guide the destinies of England . . . that England for the future is in truth to be self-governed; all her citizens taking their share, not by class distinctions but by individual worth.'[12]

The principles underlying reform, though, are barely glanced at in the Act itself, outside the preamble which directs attention to the recommendations of the Taunton Commission. It is simply clear that great changes are on foot; that from now on it will be up to school governors to make a case on historical grounds for doing what they have done without reflection – run the grammar schools as Anglican establishments; that in future the claims of girls may be admitted, regardless of what was intended in the past. The past, from now on, is to yield to the present and most of the fifty-nine clauses of the Act are in fact devoted to constructing machinery to make this possible. Thus, the new Commissioners are given power to reorganise the grammar schools far beyond any that the Court of Chancery or the Charity Commission has enjoyed.

How did it come about that such a measure went through Parliament without much trouble? Later on, when the fat was in the fire, the ease of its passage seemed disconcerting. Parliament, someone said, was 'taken on the blind side'; or, as one of the Commissioners put it, the effects of the Act 'had not been discussed and were not understood by those who passed it'.[13] At a distance it is not hard to see why. For one thing, the Bill went through in the shadow of a much more publicised, more controversial measure; it would not have passed, according to Hobhouse, 'had not people's attention been absorbed by the Irish Church Act'. And for another, though the case for reform, as presented by the Taunton Commission, was sufficiently acknowledged for Forster to claim that his Bill was not a party measure, few could visualise what reform really meant. The Taunton inquiry had been exhaustive. A countrywide investigation of the old grammar schools had been carried out, extending sometimes to cover private and proprietary schools as well. Witnesses were heard, vast data collected; and the result, in twenty-one volumes, was an indictment of the system – or rather, of the chaos that was found to exist in school education above the primary level. The ancient grammar schools, it seemed, survived where the seventeenth century had left them and not where they were most needed in the nineteenth. They were often 'languid', 'somnolent', 'decayed', some even scandalous, some at the level of an indifferent elementary school. Almost everywhere teaching was bad, statutes archaic and trustees failing in the duty that was laid upon them. A sense of waste pervaded the Report, of shame, almost, that the old foundations had been allowed to degenerate.

It would have been hard, in the face of all this, to argue that there was no room for improvement and no one tried to. The Taunton remedies – for example, that the grammar schools be graded as to fees, leaving age and curricula to suit the three strata of the middle classes, and that free schooling depend on merit – aroused little comment, possibly because few imagined what they would involve in practice.

> 'Eleven hundred schools', *The Times* said later, 'mean three or four thousand squires, clergymen, farmers and tradesmen, with as many idiosyncrasies, prejudices and traditions as the diverse neighbourhoods over which they exercise a mild dominion. Each of the little corporations thus composed had to be invited to start on a more or less new career, to abandon some exclusive rights, to make novel experiments.'[14]

There is no sign that in 1869 people like this knew what was going to hit them. Those who did know, or thought they knew, were the governors of some of the great foundations. The Greycoat Hospital trustees in Westminster petitioned for their school to be excluded from the Bill; the Duke of Richmond made a similar plea, during the debate, on behalf of Christ's Hospital; a deputation from the city of Bristol urged that their Hospital Schools should be exempt while a similar claim was made by Members on behalf of various public schools. Later, such people felt they were misled by Forster's assurance, in the House and elsewhere, that good schools had nothing to fear. But at the time, the concept of a 'good' school was not very carefully examined.

The religious question, or that part of it which created so much trouble later on, was not much argued; probably because no one yet knew where the shoe would pinch. Much would depend on the Endowed Schools Commissioners' interpretation of the relevant clause and no one knew who the Commissioners would be until the Bill had passed its second reading. Naturally this gave rise to annoyance but it also made it harder to focus opposition. The Bill, as one Member said, was simply the embodiment of the feeling that there should be reform. The whole of its working would be left to a Commission 'consisting of three persons not named who were to exercise greater functions than Parliament itself . . . in former times'.[15] A picture of this 'all-powerful triumvirate', as yet anonymous, scouring the land, ready to 'arraign and depose the trustees of the most flourishing . . . as of the deadest and most paralysed school', was painted by the arch-Tory, Beresford Hope. The Government sought to allay such fears by showing how tightly the Commissioners would be reined. Everything they did would be mere waste paper, Forster said, before it had passed 'the ordeal of Parliamentary assent'. And he described that ordeal at length: every Scheme would have to be published locally; after a statutory period for objections it would be submitted to the Education Department; only if approved would it be laid before Parliament; and only at the end of forty days, if neither House objected, would it become law.

The procedures were clear; but Members were not clear in what relation the Commissioners stood to Parliament. Assurances that they were 'but the creatures of the Government who would be responsible to Parliament for their proceedings'[16] were not necessarily reassuring. It was just this close connection with the Government that aroused Conservative suspicion: these men in fact would be Liberal nominees. Later, when their stern application of the Act had made them unpopular they were indeed arraigned as tools of a party bent on destroying all established values and especially the Church. But now there was the sense of a job to be done which should be done quickly. The Endowed Schools Bill was in any case only a temporary measure. Originally it had had two parts: a temporary part, for reform of the grammar schools, and a permanent part which would have set up a council to maintain standards in the schools once reformed by organising regular examinations and scrutinising and registering teachers. These proposals, too, came from the Taunton Commission but for some they had an authoritarian flavour and verged too much on systematic control. Forster dropped them. When the Bill was in committee it was divided and the plan for a council left to a second Bill, later forgotten. What the Commons, then, were asked to endorse was a brisk reorganisation of the grammar schools by Commissioners appointed for three years only, with possible extension of their powers for a fourth. No one seemed to give serious attention to the question whether a task of this magnitude, involving as it did some 3000 endowments, could possibly be completed in the time; indeed, no estimating was attempted, beyond the sardonic view expressed by John Walter that Commissioners had as many lives as cats 'and there was very little fear, in his opinion, that that term of three years assigned in the Act would be anything but the first of the nine'.[17]

By the time the Bill arrived in the Lords the names of the three Endowed Schools Commissioners and of their Secretary had been announced; more than that, at a public meeting held by the Society of Arts Lyttelton and Hobhouse had made quite clear that when it came to administering the new Act they would not expect to pay much deference to founders. How could they be impartial? asked Lord Salisbury. Considering their opinions, 'it would be necessary to watch very jealously the large powers which the Bill proposed to intrust to them'. Apart from this the Bill had a fairly smooth passage, again presented as a non-party measure which would achieve much-needed reform. Lord Ripon, introducing it, drew attention to the fact that it took 'particular notice' of the education of girls.

In point of fact, Section 12 was anomalous in a measure which ignored the detail of reform. Of course the Bill was meant to empower Commissioners to carry out the Taunton recommendations: to grade schools, abolish free education, break the exclusiveness of governing bodies, modernise curricula and, where possible, extend the benefit of endowment to girls. But none of these was mentioned, except the last. All the rest were covered, as that might have been, by the blanket authority to do what was needed to make endowments 'most conducive to the advancement of the education of boys and girls, or either of them'.

Why were girls singled out? The reason seems to be that Section 12 had different antecedents from the rest of the Act, which was, in general, yet another product of concern to make old charities serve modern times; or, it may seem, yet another admission of the *consequence* of the middle class, 'this class impelled to take possession of the world', as Matthew Arnold called it. Section 12 was different. The pressure to improve girls' education came from those concerned with the prospects of women.

1. The shaping of Section 1 2

It is not easy to imagine that there can be any just cause why a woman of forty should be more ignorant than a boy of twelve years of age. If there be any good at all in female ignorance, this (to use a very colloquial phrase) is surely too much of a good thing.

Sydney Smith, 1810[1]

'The education which women receive scarcely deserves the name', wrote Mary Wollstonecraft towards the end of the eighteenth century. But as we know, little was done to improve it before at least the middle of the nineteenth, and those who sought to improve it then certainly did not claim affinity with the 'hyena in petticoats'. The Owenite notions of the 1830s, according to which education was the lever to elevate Woman in the New Society, similarly ran into the sand. Those who at length took practical steps to provide middle-class girls with something better than drill in accomplishments when they left the nursery usually had practical ends in view. In 1848 when Frederick Maurice launched Queen's College, Harley Street, he took some pains to dissociate it from the 'splendid but transitory foundation' established by the heroine of Tennyson's *The Princess*. No high-flown arguments about the rights of women assailed his audience who learned instead about the misery of destitute governesses. In this cruelly congested profession where, as the *English Woman's Journal* expressed it, 'middle and upper classes meet, the one struggling up, the other drifting down', genteel women strove to support themselves without any adequate education. Maurice intended his college to supply it, enabling girls to gain certificates for teaching.

Another pioneering girls' school was launched in 1849 by Elizabeth Reid, a rich Unitarian and friend of Harriet Martineau. Bedford College opened in her house in Bedford Square and aimed to give ladies 'a liberal education'. In 1850, the following year, Frances Buss started the school in Camden which later became the North London Collegiate, offering from the first that 'sound education' which her prospectus declared to be as necessary for the daughters as for the

sons of professional gentlemen of limited means. 1854 saw the opening in Cheltenham of the Ladies' College, its promoters affirming
'that it was possible to give sound instruction without sacrificing
accomplishments, to develop the intellect without making female
pedants, to combine efficiency with economy'.[2] Four years later they
appointed as Principal the exceptionally gifted Dorothea Beale.

The pioneers' success is so well known and they put such a stamp
on girls' education that it is only too easy to forget the void that lay
between these rising stars and anything approaching a girls' school
system. When a Dorset parent in the 1880s writes to explain to the
Charity Commissioners that he has to send his girls to Miss Buss in
London in order to get them a good education we see what this
meant. 'However great the service done by a single institution its
influence was limited', was the conclusion of at least one veteran
supporter of the cause.[3] Miss Buss came up sharply against these
limits as soon as she started to look outside Camden for financial
backing to give her school the stability essential to its future. Her
failure is revealing. But just as revealing, though in a different way, is
her success, depending as it did so largely on factors which were
particular to her case: first and foremost, her own personality and
those remarkable gifts as a teacher which may be said to have filled
her school almost in spite of its intellectual range – parents put up
with the mathematics because they valued Miss Buss so highly;
secondly, the help of her father and brothers which carried her over
the major obstacle to any attempt then to make a good girls' school –
the total lack of well-educated teachers. So the school in North London created a prototype rather than even the beginning of a system.
That was bound to depend upon factors outside the range of Camden
Town.

One of these, no doubt, was the change in opinion created by concern for the employment of women. 'We go on talking', wrote Harriet
Martineau, 'as if it were still true that every woman is or ought to be
supported by father, brother or husband.' But thousands of women,
as she pointed out, were obliged to work for their living.[4] Census
figures in the middle of the century showed a marked imbalance
between the sexes. There were numbers of 'surplus' middle-class
women who must inevitably fend for themselves and one of the questions which aroused concern was how they could be fitted to do so. In
social questions, though, the critical distance is between public concern and action. If, by the close of the nineteenth century, almost

every town had its girls' secondary school modelled on the prototype created by Miss Buss this was a consequence, not of concern, but of the actual construction of machinery which made it possible to achieve such an end. For, notwithstanding the pioneers, and, in this later period especially, the work of the Girls' Public Day School Company, it was an end which could not well be achieved except by government; and what was crucial was that government should be persuaded to take it up. In this oblique, almost Fabian, process, a key role belongs to that remarkable body which came into being in the 1850s: the National Association for the Promotion of Social Science.

The Social Science Association

In many ways the 1850s were a very bright time in the women's movement. It is really from then that we can talk of a movement, for out of the committee which came into existence to campaign for the Bill on married women's property there emerged a group of talented women, most of them young and well-to-do, ready to apply themselves to any endeavour likely to benefit their sex. In these early days the field was wide open and the 'ladies of Langham Place' directed their efforts broadly across it.[5] The chief among them, Barbara Bodichon, was involved more or less simultaneously with running a progressive school, working for the Bill, publishing a pamphlet on 'Women and Work' and launching the *English Woman's Journal*. Bessie Parkes, who edited the *Journal*, had also been an active campaigner for the Bill and had written a critique of girls' education. Jessie Boucherett's great achievement was to create, in 1859, the Society for Promoting the Employment of Women which attempted, through the *English Woman's Journal*, to organise a female labour exchange. Emily Davies made contact with this group. At home in Gateshead she started a branch of the Society for Promoting the Employment of Women; in London her time was divided mainly between the work in Langham Place and trying to help Elizabeth Garrett gain admittance to a medical school.

There was, then, no lack of energy or ideas or optimism in this circle. What it did lack was effective means of making itself heard beyond the ranks of the converted, and this is where the women gained immeasurably from the Social Science Association. It had been formed in 1857, gathering up at national level the work of the earlier statistical societies, and made its reputation quickly enough to

be satirised by Peacock a few years later: 'one enormous bore prating
about jurisprudence, another about statistics, another about education and so forth'.[6] Brougham was president and its General Committee included every name in the field: Shaftesbury, Chadwick,
Southwood Smith, Farr, Kay-Shuttleworth, Kingsley, Maurice,
Simon, Mann and J. S. Mill. It also included Lyttelton, later to be
chief Endowed Schools Commissioner but at this stage a man who
had done little to bring himself forward outside Worcestershire.
Members presented papers for discussion in one or other of five departments covering law, education, penal reform, public health and social
economy. The Association's annual congress, held each year in a
different city, not only aroused great local interest but left behind a
wake of enthusiastic people 'animated with the desire to carry out the
ideas they . . . received'.[7]

As for women, it gave them a platform; the first they ever had.
Despite the active role which Barbara Bodichon and other feminists
had played in the married women's property campaign they had
never, for instance, stood up and spoken at meetings of the Law
Amendment Society. It was something, then, that the new Association, as the *English Woman's Journal* expressed it, 'assumed the right of
woman to sit in an assembly deliberating on social affairs – nay, to
express her opinion in that assembly if she chooses'.[8] And many did
choose. At the congress held in 1858 Mary Carpenter, the *Journal*
proudly noted, 'sat surrounded by the first men of England,
Brougham, Russell and Stanley among the number, raised her own
voice and was listened to with equal interest and veneration'.[9]

Mary Carpenter's claim to be listened to was, as befitted such a
gathering, that she knew a great deal about her subject. Work with
vagrant and delinquent children occupied her life and from the first
congress in 1857 when she spoke on 'Reformatories for convicted
girls', year after year through the sixties and into the seventies she
presented papers, certainly one of the most prolific of the Association's
members, male or female. Other women followed. 'The number of
the gentler sex among our list of authors' was noted as early as 1858
and seen as a sign that women were beginning to exercise more
influence for social improvement. In these first years three papers
were presented by Florence Nightingale on the subject of hospitals
and two on workhouses by Louisa Twining. The burning question of
women's employment had been discussed at the very first congress.
Later, Bessie Parkes described the experience of the Society for

Promoting the Employment of Women; Maria Rye presented an account of her Female Emigration Society; and Emily Faithfull gave a paper on the subject of the Victoria Press, which, with support from the Association, she had established to train girls as compositors. In the Association's first five years women contributed in all the departments except jurisprudence. In 1862, of the forty-one papers in the department of social economy, eight were by women, all on topics concerned in some way with female employment.

The link with education was made repeatedly. 'If they would compete for higher employments [women] must educate themselves with that view', George Woodyatt Hastings, the Association's Secretary, had declared in a paper at the very first congress.[10] 'The demand for women who had received a good practical education was becoming every day more urgent', said Jessie Boucherett, 'and it was to be hoped that means would be brought into requisition which would supply that demand.'[11] Here, in 1860, nearly ten years before such means were created through Section 12, Miss Boucherett nailed this problem to the lack, in the girls' case, of those endowed grammar schools which were such a feature of boys' education. In the Lindsey district of Lincolnshire, she said, there were ten such grammar schools for boys, all cheap and made use of by tradesmen and farmers 'and even occasionally by the clergy and professional men; but for girls of the same rank . . . no endowed school at all'. Barbara Bodichon painted a picture of the 'magnificent colleges and schools, beautiful architectural buildings, rich endowments, all over England' bestowed upon boys. Could not girls be endowed?[12] Why should not 'useless or mischievous' charities be applied to endow good girls' schools? asked Jessie Boucherett in 1862.[13] The forum in which such questions were raised was a wider one now than the *English Woman's Journal*. Here they joined the mainstream of debate on education, alongside Canon Robinson's plan, which he can scarcely have supposed he would one day be applying as a member of the Endowed Schools Commission, to make a drastic reform of the grammar schools in the best interests of the middle classes.[14] More than that, as Emily Davies acknowledged, the Association gave to the feminists 'a platform from which we could bring our views before the sort of people who were likely to . . . help in carrying them out'.[15]

No one proved the value of this more than she did; and never to more purpose than in the links she formed now with Lyttelton, Roby and Joshua Fitch, whose help in 'carrying out' feminist views when they came to apply the Endowed Schools Act is a main part of the subject of this book. At the present stage they were all involved with Miss Davies's campaign for the admission of girls to the Cambridge Local Examinations. The purpose of the Oxford and Cambridge Locals, introduced in the 1850s, was to give a standard to secondary schools. Girls' schools, in Miss Davies's view, needed such a standard even more than boys', and in 1863 she managed to persuade the Cambridge Syndicate to try a girls' examination experimentally. Her next goal was that girls should be admitted to the examinations as a regular thing and here she received invaluable help from the future administrators. Lyttelton chaired a special meeting called by the Social Science Association to discuss the results of the experiment and spoke of the hope that 'the examinations might be extended to the rest of the country'.[16] The means to achieve this was suggested by Roby who thought the Syndicate unlikely to yield 'unless urged to do so by influential memorials'. He spoke with the authority of one who had himself been Secretary to the Syndicate. Accordingly, a great effort was made to prepare such memorials. Lyttelton pledged the signature of his sister-in-law, Mrs Gladstone. He also urged the cause upon Dr Whewell and Professor Thompson, members of the council of the Cambridge Senate. As a further attempt to disarm opposition Miss Davies circulated a pamphlet in Cambridge which countered the objections to examining girls. This had been written by Joshua Fitch, an active member of the Association and at this stage an inspector of schools.[17]

The campaign succeeded. In 1865 girls were admitted to the Cambridge Locals. Meanwhile another step had been taken which revealed the Association's strength as a lobby, the splendid opportunism of Emily Davies and the value of her acquaintance with Lyttelton. In 1864 the Association's council sent a deputation to the Prime Minister pressing upon him the need for an inquiry into the state of secondary schools. The topic had been a subject of debate in the Association for years. More than one paper had reflected concern that middle-class children in many cases got a worse schooling than the children of the poor. Questions of curriculum, examinations, the use of endowments had all been chewed over. So, when Lord Brougham opened the congress which met in the autumn of 1864 with the good news that Palmerston was ready to approve the appointment of a Royal Commission, members were not slow to offer their views on the nature of the task to be undertaken. It was now that Canon Robinson proposed the drastic redistribution of endowments.[18] Joshua Fitch addressed himself to the lack of a supply of qualified teachers and the problems of a classics-based curriculum. Others spoke on how to define the middle class, how to make the grammar schools more accessible, the trustees more representative, and so on. In contrast with all this semi-expert detail was the paper presented by Emily Davies which, in essence, asked only one question: what was going to be done about girls?

It was up to women to speak out, she said, 'careless of the cost', on such a question. And she spoke out, though not in person. It was Joshua Fitch who read her philippic against the conventional up-bringing of girls.[19] What were they worth when they had been educated? 'What are they good for? What is there that they care about? How are their lives filled up? What have they to talk about? . . . I am speaking, let it be remembered, not of children but of grown-up women. Does anybody care for their opinions on any but the most trivial matters?' However things might have been in earlier times, middle-class women were relegated now to a drawingroom existence, the futility of which men could have no conception of. 'They think dulness is calm. If they had ever tried what it is to be a young lady, they would know better.' She was soon to be involved in work for the suffrage but here she very carefully avoided what would have seemed a contentious comparison between the mental powers of the sexes. 'All we claim is that the intelligence of women, be it great or small, shall have full and free development.' And she argued, as Mill did later, that the health of society depended upon it. 'I would ven-ture to urge, with the utmost insistence, that it is not a "woman's question". Let me entreat thinking men to dismiss from their minds the belief that this is a thing with which they have no concern.' As to the inquiry now before them, 'We are taught to expect great things from a reform in secondary instruction, and this being so it is surely reasonable to ask that such reforms . . . shall be on the widest basis, not omitting any really important section of society.' Her paper ended with the practical proposal that some of the ancient grammar school endowments might be used to establish girls' schools.

The Social Science Congress had barely ended when Emily Davies took steps to make sure that girls' education would be included in the terms of reference of the Royal Commission. Lyttelton, with whom she was already involved in the fight to have girls admitted to the Locals, was a promising contact, for he had been appointed as one of the Schools Inquiry Commissioners. Presumably, she wrote to him now, there could be no objection to including girls' schools;

> but we are anxious that they should not slip thro' by inadvertence and in some similar cases it has been found that the whole question has turned upon a doubt as to whether certain pronouns are to be interpreted as masculine or common. We were very desirous, therefore, that the Instructions should be framed as expressly to include girls, and we should be greatly obliged if you would have the goodness to bring the matter before Lord Granville.[20]

Lyttelton replied that he had no doubt 'girls are to be included in our Commission which is to enquire into the "education of the middle class" generally: but I will mention it to Lord Granville'.[21] He did so the same day.

When Lyttelton's friendliness did not produce an immediate result Emily Davies wrote to Acland, to Matthew Arnold and to Grote on the same subject.[22] In January, with others, she prepared a memorial to the Schools Inquiry Commissioners, urging that 'the Education of Girls and the means of improving it are within the scope of your inquiry', and at long last she received confirmation. It was preceded by a personal message which augured very well for the future. Her ally in the Cambridge Locals campaign, Henry Roby, had been appointed Secretary to the Commission. Now he showed his colours by promising Miss Davies all possible help on the girls' school question.[23]

So, through the enterprise of Emily Davies the first of two essential initiatives in getting grammar schools for girls was taken. The second, the inclusion of a specific clause relating to girls in the Endowed Schools Act, followed on the work of the Taunton Commission.

The Taunton Commission

The choice of those who, under Lord Taunton, were to investigate the secondary schools could hardly have failed to appeal in the main to Emily Davies or anyone in sympathy with the Social Science Association. That one headmistress believed the Commissioners were actually a *branch* of that Association[24] probably says more for her fear of their proceedings than for her knowledge of their membership, but in point of fact, about half the Commissioners had presented papers, sat on committees or in other ways exerted themselves in 'the very parliament of social causes'. So far as her particular cause was

concerned, the Commissioners struck Emily Davies as 'favourably disposed towards women generally'. Lyttelton had shown this in practical terms; W. E. Forster was interested enough for his brother-in-
law, Arnold, to send him a copy of Miss Davies' paper on girls'
education[25] while Thomas Dyke Acland had dealt with her kindly on
the question of girls and the Oxford Locals.[26] Frederick Temple
appears to have been 'decidedly in favour' of investigating girls'
schools,[27] Sir Stafford Northcote was another sympathiser[28] as, it
might be assumed, was Lord Stanley, who had shown interest in
revision of the law regarding divorce and married women's property.[29]
Among the Assistant Commissioners appointed was Joshua Fitch, the
inspector of schools who had taken a large part in the Cambridge
Locals campaign, spoken for Miss Davies at the Social Science Congress and was by now her friend.

When proceedings opened, Henry Roby, despite the pressures
which were now upon him for the organisation of this broad inquiry,
made good his earlier pledge of help by keeping Miss Davies minutely
informed on every matter that could possibly concern her. She was
sent a list of Assistant Commissioners and a copy of their Instructions
('You will see that it is marked *confidential*').[30] She was invited to propose the names of witnesses 'best able to speak and able to speak best'
about the state of girls' schools. A few days later Roby wrote that he
would be glad to discuss with her, if she could spare the time, the kind
of questionnaire which might be sent out to girls' schools.[31] Miss
Davies was busy now with another paper to be presented to the Social
Science Congress on the theme that 'children' in ancient charters had
been intended to cover girls. She consulted Roby and he read her
draft and offered criticisms, all at a time when he described himself
as 'more than usually occupied with the despatch of forms and of the
Assistant Commissioners'.[32] They discussed witnesses and Roby
explained that he had put down Mark Pattison and Huxley; also
that he hoped to get Mill examined. His courtesy was inexhaustible.
At the end of April 1865 he wrote, 'you must not consider it a dis-
paragement of the importance of the schools for girls that I have not
yet sent out the Circulars to the Endowed and Proprietary Schools
for Girls. I shall get the proofs from the press today or tomorrow and
the papers will be sent out next week I believe.'[33]

The first witness to be examined at any length on girls was Dr
Hodgson, who had been instrumental in starting the girls' school
attached to the Liverpool Institute. Roby let Miss Davies see the

evidence, which brought from her the comment, 'the Commissioners seem better disposed than I had imagined'. She went on to make half-humorous suggestions about the priming of possible witnesses, adding, 'I have thought of several things since seeing you that I should like the Commissioners to recommend if they are likely to do it'.[34] Her own evidence was called for 30 November and Roby was solicitous on every detail. 'If you will draw up some list of heads under which your evidence could best fall, it will contribute much to the good order of the Examination. You must be able to form a better idea than I can as to the points of most importance, but at any rate I shall be glad to do anything I can. Would you prefer the 12 December? I think perhaps I could manage that.'[35]

He had asked her to propose a witness to follow her and Miss Davies suggested Miss Buss. Their examination 'went off capitally' he told her later. Indeed, so far as girls were concerned, all the evidence was capital for it pointed plainly to the need for far-reaching reform. The superficiality of girls' education, its lack of purpose and obsession with accomplishments, the apathy of parents and the ignorance of teachers all came up again, indeed so abundantly and with such consensus that there was some difficulty in selecting references when it came to writing up the final report. If little was said that would have surprised a member of the Social Science Association, the people who said it were not always those who might have figured there. Miss Davies, of course, was well known in such circles; Miss Beale, by the time she appeared before the Commission, had already addressed the Social Science Congress on the subject of Cheltenham Ladies' College. Miss Wolstenholme, the Manchester teacher and suffragist, had also presented a paper there. The views of such witnesses could be predicted. What perhaps could not was that William Torr, a gentleman farmer from Lincolnshire, should admit a greater want of education in farmers' daughters than in their sons; or that Mr E. Edmunds, an ironmonger from Rugby, should concede that girls' education was imperfect. The view that girls' schools mattered was perhaps less surprising in Dr Hodgson of the Liverpool Institute than in Mr Twells of Godolphin School, Hammersmith, or Mr Evan Davies of a private school in Swansea.

The question of endowments was raised many times. Emily Davies had a chance to reiterate her view that it had never been intended to exclude girls from foundations for 'children'. 'Girls should have some share in the endowments,' said Miss Buss.[36] 'I think,' said Miss

Wolstenholme, 'that female education needs the help of endowments most, because parents and the public care least about it.'[37] 'I regret extremely,' said Dr Hodgson, 'that in the endowments for education . . . girls have been deprived of their fair share of the benefits.'[38]

Support for this view came also from others who brought to it the weight of their official personae.

> 'Do you believe,' said Lord Taunton to Lingen, Secretary of the Education Department, 'that it would be reasonable and right that the benefits of endowments should be extended much more to girls than they now are?'
>
> 'Yes, I think so certainly. They are half of the community. I cannot understand, if these endowments are treated at all as public funds, why the girls have not as good a right to share in them as the boys.'[39]

The legal aspect was put to Lord Romilly, Master of the Rolls.

> 'In any deed of endowment where sex is not mentioned, and where perhaps the more general term "children" is used, would that exclude the claims of girls?'
>
> 'No, certainly not.'[40]

From his experience in Chancery Sir William Page Wood, Vice-Chancellor, suggested that the time must come when small dole charities were converted to education. When that happened, 'if you do apply any part of them to the middle class teaching at all, then I say do not forget the girls'.[41] From the women's point of view, then, the oral evidence could hardly have gone better.

> 'I feel very hopeful about things in general', wrote Miss Davies to Barbara Bodichon, 'we had a gathering last week to meet some of the Commission people. We put Dr Hodgson in the Chair and he conducted very nicely. To my surprise, several of the school-mistresses spoke, and did it very well. The best speech was from Mr Roby, Secretary to the Commission. He said he thought there was a great ferment going on about the education of women, and he hoped it would go further and be helped by the investigations of the Commission.'[42]

The mainstay of these investigations was the work of the Assistant Commissioners who inspected every endowed grammar school in England and many proprietary and private schools too. In the case of girls' schools it was left to the discretion of the individual Assistant Commissioner to pick out the most important in the district for which he was responsible. This meant private schools – for girls there were no other – and breaching their privacy seems to have been an enterprise comparable with that of the young men in *The Princess* who penetrated a female university.

> 'It is . . . touching', commented the *Quarterly Review*, 'to read how the first advances of these "heralds of progress" were received by the fluttered mistresses when their secure repose was first startled by the Assistant Commissioners, as by something dropped from the clouds. Was it quite wise to put this delicate task in the hands of so many young Fellows of Colleges fresh from the University, and knowing little more about girls than they could gather from novels?'[43]

Miss Pinkerton's Academy invaded by questionnaires, examination papers for Amelia and Becky! This was more or less what actually happened where headmistresses were willing to allow it. Many would not. 'We have always been private in our home', wrote one, 'and desire so to remain, in spite of the march of intellect in the nineteenth century.'[44] Another told Fitch that the circulars he sent her were 'inquisitorial and irrelevant'. Hammond's application to inspect a school in Yarmouth met with 'undisguised derision'.[45] Stanton, who had expected some resistance, 'was not prepared for its intensity'.[46] What was accomplished depended on tact; they had no kind of compulsory powers. Joshua Fitch, who was concerned with Yorkshire, sent circulars to over one hundred and fifty girls' schools; about half replied and he visited thirty.

It was an extraordinary new departure. 'Nobody knows enough of the interior of girls' schools to speak with authority about them', Emily Davies had complained.[47] Such a thing could never be said again. In the history of girls' education the reports that were made now ought to have the standing of Chadwick's great *Report* in the field of public health; for the first time they presented hard data, combined with those impressions gained from first-hand experience which can be more persuasive than any statistic. They vary in eloquence but scarcely in conclusion: that the education provided for girls was just as bad as the critics had made out. What is of special interest to us is that, when the time came, the Endowed Schools Commission was served by the very men who had carried out this investigation for Taunton. D. R. Fearon, J. L. Hammond, C. H. Stanton and J. G. Fitch were employed once again as Assistant Commissioners, this time under the Endowed Schools Act, to cure the imperfections they had helped to define. And so the duty, among much else, of convincing trustees of the need for girls' grammar schools, fell in due course to those who had suffered personally from *Mangnall's*

Questions and pianos which 'resounded all day long'; who had been informed that cotton came from Scotland and that 'Lord Beacon' had invented gunpowder; who had watched young ladies carefully compiling histories of the world that went back to the Creation.

'The Assistant Commissioners, with scarcely an exception, go in for the girls', wrote Emily Davies.[48] This was quite true, and of two of them especially. The exclusion of girls from educational endowment seemed to Fearon 'a cruel injustice'. He ends his report by consoling himself that a movement to improve girls' education has begun and is being pushed with so much vigour that it is not likely to die out.[49] So anxious was he that the force of his conclusions on the need for good girls' schools should reach a wide public that when the Taunton Report had been published he summarised them in the *Contemporary Review*, believing that the question was so important that 'it is better to run the risk of being accused of needlessly reproducing parts of a public document than to lose a fresh chance of enlisting sympathy . . . in the great cause of . . . women's education'.[50]

Fitch was even more committed to that cause. It is not that the tone of his report is polemical but that, among the tables and other hard data appropriate to a government Blue Book, he does not shrink from professions of faith. 'Some day perhaps we may be in a position to map out the whole region of human knowledge, and to say how much of it is masculine, and how much feminine. At present such an attempt would at least be premature.'[51] Fitch, as we know, had written the pamphlet employed in Miss Davies's campaign for the Locals. He had written, too, a powerful article in the *Victoria Magazine* to urge the improvement of women's education. 'After all, intellect is of no sex.'[52] The man who could write that in 1864, who could affirm 'there is . . . no sort of right knowledge . . . which is in its essence unfeminine', did not scruple to declare himself in the bleaker text of an official report. While others are tempted to link the faults of girls' schools with the apathy of parents and leave it at that Fitch contemplates the whole middle-class ethos in a way which anticipates Matthew Arnold.

> There is no hope for the middle classes, until the range of topics which they care about includes something more than money-making, religious controversies and ephemeral politics: nor until they consider that mental cultivation, apart from its bearing on any of the business of life, is a high and religious duty. When they come to consider this, they will set as great a value on evidences of intellec-

tual power or literary taste when they are put forth by a girl as by a
boy; and they will feel that the true measure of a woman's right to
knowledge is her capacity for receiving it, and not any theories of
ours, as to what she is fit for, or what use she is likely to make of it.[53]

It is little wonder that Emily Davies thought so well of the Assistant
Commissioners.

The *Quarterly Review* detected feminist bias in chapter VI of the
Taunton Report which summarised the evidence on girls' schools.
Lyttelton wrote it and the only problem seems to have been to know
what to leave out, so abundant and consistent was the material. As it
is, chapter VI stands out from the rest for its dense footnotes – in which
the Transactions of Social Science Congresses are well represented –
and its unanimity. Everyone agreed on the 'want of thoroughness and
foundation', 'want of system', 'superficiality' of girls' schools and on
the great disadvantage they suffered from being so small and having
such poor teachers. Fearon's opinion of the 'cruel injustice' of exclud-
ing girls from endowments is cited and it is recommended that in any
Act passed 'the principle of the full participation of girls in endowments should be broadly laid down'.

Parliament, we saw, with comparative ease had endorsed the
Taunton case for reform and had raised but little objection to a Bill
which empowered Commissioners to reorganise endowments so as to
render them 'most conducive to the advancement of the education of
boys and girls, or either of them'. The claims of girls were indeed
'broadly laid down', and nothing more. There was no specific clause
singling out their interest. Nor would there have been, so far as can
be told, without the strenuous efforts of the young Member for
Stroud, Henry Winterbotham.

Getting Section 12 into the Act

It is not clear how he came to be involved. Winterbotham's is the
classic example of a career cut short by death, of a man whose entry
into public life seemed to cast him as a subject for biography but who
earned only premature obituaries.

He was thirty-six when he died in Rome quite without warning in
1873. He came of a distinguished Dissenting family and was in practice at the Chancery Bar before entering the Commons in 1867 as an
Independent Liberal representing Stroud. The eloquence and frankness of a maiden speech on the plight of Dissenters at Oxford and

F.A.B.—B

Cambridge marked him out: here was the man of culture pleading against cultural deprivation, the barrister putting an unanswerable case and, above all, the Nonconformist whose intellect, temperament and heredity drove him to a bold declaration of rights but not to bitter war on the Established Church. This able, passionate yet moderate Dissenter was picked out by Gladstone in 1871 and made Under-Secretary of State at the Home Office. Some of his friends regretted the promotion. Preoccupied with administrative matters he came to be very little heard in Parliament. He had, they thought, lost his independence too soon. Two years later this 'rising young states-man', this Radical who also 'dared to be free from the slavery of Radicalism', this man of 'calm, orderly, sagacious judgement' in whom some recognised a second Cobden, suddenly died.[54]

The obituary writers, busy with their theme of unfulfilled promise, make no reference to the service which Winterbotham rendered girls' education. Yet, for girls, it was lucky the reform of endowed schools came into the realm of practical politics in 1869 when he was still a freelance. In May, as a member of the Select Committee appointed to scrutinise the Bill, Winterbotham proposed a new clause: 'In framing schemes under this Act, provision shall be made, so far as conveniently may be, for extending the benefits of endowments equally to boys and girls.'

Special interests are not hard to identify in the Committee minutes, as one might expect. It is no surprise to find Mr Goldney, a governor of Christ's Hospital, proposing an amendment highly favourable to governors of Christ's Hospital, nor that ardent Churchman, Beres-ford Hope, proposing an amendment which would favour the Church, nor, for that matter, the Dissenter, Winterbotham, proposing one which would not favour it so much. But it is not clear if his proposal now of what became effectively Section 12 reflected simply that sense of justice and feeling for the wretchedness of unsupported women which Winterbotham later expressed in debate, or if he had links with the women's movement.

Time had not stood still in that quarter while the Taunton Com-mission was deliberating. Emily Davies, so involved at the start, had become involved in a great many other things: in electioneering for John Stuart Mill, in the work of a women's society in Kensington which began to interest itself in the suffrage and in the presentation of a suffrage petition. As for education, though in 1866 she had launched the Schoolmistresses' Association, her thoughts were turning now towards the universities and plans for a college. The Taunton Commission's 'cordial approval' of this idea was exceedingly welcome and her women's college at Hitchin opened in October 1869. Understandably, then, it was not to Miss Davies that Henry Winterbotham looked for support in June of the same year over Section 12.

The Select Committee had approved the clause in substance but the efforts of Winterbotham and of Northcote had not brought them to accept that endowments should go *equally* to boys and girls. Winterbotham was determined to fight and now sought backing from the likeliest centre of interest in the secondary education of girls: the North of England Council launched in 1867 to promote the higher education of women.

The Council had been the inspiration of Anne Clough, sister of the poet, and many of its members were either teachers or interested in teaching. It was by no means confined to women: Fitch took an active part, as did James Bryce, George Butler, Principal of Liverpool College, T. H. Green and other academics sympathetic to women's education. Its main object was to organise lectures in the northern cities where girls could advance somewhat beyond what they learned at school, but not surprisingly it soon became involved in the wider problem of how to raise standards and especially in the question of examinations. In these years, at almost every juncture, the women's movement was forced to make a choice between what they wanted and what they thought attainable, and where examinations for women were concerned the Council and Miss Davies were poles apart. In her view girls should take the same examinations as men, but the Council had asked Cambridge for a form of Higher Local which would be intended specially for girls. Their request was granted. In 1869 they awaited the first trial of this examination and now Henry Winterbotham asked for their support on just such another all-or-nothing issue. Indeed, he put it to them rather in those terms. The Endowed Schools Bill had returned from committee and Winterbotham asked for a memorial from them to support the inclusion in it of *equally* 'on the ground that if we do not gain that we gain nothing'.[55]

The Council discussed it, reminded by their president, Josephine Butler, that 'a word too much . . . may be in danger of damaging our cause'. James Bryce pointed out that 'equally with boys' had already been thrown out in the Select Committee. T. H. Green thought the Commissioners appointed under the Act would have all the power they needed 'if they would exercise it – the main drift of the memorial should be simply to urge Parliament to pass the 12th clause'. Fitch supported this. Without more detailed information he thought they could hardly know what was feasible and from his experience of the Taunton inquiry he told them that endowments were usually too small to allow of their being divided. In his view Parliament should be asked to confer large powers on the Commissioners as a whole, 'without defining any proportion . . . between boys' and girls' schools'. So they gave up *equally*.

But Winterbotham did not. On 14 June, when the Bill returned from the Select Committee, he moved to insert the phrase 'equally with boys' on grounds of common justice and urged it with an eloquence reminiscent of his great speech on Dissenters, sometimes dwelling on the value of education for its own sake, 'for the mental wealth, for the dignity of character, for the intense yet pure enjoyment it confers'; sometimes recalling the 'thousands of women . . . sent adrift every year to struggle for themselves' and sometimes the crying need for teachers. He quoted census figures and he looked to a future where the country's greatness could only depend on 'the intellectual culture and moral elevation of the people' for, as to commerce, 'younger and more favoured countries must sooner or later pass us in that race'. The matter before them was no trifle, he said. 'It is the education of half the people.' And the present Bill was 'only half a measure. Hudibras wore but one spur because he thought if he could make one side of his horse go, the other would not be far behind. That is what you are doing here. You think if you educate the men the women will not be far behind. But history belies your expectation.'[56]

Reactions to all this ran true to form. Fawcett and Bright were sympathetic. Beresford Hope took fright at the notion of 'arithmetical equality'. Stafford Northcote pointed to the danger of forcing a division on such an issue, though he was insistent that they should not be satisfied with merely 'throwing a few crumbs to the girls'. Perhaps the most telling intervention came from Forster who, as he explained, 'was bound to consider how they could get this measure . . . carried out'. Most of the endowments were already appropriated. If they were dealing with a fresh fund, he admitted, 'they ought to divide it between girls and boys; but at the present the endowments were, for the most part, possessed by boys'.

Winterbotham withdrew his amendment. The share of endowment

to be given to girls was, as a feminist journal perceived, to be 'left to the judgement of the Commissioners appointed to carry out the Bill'.[57] The chief of these was Lyttelton. And whether from an ingrained sense of justice, or from a perception that the girls' clause would need to be very strong indeed to have any value, he urged in the Lords, as Winterbotham had done in the Commons, with no more success and much less eloquence, that endowment should go to girls 'on equal terms with boys, so far as the circumstances of the case shall admit'.[58] Eloquence, perhaps, was not a negligible quality in the task that lay before him. But it was less significant than courage, and, like Winterbotham, he had plenty of that.

2. The men who rejected the dead hand

'Here is money for the relief of Barbary captives', says the court, 'but there are no
Barbary captives. Then let us see how near we can go to a Barbary captive.'

J. G. Fitch, 1869[1]

The Commissioners are appointed

No particular interest was shown in the Commons when it was
announced in June 1869 that the three Commissioners appointed to
administer the Endowed Schools Act would be Lord Lyttelton,
Arthur Hobhouse and Canon Hugh Robinson. No one voiced alarm,
though Lyttelton had spoken in draconian terms at the Social Science
Congress the previous year on the need to reanimate school endowments, at present 'lying crushed under . . . a mass of stupidity,
ignorance and maladministration'. He had referred, of course, to the
Taunton Report and everything he said about incompetent trustees,
or taking power to transfer endowments from one part of the country
to another or, above all, of the need to depart from slavish deference
to founders' wishes, could be found there. But he left no doubt of his
own entire adherence to these views, borrowing the phrase of Arthur
Hobhouse, the Charity Commissioner and law reformer: 'Property is
not the property of the dead but of the living.'[2]

Nine months later, he found himself appointed as chief of the
Endowed Schools Commissioners who were to reform the grammar
schools. He had not changed his earlier opinions. On the contrary, he
held them so strongly that he felt obliged to make a clean breast of
them lest he seem to act under false pretences. At a meeting held by
the Society of Arts in July 1869 to hear a paper from Arthur Hobhouse on the subject of endowments Lyttelton drew attention to the
fact that they were both to be Endowed Schools Commissioners and
that 'if they were to be allowed to do what they certainly would feel
it their duty to attempt, in very many cases the "pious founder"
would go the wall'.[3] The alarm bells rang now. At this time the

Endowed Schools Bill was making its way through the House of Lords and the Chief Commissioner's formidable honesty, his inability to temper the wind where matters of principle were concerned provoked consternation. The Dukes of Richmond and of Cambridge expressed alarm for the fate of Christ's Hospital, of which they were governors. Lord Salisbury, moving an amendment to the Bill, admitted that he wished 'to restrict the area over which the destructive action of his noble Friend was to range'. And Lyttelton, far from reassuring them, harangued them frankly as if they were members of the Social Science Association, admitting that there was 'much force' in what they said. 'He could not pretend . . . that he had changed his opinions.' Indeed, he reminded them that for this very reason he had at first refused the appointment.[4]

'I do not think I can accept this office', he had written to Gladstone. It seemed to him clear that the fact that he had sat on the Taunton Commission was a great obstacle since its members were committed to 'a great many very strong and sweeping views' on questions with which the new Commission must deal. 'It seems to me essential', he explained, 'that the new Commissioners should set about their numerous and very delicate negotiations with minds unfettered and free from all previous conclusions.'[5] But Gladstone pressed him and Lyttelton accepted. He had had a run of educational Commissions, having served not only on Taunton (of which he was originally asked to be chairman) but before that on the Clarendon Commission which inquired into the public schools. They were 'great bores', he said, 'and unpaid bores but . . . the only quasi-official work I shall ever do'.[6] At the Endowed Schools Commission he was in fact to receive a salary of £1500 p.a. and this was very welcome for he was not rich by the standards of his class and had a large family.

He was fifty-two when the appointment was made. Unceremonious, he took the view that he and his colleagues were 'entirely on a level'[7] but, officially, he was Chief Commissioner. Lyttelton and Gladstone had married two sisters at a double wedding in 1839 but since that occasion, though their friendship was close, it could hardly be said that their careers had run parallel. Lyttelton, considering his rank and intellect, had made small mark in national affairs. When he was young, his performance at Cambridge, where he was bracketed as senior classic with Vaughan, the future headmaster of Harrow, had inspired the Bishop of London to remark on 'talents which may enable you to render important service to your country in the station

which you are about to occupy'.[8] Lyttelton had just come into his
inheritance and the station he was about to occupy was that of Lord-
Lieutenant of the county of Worcester. Perhaps this was what the
Bishop meant. At all events, he did nothing in politics. Apart from a
few months in 1846 when he was Under-Secretary of State for the
Colonies, he never held office. He pursued no career. But he had that
high conception of the duties of a landowner of which his colleague,
Hobhouse, wrote that there was 'no more noble or useful life . . . Such
men are the very cement of the society in which they live.'[9]

From his estate at Hagley, near Stourbridge, Lyttelton fulfilled all
the conventional obligations of a local magnate and went far beyond
them in his concern for the education of the young miners and factory
workers of north Worcestershire. He started numerous clubs and
societies; he lectured; he spent long hours on committees to get support for night schools and working men's institutes. 'One of the most
earnest labourers on behalf of the working class', said Henry Solly,
'that ever sacrificed time, ease and self-gratification to a great cause.'
What impressed Solly was that hard work did not come naturally to
Lyttelton. He had to fight an indolent and pleasure-loving nature.
Indeed, his life appeared one long conflict 'in which conscience was
incessantly victorious'.[10]

Lyttelton certainly grumbled about work. He used to say that he
envied the men he saw lying in the sunshine in St James's Park with
their hats over their faces. The equivalent, for him, might have been
to spend his time on the cricket field; or hunting, or composing Greek
verse, or both these together – a son of his recalled his remarkable
talent for combining the two: 'While cantering towards the largest
fences . . . he was translating Milton into Greek Iambics. If there was
a good deal of running he would get about fifteen lines done in the
day.'[11] As a classical scholar he rivalled Gladstone. Scraps of Greek
verse went back and forth between them and they published a volume
of translations together.

To Lyttelton, the hours spent sitting on Commissions were hours
away from all this and from a much-loved family. But it must be done.
'I have been near six years on these things', he told Gladstone,
meaning the Clarendon and Taunton inquiries, 'and on neither . . .
have I ever missed a day.'[12] The offer of the Endowed Schools Commission came at a time when he had recently remarried after a long
widowerhood; on personal grounds, he said, the work would be in-
convenient. 'It would take up nearly the whole of my time for a year,

and keep me in London a very large part of the year.'[13] But he agreed to do it; in the spirit, it seems, in which he taught in the parish Sunday school: he felt it was his duty.

Like Gladstone, he was a devout High Anglican. It was not duty but devotion which brought him tramping up the aisle at Hagley, splashed from the hunting-field, to take communion. The far recesses of his spiritual life can hardly be explored; they may well have been dark, for Lyttelton suffered swings of mood from great high spirits to the fearful depression which in the end led to his suicide. But Christian faith was always at the centre and if moral conflict left its mark upon him so too did moral certainty: George Otto Trevelyan, meeting him as a stranger on a train, actually took him for an eminent churchman 'on account of the great power and goodness of his face'.[14]

Robert Lowe thought Lyttelton a bigot[15] – a natural verdict on obsessive high principle from one who might himself be called a great opportunist. How Lyttelton fits into the gallery of bigots or 'zealots' in Victorian administration is worth considering later. For the moment it is more to the point to observe not only that his friends admired him for 'his singular freedom from . . . dogmatism'[16] but also that he showed a marked lack of bigotry in areas where it might have been expected; in religion, for instance. Here we have a man who was not only deeply pious but devoted to the Church at all practical levels, from its village schools to its bench of bishops; a man who almost turned down the chance of office in 1846 because the Government proposed to join the bishoprics of Bangor and St Asaph. Yet he was a strong supporter of conscience. He voted for Jews to be admitted to Parliament. He did not go along with Archdeacon Denison and other High-Churchmen in wishing to exclude Dissenting children from Anglican schools. He believed – better still, *came to believe*, in the course of his experience on the Taunton Commission – that parents should be free to withdraw their children from religious teaching.[17] And, above all, in the business of working the Endowed Schools Act he was far from tender of Anglican interests. In his opinion, Section 19, according to which it was possible for schools to remain exclusively Anglican if the founder had made certain requirements, was just another aspect of the dead hand.[18]

For a man who thought in Greek on the hunting-field, Lyttelton was surprisingly open on the great curriculum question of the day. Of course he favoured the prestige of the classics; but, as he told the

Social Science Congress, considering the conditions of modern society 'the multiplied demands on our time, the absolute need of much . . . information apart from the old learning . . . I cannot bring myself to the conclusion that . . . the knowledge of Greek and Latin, or even of Latin alone, is indispensable'.[19] He understood the narrowing effect on the schools of the ancient universities' insistence on Greek as an entrance requirement; as Endowed Schools Commissioner he did his best to persuade them to change it.[20]

Change did not go against the grain, then, with Lyttelton; he readily subscribed to that break with the past implied in the proposals of the Taunton Commission and was well fitted to carry them out. Whether he would have been appointed to do so had not the work been regarded as temporary is another question. The Endowed Schools Commissioners were certainly not the current stamp of civil servant. To contrast Lyttelton with the uncommitted, professional administrator, Lingen, of the Education Department, is to juxtapose two different worlds. Indeed, the Endowed Schools Commissioners-designate were welcomed by the veteran Edwin Chadwick as if the clock had turned back thirty years. Chadwick was present at the famous meeting organised by the Society of Arts at which Lyttelton and Hobhouse owned to the principles on which they would feel themselves bound to act and he found their frankness 'highly refreshing'. He talked of public servants in education and other departments who were 'uninformed or half informed' of the principles they were trusted to apply, or 'apathetic or positively antipathetic to them or to anything but the official salary'.[21] This was a prejudiced but not unrealistic view of the bureaucracy then emerging and Chadwick voiced it after listening to Hobhouse deliver his polemic on the charity laws.

Hobhouse had made this subject his own. For him the appointment as Endowed Schools Commissioner was a sideways move from the Charity Commission on which he had served for the past three years and where he had become thoroughly dissatisfied with the limited powers which that body possessed to reorganise charitable trusts. He had joined the Charity Commission in the first place because ill health forced him at the age of forty-seven to give up his career at the Bar. For a promising barrister it was a backwater. If in some ways it marked an advance on the procedures of the Court of Chancery no moving spirit could fail to chafe at its very small powers to initiate reform and at the way in which its efforts were hobbled by the principle of *cy près*.

In 1868, in a paper given at Sion College, and the next year, speaking at the Social Science Congress, Hobhouse pleaded for a change of attitude to public bequests. He vehemently attacked the 'misplaced and superstitious worship of the Founders' which hindered progress; the facile assumption that, in their generation, such men had been particularly wise or even benevolent. Even if they had, 'Property is not the property of the dead but of the living', Hobhouse declared. The law of charities should be changed. The mission which he seemed to assume now to change it was warmly welcomed by Benjamin Jowett.

> 'I hope that this is only a beginning', he wrote, 'and that you won't let the matter drop . . . It has often seemed to me that it was not worth while for you to give up the prospects of the Bar unless you meant to undertake something of this sort . . . You have the knowledge of the law, and the experience of the facts, and the liberal mind that is not enslaved by long practice of the law. These meet in very few persons.'[22]

In a sense, then, the Endowed Schools Commission offered Hobhouse the ideal opening. Before any question arose of his appointment he had seen the Endowed Schools Bill as symptomatic of a change of spirit. It would, he said, 'apply to certain classes of Foundations authority enough to make them really useful, according to the needs of the present day'.[23] In fact it had not quite become law when he gave his much-publicised paper 'On the limitations which should be placed on dispositions of property to public uses' at the joint meeting of the Society of Arts and the Social Science Association in July 1869. It was this, and Lyttelton's agreement with it, that pleased Edwin Chadwick but impelled Lord Salisbury to warn of the risks in the Commission for reform, 'considering the known opinions of two out of the three Commissioners'. Later, from the standpoint of 1873, looking round on what he regarded as the depredations of Lyttelton and Hobhouse, an angry critic asked, 'was it fair to Parliament, to the country and to their intended victims to appoint them Commissioners? This was not putting reformers to work but revolutionists.'[24]

It is significant that, even in 1873, no one called Robinson a revolutionist. He always attracted less attention than his colleagues and certainly he did not flaunt his views as they did. In substance, however, it may be doubted whether he was very far behind them in his readiness to reject the dead hand. Like Arthur Hobhouse, Hugh Robinson was fifty when he became an Endowed Schools Commissioner, 'called . . . from the seclusion of the Rectory of Bolton Abbey', as a journalist put it. His life, though, had not been utterly secluded. For nearly ten years he had served as Principal of the Training College at York and he submitted an important statement on training colleges to the Newcastle Commission appointed in 1858 to inquire into the state of elementary education. He became interested in secondary schooling through his connection with the school for farmers' sons associated with the training college and had turned his mind to the wider problem posed by the deficiencies of the grammar schools well before the Taunton Commission was appointed. In 1864 he presented a paper, 'Suggestions for the improvement of middle-class education' at the Social Science Congress in York. Opening with the familiar argument that the middle classes were worse provided for than those above or beneath them in society, he examined various means of improvement, including the reorganisation of endowments. There was nothing timid about Robinson's proposals for the better use of what he called the 'surplusage' of grammar schools. They might well have been dubbed 'phalansterian'. He envisaged the country divided into districts, in each of which the best school would provide a high-grade classical education while the rest would be converted into middle schools 'and organised on the plan best suited to the circumstances of the classes who would make use of them'. It might be necessary to amalgamate endowments and Robinson was ready to take in his stride the 'apparent infringement of local claims' which this would lead to, on the ground that 'where the national interests are involved, it is possible to be too tender of local privileges'. He was not in favour of a secondary school system controlled by the Government but he understood that reorganisation on the scale he had in mind must involve 'legislative interference'.

Less than a year later he had the chance to expound his plan to the Taunton Commission. In the existing grammar schools, he told them, lay the country's very best resource for building up good middle-class education; 'there is a fund of opportunity there that has never been sufficiently thought of or realised'. He described again his division of the country so that each district had its leading grammar school giving a classical education and its cluster of minor grammar schools serving the needs of the lower middle class.[25] Here, in short, is the gradation principle which in due course the Taunton Commissioners were to recommend as the basis of reform, and which Robinson himself, as an Endowed Schools Commissioner, eventually tried to put into practice; with what difficulty we shall see. It was a highly bureaucratic notion, scarcely compatible with deference to founders. And indeed, Robinson talks of endowments not at all as if they lay beneath the dead hand but as if they could be manipulated in any way one pleased. When asked by Lord Taunton how he would deal with very small charities, producing only a few pounds a year, he answered 'If they were in towns I should be disposed to get rid of them altogether and raise a capital sum in lieu of them and build a good model school-room with that sum.'

W. E. Forster pressed for the appointment of Robinson as the third Endowed Schools Commissioner and so the 'all-powerful trium-virate', as an opponent called it, was complete. Despite great differences of temperament and background all three men were committed to their task. 'I do not know that, at first at any rate, there was marked difference between one . . . and another in their general view on the reform of the schools or on the application of the Act in detail.'[26] This was the opinion of Henry Roby, the man who shared with Lyttelton in 1874 the odium of the Commission's disbandment, as Hobhouse at the start had shared the notoriety of having pub-licised provocative opinions. Roby was made Secretary to the Com-mission when it was set up, but in 1872 he became a Commissioner in place of Hobhouse who gave up the post to serve on the Viceroy's Council in India.

Roby was a reformer through and through. As a young Fellow of St John's College, Cambridge, he had published *Remarks on College Reform* attacking the system of isolation under which the colleges, whatever their resources, strove individually to educate their members. Having to resign his Fellowship on marriage he became a master at Dulwich College and embarked on writing a reformed Latin Grammar which was highly praised. From his Cambridge days, when he was involved in that new departure, the Cambridge Local Examinations, as Secretary to the Syndicate, he had been interested in middle-class schooling. Frederick Temple praised him so warmly to Lord Granville that, for a moment, he seems to have been considered as a possible member of the Taunton Commission; then it was decided that he was too young and of not quite sufficient standing, nor in a position to work unpaid.

They made him Secretary instead. In addition to the massive task of running an inquiry into eight hundred grammar schools, he wrote what were perhaps the two most significant chapters of the Taunton Report: chapter II, which makes the case for reform by summarising all the evidence on 'The present state of schools for secondary education', and chapter IV which demonstrates the weakness, as it stands, of 'The law of charities affecting endowed schools' in face of the power of 'posthumous legislation' exercised by founders. These two chapters, it was said later, 'furnished the brief on which Mr W. E. Forster convinced the House of Commons of the necessity for the Endowed Schools Act, 1869'.[27] Indeed, in one sense, the entire Report, which it fell to Roby to assemble, constituted a twenty-one-volume indictment of the dead hand.

The strength of that indictment lay in the reports of the Assistant Commissioners who between them had inspected every endowed grammar school in England and Wales. Five of these men – C. I. Elton, D. R. Fearon, J. G. Fitch, J. L. Hammond and C. H. Stanton – were now appointed as Assistants to the Endowed Schools Commission. The advantage to be gained from their special experience seemed to Lyttelton obvious enough, as it would have done to Edwin Chadwick. 'In fact, we did not select them at all, they were, so to say, ready to our hand if we were fortunate enough to obtain them.'[28] The Assistant Secretary to the new Commission was D. C. Richmond, another who had worked as an Assistant Commissioner for Taunton, while the chief members of the clerical staff had also been employed by the Taunton Commission. In short, the new office in Victoria Street, from the Chief Commissioner to the junior clerk, abounded in what Chadwick called the 'special aptitudes' – that is, the expertise and commitment – which he sought in vain among other public servants of the late sixties. Between the new Commission and the Education Department there was certainly a very sharp contrast. Both were staffed by very able men, educated in leading schools, who had taken high honours at Oxford or Cambridge. But whereas the main department's examiners brought to their work no relevant experience nor the slightest interest in elementary schools, the Assistant Commissioners came steeped in contact with the old grammar schools; and whereas the examiners' duties were routine, and often seen by them as little more than the means to support a career in letters, the Assistant Commissioners had the critical task of advising, school by school, on the changes to be made, in line with principles which they had helped to formulate.[29] As Lyttelton said later, 'The Assistant Commissioners are so entirely in our confidence, and so thoroughly understand the work, and we work so very much through them.'

Among them, Joshua Fitch was outstanding. He was the oldest – forty-six – and lacked the conventional upper middle-class, public school, varsity background of the others. Fitch had been an elementary school teacher and took his degree at London University. He joined the staff of Borough Road Training College and became its Principal in 1856. In 1863 Matthew Arnold recommended him for appointment as an inspector of schools and from this work he was later seconded to assist in the inquiry of the Taunton Commission. Fitch had already given serious thought to the problems which would face that Commission and made this his subject in a paper presented to the Social Science Congress in 1864.

As the Assistant Commissioner sent to investigate the grammar schools of Yorkshire, he submitted possibly the most outstanding of all the reports to the Taunton Commission, a study sharp with practical comment based on personal experience of teaching and enlightened by high ideals. The standing he had gained by 1869 is plain from the fact that he was one of those whom Forster thought worth considering for the post of the third Endowed Schools Commissioner.[30] In the event he did not yet rise so high. If he had, it seems unlikely that his views would have been more acceptable than Lyttelton's or Hobhouse's in certain quarters. Fitch could be scathing about the dead hand and that convoluted obeisance towards it which he once summed up in the idea of lawyers struggling to apply the dogma of *cy près* to funds bequeathed to ransom Barbary captives.[31]

In 1869 girls suffered more than anyone from the dead hand in education. Emily Davies had chosen to argue that references to 'children' in ancient charters had been intended to cover both sexes. This was not only a doubtful starter but at best simply a version of *cy près*, having, in the words of the Taunton Commissioners, 'little but an antiquarian interest'. Wisely, they preferred to base the claim of girls to some share in the grammar school endowments on grounds of justice and the needs of the age. In various ways the attempt had to be made to adapt the old system to modern requirements and the men whose task it was to make that attempt stood as firm behind the principle embodied in Section 12 of the Endowed Schools Act as behind every other Taunton principle.

When the Commissioners' names were known Lyttelton's won immediate approval from the *Englishwoman's Review*; as well it might, considering the effort he had made to get girls admitted to the Cambridge Locals and to the inquiry of the Taunton Commission. He it was who wrote the chapter on girls' schools which appeared in the Taunton Report and while such authorship was not attributed he did not conceal that the subject was one to which he had had to pay 'particular attention'. His genuine concern for it comes across in the whimsical announcement made to his family when he had completed the draft:

> Births
> At 21 Carlton Terrace, on July 11th, after a painful and protracted labour, Lord Lyttelton of a chapter on Girls' Schools. Friends at a distance will be glad to hear that this long expected event has taken place and that parent and child are charming well.
>   The Infant Chapter has a strong likeness in features and deportment to its parent. It is uproarious – squalls incessantly – and hopes to make much noise in the world.[32]

In a different vein, at the Social Science Congress, he expressed the hope:

> that if nothing else follows from the Schools Inquiry, this may follow: some substantial measure of rectification of what I conceive to be one of the grossest instances of injustice – one of the most unrighteous deprivations, that can be mentioned, that of, it may almost be said, the whole female sex of England, for a very long time past, of any benefit from the ancient educational endowments of the country.[33]

When 'the substantial measure of rectification' – Section 12 – was being debated, he tried, as we have seen, to strengthen the wording.

Acknowledging that Lyttelton approved the girls' cause and that 'Canon Robinson is certainly not opposed to it' the feminist *Review* was doubtful about Hobhouse. 'Mr Hobhouse is a Charity Commissioner, and the Charity Commission has hitherto done very little to promote the education of girls, we therefore feel somewhat afraid of this gentleman.'[34] They did him less than justice. The limited capacity of the Charity Commission to promote action of any kind was, of course, one of his reasons for leaving it. As for girls, he should have gained credence, if not for his polemics against the dead hand then from his efforts to change the law regarding married women's property. In a splendid paper on the property question at the Social Science Congress in 1868 he declared his view that male superiority had been 'very much overstated'.

No one could doubt Roby's sympathy for girls who knew the remarkable exertions he had made on behalf of Miss Davies at the Taunton Commission, nor that of the body of Assistant Commissioners, if their reports on girls' education in that inquiry were anything to go by. All in all, if the Endowed Schools Commission had been staffed with no other end in view than to administer Section 12 it could hardly have turned out better. How this Section was to be applied, indeed, how the Act would be worked in general, was something about which, till it came to be attempted, nobody had the faintest idea.

The Commissioners at work

If the powers conferred by the Act equipped the Commissioners to ride into battle against the dead hand with trumpets sounding, the legal procedures it obliged them to follow, whereby each endowment had a separate Scheme and every Scheme, before becoming law, could be formally objected to by the public, the Education Department and by either House, ensured that, in practice, every onslaught turned into a campaign. The seven or eight hundred grammar school foundations were sustained by something like three thousand endowments.[35] That it should ever have been supposed that the Herculean task of reorganising these could be finished in three years – or at the most, four (the Endowed Schools Act extended no further) – shows how little thought was given to the problem.

Where should they begin? In one area at least they did begin with flags and trumpets. 'A number of wealthy endowments in Westminster, within a stone's throw of the Commissioners' office . . . seemed to me', wrote Roby later, 'to invite large and early reform. Mr Hobhouse readily took the suggestion and commenced proceedings.'[36] The foundations in question were the Emanuel and Greycoat Hospitals and in no time at all the Commissioners were involved in a struggle publicised all round the country. They had thrown down the gauntlet to powerful trustees – in the case of Emanuel, the City Corporation – and they came badly out of it, their Schemes rejected and themselves fixed as plunderers in many people's minds. Among the many issues involved in this struggle was the provision to be made for girls and we must return to it. But an impression of the everyday working of the Act, and especially of the way in which the girls' claim had to be balanced against many others, is more easily gained from

observing the Commissioners engaged in run-of-the-mill administration.

At the outset they decided that their formidable task could best be
tackled by selecting certain districts and attempting to reorganise
them thoroughly. Whether they would indeed have liked 'to cut up
the country into so many squares and have so many schools in each
square', as some people feared, they lacked the means to do it. Apart
from the Commissioners and the two Secretaries the Victoria Street
office in 1870 consisted of only four clerks and a messenger. Out in the
field were the Assistant Commissioners, each with his clerk, but there
were never more than five in full-time employment.

The Commissioners began by drafting a statement intended to set
out for the benefit of trustees, the principles on which they meant to
proceed.[37] These were Taunton principles. The Taunton Report, as
they explained here, was their guide 'on those points on which the
Act itself does not speak'. They described how they wished to classify
the schools 'to meet the differing demands for education existing in
society'. First grade schools would have a leaving age of nineteen and
prepare boys for the university. The leaving age and the standard of
curriculum at second and third grade schools would be lower. They
spoke of reconstituting governing bodies and of the functions of
governors and headmaster and of abolishing free education, except
where it was given as the reward of merit. In these general remarks to
trustees they said nothing about girls' education but their 'Instructions to Assistant Commissioners' direct that 'the express provisions
of the Act on this point must not be forgotten . . . the Assistant Commissioner must seek to ascertain in each case what is required in this
respect and what in his judgement can be done'. This comes towards
the end of twenty-seven paragraphs designed to guide the Assistant
Commissioners in those very delicate dealings with trustees from
which would be determined the grade of the school, the composition
of the governing body, the income, the settlement of vested interests
and everything pertaining to the making of the Scheme.[38]

They worked, of course, to the Commissioners' instructions. When
the Commission was well under way, with five regular and two occasional Assistant Commissioners, North Wales and the north of
England were assigned to Canon Robinson, South Wales and the
Midlands to Lyttelton and the south, including London, to Roby. Of
the five regular Assistant Commissioners, Fearon and Hammond
worked to Robinson, Stanton to Lyttelton and Fitch to Roby, while

White was mainly employed on legal work.[39] But in the early days, at the beginning of 1870, the Commissioners started with two districts only, Somerset and Dorset, and the West Riding of Yorkshire, chosen simply because one or other of them happened to know these parts of the country.

While it lacked the notoriety of the battle with Emanuel, Robinson's attempt to apply in Yorkshire the kind of systematic grammar school plan which he had outlined to the Taunton Commission provides as good, if not a better illustration of the many obstacles to be overcome in breaking with the past, and of the very limited room for manoeuvre available in trying to make provision for girls. Subject to the general principles referred to, the Commissioners exercised a pretty free hand in their own districts, deciding individually which foundations to deal with first and what particular advice to give their Assistants. When, as a result of his local inquiries, the Assistant Commissioner was able to draw up heads of a proposed Scheme, these were submitted for the approval of the whole Board, which would also authorise each important stage as it came along: the publication of the draft Scheme locally, amendments of it in response to objections, and, eventually, its submission for approval by the Education Department. If it was approved there, it would again be published and a petition could be made against it. If none was made it must lie for forty days before both Houses, and only after this, if no Address was presented against it, did it go forward for the Royal Assent.

Canon Robinson knew the West Riding from his charge of the parish of Bolton Abbey which, rather surprisingly, he retained until 1874; but his principal source of information in regard to the grammar schools was, of course, the report made by Fitch to the Taunton Commission some four or five years back. Fitch could be eloquent, but nothing he wrote then said more about the problems that awaited Robinson than the map he had included to show the distribution of grammar school endowments in Yorkshire.[40] They were where they might have been expected to be in the seventeenth century but not exactly where they were most needed two hundred years later. While there were large towns without endowment – Huddersfield and Dewsbury had none, while Sheffield, with 185,000 people, had endowments worth only £300 p.a. – the village of Horton with 400 people had endowments worth £200 p.a. Half of the sixty or more endowments in the West Riding were very small, bringing in less than £80 a year, and a quarter of them less than £30. As for the state of the grammar schools, Fitch had found this 'unspeakably disheartening'. Travelling up the valley of the Aire to inspect the grammar schools of Bradford, Bingley, Keighley, Skipton, Giggleswick and Sedbergh he had found that, with a total revenue approaching £5000 p.a., the number of scholars in all six schools was less than two hundred.

Robinson, we saw, had long ago worked out the principle of classification by means of which he thought the old endowed schools could be adapted to serve current needs. The Taunton Commissioners had endorsed this and the large powers of the Endowed Schools Commissioners were intended to make it possible, as it had never been before, to organise schools in relation to each other over a whole district: in short, to form a system. Robinson now proceeded to attempt this in the West Riding. To Daniel Fearon, his Assistant Commissioner, he gave a memorandum setting out 'a complete scheme for the organisation of that division of the country; it was a scheme which was not official at all; I was personally and privately responsible for it, and I drew it up for his use and my own'. Apparently Robinson divided the Riding into seven districts, for each of which he set out 'a general view of the grade and character of the schools which prima facie it appeared desirable to establish'.[41]

The first of Robinson's districts was Bradford, or rather, what he called 'The Bradford Circle', a model in which he precisely exemplified the theory of gradation.[42] As he describes it, Bradford Grammar School is to be the centre, a first grade school; around it he envisages the 'chief affiliated schools' of the second grade established at Keighley, Bingley and Otley, with third grade schools at Thornton, Drighlington, Guiseley, Ilkley and Haworth. He notes down how far these are from the 'centre', their population, endowment income and the provision they ought to supply. This includes substantial provision for girls. There was, as Fitch's report had shown, no endowed girls' secondary school in the Riding. Robinson proposes that all five third grade schools be mixed, while second grade schools for girls shall be established on the Bradford, Keighley and Bingley foundations.

Eight schools for girls! When one thinks how Miss Davies had had to pester the Taunton Commissioners to get them to take in girls' education and how Miss Buss, at that very moment, was struggling vainly to raise endowment, there is something remarkable, even touching, about the idea of a civil servant taking up his pen in 1870 and writing in provision of eight schools for girls in one small part of Yorkshire alone. Of course, they did not get eight. In several places the readiness of the Yorkshire dales to sustain the idea of girls' education was never tested, for lack of money. Robinson had been much too sanguine about what could be achieved with very small endowments. Apart from Thornton, all the foundations which he had earmarked for third grade schools had incomes of less than £100 p.a. How far such modest resources could be stretched depended not only on local demand – the probable income from grammar school fees – but also on the state of the buildings. If these were decrepit, as at Drighlington, and the endowment could not pay for new ones, what was to be done? These were the kind of questions which exercised Fearon, the Assistant Commissioner, as he moved around the Bradford Circle. What happened in the end was that it proved impossible to establish grammar schools at Haworth and Drighlington; the money was used for exhibitions instead. At Guiseley no effective action was taken. At Ilkley the original idea of a mixed school was given up in favour of a school for boys. The only mixed school established was at Thornton.[43]

These early dealings with meagre endowments show, then, that whatever the principles involved, reorganisation was a question of money. It was pointless for Robinson to stipulate that Otley was 'entitled to have a second grade school' when its income was only £60 a year. This was another instance of endowment converted, in the end, into exhibitions. At Keighley the school for girls he proposed became practicable only because Fearon contrived a means of achieving it without extra building: the Mechanics' Institute housed a trade school far more highly esteemed than the grammar school and it was decided to subsidise that and use the old grammar school buildings for girls. At Bingley a not dissimilar arrangement provided for a girls' school in the Mechanics' Institute. In both cases it was touch and go whether enough money for girls would be found. At Keighley the amount assigned to girls was halved in the course of the negotiations. At Bingley the settlement reflected not only the conflicting attitudes of the Mechanics' Institute and the Grammar School trustees towards the girls' school project – the first by far the more enthusiastic – but the financial liability imposed by the need to pension off the Grammar School headmaster and the bonus gained by pulling into the kitty the endowment of a small non-educational charity.[44]

'The principle of Girls' education is approved of but the Governors consider it of much more importance to have a first-rate boys' school and until that is established would prefer not to cripple the funds.'[45] This response, from Bradford Grammar School, illustrates a very common reaction to the relative claims of boys and girls, and at Bradford there were other reasons why the girls' claim was secondary: the settling of the Scheme resolved itself into a tremendous battle about the way the school should be graded.

Robinson had made it the centre of his Circle. 'What does Bradford want?' he had asked. 'It wants and can well afford to pay for high Education but it must be *adapted*.'[46] This northern metropolis seemed to him ideal for a first grade school with a 'modern' curriculum, one where science and European languages would have pride of place instead of Latin and Greek. The Taunton Commissioners, uneasily regarding the classics-ridden schools of a scientific age, had proposed not only that lower grade grammar schools should do much less classical teaching but that an experiment might be made of some truly modern schools at the highest grade. 'The arguments in favour of a Classical School are not likely to be very strong', wrote Robinson in his instructions on the Bradford case. He was never more mistaken. Bradford was outraged. In vain did the Commissioners urge upon the Governors that 'a District teeming with modern industries . . . full of the life of the present age' needed a school of a scientific type. In vain was Bradford pressed to 'accept the mission of proving the value of an Education based mainly on Modern Languages and Literature and Natural and Modern Science'.[47] Bradford did not want it. Some very powerful arguments were fired back at London. One was that Greek was still an entry requirement 'for any British or Foreign University';[48] another, that in terms of its rates and taxes Bradford was a wealthier place than Leeds and Leeds had a first grade school teaching Greek; why also should Bradford be denied the kind of school 'found in every third and fourth rate town in Germany'?[49]

Despite his many years in the north Robinson had very greatly misjudged the temper of one of its leading cities. There was a demand for a public inquiry. This was held early in 1871 and a string of witnesses – clergy, doctors, manufacturers, even one working man – came forward to attest the demand for Greek in Bradford.[50] The Endowed Schools Commissioners had to back down. Bradford got its first grade classical school and so ended one attempt at breaking with the past.

Its importance for girls' education is simply that the need to resolve this conflict dominated the making of the Scheme. Long before it came to an inquiry the Endowed Schools Commissioners made various concessions in the hope of reaching a compromise. One of these concerned the amount of money to be assigned to girls' education. The need to launch a girls' school on this foundation had been stressed by Robinson from the start. In a paper he presented to the rest of the Board early on in the negotiations he talked of assigning three-eighths of the income, which would have been about £300 p.a. By the time the draft Scheme was published the figure quoted was £250 p.a.; the governors protested that this was too much; they suggested £200 and a few months later they pressed the Commissioners to postpone the girls' claim altogether until the boys' school was firmly established. This was in October 1870, in the thick of the debate over Greek. The Commissioners agreed. They offered this concession, along with others, 'as a proof that . . . while insisting on principles which they regard as vital and essential' (by which they meant the Greek question) '[they] are desirous of giving all due weight to representations made to them by . . . the locality'.[51] The Scheme as it was finally approved set aside for girls £200 p.a. and provided that payment might be deferred for three years after the Scheme took effect. The concessions which the Commissioners offered did not buy off the governors' opposition, yet they had been made and the girls lost by it.

Robinson's interest in the novel idea of a first grade modern school crops up again in his dealings with 'Sedbergh and Giggleswick', as he called the second of the districts into which he had divided the West Riding. Again, one could say he was defeated by the past. The two foundations presented a great contrast. Both were substantial: at Giggleswick the income was £1200 p.a., at Sedbergh £800 and the Sedbergh school had also an extremely valuable endowment of exhibitions to St John's College, Cambridge. But apart from this they had little in common. Giggleswick was one of the most thriving schools in Yorkshire with active governors, handsome new buildings and a recently modernised curriculum; Sedbergh, Fitch had found too painful to dwell on, having soon abandoned all attempts to examine the handful of boys in its dirty schoolrooms. Things were no better in 1870. Though the headmaster was a scholarly man he had somehow failed. The school was 'almost in abeyance'.[52]

In Taunton terms it was essential to view the two schools in relation to each other and the Instructions issued to Fearon explored the idea that, while both should be first grade, one should be classical, the other modern. As the condition of Sedbergh was so poor it might 'without impediment from existing arrangements be reconstituted on the modern system'. On the other hand, it was a fact that Giggleswick had lately been rebuilt 'with a view to its being a leading modern school'.[53] The Giggleswick governors, when approached, were not enthusiastic about this idea. However, they were ready to consider the next one, which was that the two foundations should be joined to provide a notable school on one site. They assumed it would be the Giggleswick site. The Sedbergh governors were furious at this. They would not hear of an amalgamation. Though their school was in such low water they declared 'the whole parish will resist its removal'.[54] In the end the idea was dropped and the two schools were dealt with independently.

But there were other problems obtruding from the past. The governors of Giggleswick were eager to develop it as a public school but had so far been frustrated by its obligations to the locality. For three hundred years the inhabitants of Settle had sent their sons to Giggleswick free and such boys drove away the higher class of boarders. If the school was to advance the Commissioners acknowledged that the local people would have to be bought off. The Scheme they made for Giggleswick in 1872 did this by providing for a third grade mixed school in or near Settle; and since every Scheme was a matter of arithmetic, admission of this claim must be seen in conjunction with the assignment to girls' education of only £100 p.a. from an income of £1200. This did not constitute enough to start a school. It was hoped to add to it money from Sedbergh but here the past loomed even more dauntingly. Not only were the Commissioners obliged once more to meet local claims with a third grade school but they were forced to buy out the headmaster. Though his incapacity had pulled the school down, the Sedbergh headmaster had a vested interest, which meant that he could not be dismissed without a pension. Thus the Sedbergh Scheme made in 1874 pensioned him off at £400 p.a. – half the value of the endowment – and all that could be done for girls was to assign £200 p.a. for their education when the pension ceased. This was long awaited. The headmaster lived for another thirty years. He cost the endowment £12,000 and the girls £6000.[55]

Like the Bradford district this part of the Riding had its scatter of small endowments. It is hard to see what Fearon could have done

with the £10 at Arncliffe, the £15 at Cargrave or the £30 at Linton
and Long Preston. There is in fact no evidence that he did anything,
which would be in line with the general Instruction issued to Assistant Commissioners to postpone inquiry into small village schools.
The larger endowments of Horton and Bentham were viewed initially
in the light of their bearing on the Sedbergh–Giggleswick proposals;
indeed, it was hoped that other foundations might 'join the con-
federacy'.[56] This is pure Taunton, the appraisal of endowments in
relation to each other and to the district. But nothing came of it. At
Horton, for instance, progress was impeded by the vested interest of
the headmaster.

Equally intractable problems arose in 'Leeds and Ripon', Robinson's third district. Harrogate was quite without grammar school
endowment; nothing could be done there. Knaresborough Grammar
School had an income of only £20 p.a. At Ripon there was opposition
over grading. Taunton planning pointed to a second grade school
because the schools at Richmond and York, in the North Riding,
were near enough to meet the expected demand in this area for a
classical education. But the governors of Ripon Grammar School
were no more eager than anyone else to lose the cachet of teaching
Greek and they pressed for their school to be first grade. The Commissioners gave in, influenced perhaps by the outcome of the Bradford Inquiry which had just taken place when the Ripon Scheme was
published, or perhaps with an eye to disarming opposition to other
very unpopular changes – the abolition of free education and the
introduction of a boarding house. At the beginning they had
intended also to provide something for girls at Ripon but references
to this seem to disappear with acceptance of the idea of a first grade
school – not surprisingly, for the higher the grade the higher the
income needed to sustain it.[57]

An out-and-out refusal to do anything for girls came early in 1870
from Leeds. With an income of £2500 p.a. this was the second richest
grammar school in Yorkshire. Fitch in his report had written
admiringly of its stately and commodious buildings, excellent staffing
and broad curriculum. Leeds was prompt now to exercise the right
which the Act gave to wealthy foundations to submit their own
Draft Scheme to the Commissioners and the Commissioners returned
a long commentary, full of Taunton principles, advising the governors,
among much else, to reflect on the need to make provision for girls.
The governors came back sharply with their view that the school's

income would all be needed 'for the proper support of the school . . . and that it is not possible to make any provision for girls'.[58] Whatever concessions might be forced on the Commissioners during the course of negotiations – and we have seen how the girls' claim was vulnerable – they regarded such an answer as quite unacceptable at this early stage, in regard to such an income. The next year Fearon was launched on Leeds and instructed that 'so wealthy a foundation ought to do something for the education of girls and you will take the opportunity of discussing this matter with the governors, and ascertaining how it can best be carried into effect'.[59] For the moment the action stops here. Once again, there is reason to believe, progress was frustrated by the vested interest of a headmaster hostile to change. At all events, no more was done with Leeds in the seventies. When the case was taken up again later the main point at issue was provision for girls and the struggle lasted till the end of the century.

Leeds of course was not the only place where inquiries were begun and then deferred. There were many loose ends and the work overlapped between one of Robinson's districts and another. In the spring of 1871, for instance, Fearon had not shaken off the Bradford Circle yet he had made a start with Leeds and Ripon and was well advanced with initial inquiries in the Halifax area. 'Halifax and Huddersfield' was how Robinson defined his fourth district but no definition could alter the fact that Huddersfield entirely lacked grammar school endowment. For Halifax, however, a plan was worked out somewhat reminiscent of the Bradford Circle. The Heath School at Halifax was to be first grade, and for that a Scheme was settled by 1873.[60] A second grade school 'with prominence given to scientific subjects' was to be provided by nearby Hipperholme.[61] This outraged the Hipperholme trustees. Why should their grammar school be downgraded? They wished to develop its boarding side. The second grade school could be at Halifax, they said. Further, there developed a kind of sub-plot: two factions emerged in Hipperholme, the conservative element led by the trustees and another group of townspeople keen to see the school made less exclusive and open to both sexes. Fearon was in no doubt where progress lay. 'The issue', he wrote to Victoria Street, 'can be very simply put viz . . . aristocratic Governors and an unpopular Headmaster with their boarders, their Greek and their high fees versus middle class education and moderate fees for the benefit of the Township, with local governing body and extension of the foundation to Girls.'[62] It seemed to him a classic opportunity to fight for Taunton at a public inquiry, but none was held. The Hipperholme case dragged on well beyond 1874 when the Endowed Schools Commission was disbanded.

For further provision of second grade schools the Commissioners looked to Rishworth, but here they had problems. The Wheelwright foundation was the richest in Yorkshire but it sustained a Hospital School, one, that is, where children were clothed and boarded as well as educated. The peculiar obstacle which such schools offered to Taunton reforms, and especially to the advancement of girls' education will be considered later. For the moment we should note, though, that the dead hand lay more heavily upon them than upon any other kind of school in England. And indeed the chairman of the Wheelwright governors captured this exactly when he said to Fearon that 'all the explanations in the world would not make it right to violate a founder's will'.[63] Wheelwright resistance had more than half an eye, too, to the battle going on in London with Emanuel Hospital and no surrender was in sight at Rishworth by 1874. This was yet another problem which the Commissioners passed on to their successors.

In the Halifax–Huddersfield district third grade boys' schools were established at Rastrick, Mirfield and Sowerby, the Scheme in each case authorising the admission of girls.[64] But Robinson's attempt at Elland to utilise two small foundations for a boys' and a girls' school respectively only half came off: the boys' Scheme went through but the Ramsden trustees objected strongly to their foundation being used for a girls' school because 'the clear and positive intentions of the Foundress' related to the teaching of poor *boys* only.[65]

Immense time was taken up on all such cases. It is not in the least surprising to find that whole tracts of the districts defined by Robinson had scarcely been touched by 1874 when the Endowed Schools Commission was disbanded and the work handed over to the Charity Commissioners. Little had been done in the Sheffield district: Sheffield itself had an awkward headmaster and at Rotherham where the need was great the endowment, as Robinson said, was 'very trifling'. The Doncaster district fared no better; it seems that Fearon never got round to it. In the seventh district, 'Dewsbury and Wakefield', Schemes went through for Wakefield and Batley, each of them making provision for girls, but very little else was accomplished.[66]

'We had very little opposition in Yorkshire,' Robinson told a Select Committee in 1873.[67] This was perfectly true. Compared with

Emanuel the north was well managed. The marathon fight with Leeds lay in the future, as did the real confrontation with Rishworth. Meanwhile, there had been the Bradford Inquiry, a number of Parliamentary references to Ripon and protests here and there – the angriest, perhaps, coming from the Ramsden trustees at Elland, who appeared every bit as loyal to their foundress as were the City Aldermen to Lady Dacre, but who, on an income of £70 p.a., could scarcely rouse the nation in her defence.

The Ramsden protest was a matter of principle; but what comes over clearly from the work in the West Riding is that there were many hindrances to change other than principled opposition and what most of them came down to was lack of money. The dead hand had financial implications, in the uneven distribution of endowments, in the vested interests of individuals and of localities, requiring compensation, and all this restricted the potential of the grammar schools to form a coherent secondary school system on the lines conceived by the Taunton Commissioners. As we saw, four of the contributory schools which Robinson included in his Bradford Circle remained non-starters for want of money. Where there was money there was room for manoeuvre but even large funds could not obscure the fact that a Scheme was an assignment of limited resources. It is in this context that we have to appraise the provision the Commissioners made for girls.

They found no grammar school for girls in the Riding. They established four, at Keighley, Bradford, Bingley and Wakefield, as well as a school for both sexes at Thornton. Further, the endowments of Sedbergh and Giggleswick were to be 'taxed' for girls' education and at a number of minor grammar schools it was provided that girls might be admitted. All in all, eleven of the sixteen Schemes for secondary schooling in this part of Yorkshire included some kind of provision for girls and not one of them had been prepared without reflection on what might be provided, by that Scheme or another in the area. The most ardent feminist could hardly have expected a more zealous attempt to apply Section 12. As Forster said to a sympathetic audience at the formal opening of Bradford Girls' Grammar School, 'They had dispelled the popular notion that, in meddling with ... the pious founder, they were killing the goose with the golden eggs.'[68] They had perhaps dispelled that notion in Bradford. But there were not many eggs to go round and it remains to be seen how many came to girls, and with what difficulty, elsewhere in England.

3. The money problem

Money, money, where is it to come from?

Miss Buss, 1871[1]

Endowment for Miss Buss

In theory the Commissioners' very large powers were, as was said, sufficient to enable them 'to take a girls' school in Northumberland and make it a boys' school in Cornwall'[2] or vice versa. In practice, as their Yorkshire experience makes plain, they worked very much in terms of locality, applying Section 12 as a means of extending the range of Charles II's foundation in Bradford or John Drake's bequest to the people of Keighley. But there was one exception: from the very beginning the Commissioners were resolved to find endowment for Miss Buss.

Nothing shows the weakness of the girls' school lobby more than the predicament in 1870 of the very successful North London Collegiate. The idea of converting her private venture into a public school had grown on Miss Buss from the time she appeared before the Taunton Commission and she tried now to assure its future by putting it under the control of a trust. Financial security was another matter. The rich might be ready to pay through the nose to anyone prepared to teach their daughters accomplishments, but when it came to subscribing the endowment which would enable a serious girls' school to offer scholarships and keep up its premises, they were not interested. Appeals went in vain to City companies and people of influence. Maria Grey wrote letters to *The Times* urging support for the Collegiate School and for its Lower School in Camden which Miss Buss started in 1871 to meet the demand for a less expensive but equally sound education for girls. The response was pitiful. And while Miss Buss was scraping around to find desks and inkwells an almost insupportable affront came from the City: money subscribed there for a girls' school was diverted to a school for boys. In 1871 the sum of £60,000 had been offered overnight by the merchants and bankers who formed the Middle Class Schools Corporation to build a new boys' school in the City. Further application for a similar girls' school after some months produced £5000. But at this point attention was drawn to the possibility that Datchelor's Charity might be prepared to establish a girls' school. Those who had subscribed the £5000 decided it was no longer needed for girls and could be added to the boys' school fund. Was this not, as Maria Grey put it, 'like taking the poor man's one ewe lamb to garnish the rich man's feast?'[3] It was certainly painful to Miss Buss. £5000 was the sum she had hoped for to endow her Lower School in Camden. Clearly, her own impressive reputation, the fact that her schools were overflowing, that they exemplified the Taunton ideal of what girls' education ought to be, even the fact that the Princess of Wales had consented to be their patron could not give them financial stability. 'Really', she wrote, 'I am very despairing.'[4]

Miss Buss's biographer, reliving the anxiety of the early seventies, recalls, in a chapter headed 'Triumph', how 'things suddenly assumed a fresh aspect' with news of help from the Endowed Schools Commission in August 1872. This sudden change, though, was born of a commitment going back as far as the Taunton Inquiry. It was this Inquiry which established Miss Buss with the men who were now in charge of endowments. Roby, as we saw, in his capacity as Secretary, had arranged with Miss Davies for Miss Buss to give evidence. Lyttelton was one of the two or three Commissioners who involved themselves in her interrogation, while Fearon was the Assistant Commissioner who visited and reported on her school.

The Inquiry ended but the links remained. 'I am sorry it will be impossible for me to attend your distribution of prizes', wrote Roby to Miss Buss in 1872, assuring her, however, of his 'hearty sympathy'. 'Public schools . . . are, I believe, quite as useful for girls' education as for boys', and far more needed because at present they are so few. You and your coadjutors are highly to be praised for your energy in developing the Camden schools and sincerely to be congratulated on the success which you fully deserve.'[5] Joshua Fitch had appeared on the platform at the first prizegiving of the Lower School. On another occasion, Miss Buss's girls received their certificates from Lyttelton himself; and in 1871 Miss Buss had the pleasure of hearing the chairman of her governors read out 'a private but very encouraging note from Lord Lyttelton, saying that we should have some endowments as soon as they can lay their hands on any'.[6]

Laying hands on endowments was not easy but by 1872 the Commissioners saw their way. The Brewers' Company, trustees of Platt's Charity which governed Aldenham Grammar School, had been recently enriched by the sale of land to build St Pancras Station and were not unwilling to make some contribution for the benefit of girls. Roby hastened to inform Miss Buss and from this point to that other, three years later, when Fitch wrote specially 'with the kindest good wishes' to say that all was settled,[7] the endowment for Camden was nursed along by the Endowed Schools Commission.

William Latham, the Assistant Commissioner who was instructed to handle the case, was a practising barrister and, unlike his colleagues, had had no links with the Taunton Commission. But he had had experience analogous to it, as Lyttelton at one point thought fit to explain, having worked on the reform of the statutes of Christ's Hospital.[8] And whether this had given him a taste for change or whether his was simply a progressive disposition, no one could have brought more diligence and zeal to the application of Section 12 than Latham did now for Miss Buss's schools.

The first thing had been to put it to the Brewers that some of their money might go in this direction. Their own ideas – and the wealth of the foundation entitled them to send in a Scheme of their own – did not really look beyond Aldenham. Thus, they were eager to spend freely on the grammar school to lift it up into the public school class. A large new wing had recently been added and everything was done to encourage boarders. The Brewers were also supporting almshouses and two elementary schools in the locality. It was Latham's task to try and persuade them to be less parochial with their £4000 a year. There was no objection to Aldenham School being raised to the first grade but neighbouring towns – Watford, for instance – had no endowed grammar school, and there were the exigent claims of girls. The trustees must be reminded, wrote Lyttelton, instructing Latham for his meeting with the Brewers, of what the Taunton Commissioners' Report and the Act said about female education. 'And the Commissioners must say plainly that they cannot consider it consistent with their duty, when dealing with so wealthy a foundation, to overlook those claims. They must indeed assign to them a substantial share in its benefits.'[9] Lyttelton proposed to turn the Company's attention to St Pancras, that 'large and poor' parish whence their wealth derived. The Brewers had in mind to aid the elementary schools there; but 'from circumstances within the Commissioners' knowledge it appears highly probable', wrote Lyttelton, 'that a substantial sum might be most advantageously spent in establishing and permanently supporting Schools for Girls in that quarter'.

The Brewers' response was sympathetic and it was when she heard of this from Roby that 'things suddenly assumed a fresh aspect' for Miss Buss, as well they might. He told her nothing was settled, 'but I hope to get a handsome sum towards building, so as to complete, with what you have collected, all that is necessary, and also some annual endowments'.[10] *I hope to get . . .* This vein of personal commitment was Latham's too. He exerted himself, from his first meeting with Miss Buss and her governors, to secure the future of these 'two most successful Schools, both of which are carried on in hired houses'.[11] £20,000 he thought might come from the Brewers towards the cost of buildings for them. The Commissioners had at first proposed double that figure but Latham represented that to some of the Brewers this seemed 'a *monstrous* demand on the Trust'.[12] So £20,000 was assigned in the Draft Scheme, a 'handsome sum' indeed, and far exceeding Miss Buss's original aspirations. In addition £600 p.a. would be paid to the North London Collegiate School; and still further help might be forthcoming, said Latham, when the Commissioners dealt with Dame Alice Owen's Charity, of which the Brewers were trustees also.

His forty-year devotion to the schools was just beginning. Over the years he was to give Miss Buss crucial advice on siting problems, and to play his part in the decision of the Clothworkers' Company, of which he was a member, to donate an assembly hall. Later he became a Camden trustee. By the time he died in 1914 the North London girls had become 'my girls' and for eighteen years he had been chairman of the governors. But all this was rooted in the early seventies when he dealt with the schools as an Assistant Commissioner. The tenor of his letters then to Miss Buss is reminiscent of Roby's correspondence with Emily Davies in the Taunton era: there is a strong sense of alliance.

'The Brewers, as I think you are aware, are with us; and . . . will be probably in time of need, not only neutral but active supporters. I think we can rely on them.'[13] What he had in mind, writing this in March 1874, was serious obstruction of the Scheme by local interests. The Endowed Schools Commissioners, the Camden trustees, even the

Brewers' Company might be happy with the assignment to girls' education, but the headmaster of Aldenham Grammar School was not. When the Scheme was published in 1873 he formally objected to the proposal to allocate £20,000 to Camden and £13,000 to start grammar schools in Watford. 'Lavishing such sum on Schools in no way connected with Aldenham is not warranted by the Act as I read it.'[14]

The headmaster's motives were probably complex for he was at odds with both Brewers and Commissioners over the question of his own vested interest. However that might be, he came forward now to champion the cause of the lower schools in Aldenham. The Scheme assigned them £5000 from the foundation; the headmaster suggested £20,000. The vicar, ratepayers and inhabitants of Aldenham also urged that the proposed allocation was 'unequal and unjust' towards the elementary schools and 'excessive and unnecessary' towards the North London Collegiate.

Latham saw cause for anxiety here. For while he considered the headmaster's demands 'more than can in reason or decency be granted', and thought the Scheme treated the people of Aldenham 'with exceptional liberality', it could be blocked by an appeal against it. There were problems, too, on political grounds. In February 1874, the month before this letter to Miss Buss, the Liberals, who had fathered the Endowed Schools Act, had gone out of office and Disraeli's party was known to be bent on some drastic alteration.

> With the present Ministry in power the great thing to be gained is to send up *unopposed* Schemes. If the Aldenham Scheme is opposed by the Headmaster and parishioners I cannot avoid a doubt whether the Duke of Richmond will approve it. If on the other hand we endeavour to *convince (or convict of error)* the parishioners, the process will be long.[15]

But he had faith in the Scheme. And 'if the worst comes to the worst . . . our good friends the Brewers are governors of another trust out of which I hope we might obtain you compensation'.

Latham's anxiety comes to the fore in another letter written ten days later. He admits he does not know what the Government will do. 'If they mean to approve none but unopposed Schemes, Aldenham is doomed.' Yet he advises against action.

> I do not think you can do any good at present by moving. If it ever comes to a contest in either House of Parliament you and your friends can then do good service. At present the struggle lies between the

'interest' and the Commissioners, the Brewers being clearly on the side of the Commissioners. If the local interests can be defeated your claim . . . is not only undisputed but warmly supported in most quarters.

Meanwhile he thought the Brewers should not be pestered.

Dealing with Companies is slow work because they meet but seldom. The Brewers are trotting along so steadily in the right direction that I am for leaving them alone . . . My own impression is that we shall carry the Aldenham Scheme but it needs good generalship and in Carnot's phrase *surtout point de zèle* – that is to say, until we reach the moment for fighting. Then we must all do our best.[16]

The Aldenham parishioners, as he had feared, tried to block the Scheme. Their earlier objections had led the Commissioners to increase the elementary school allocation from £5000 to £8000 and in June 1874 the Scheme, thus amended, had gone on to the Education Department. This Department now received the Aldenham protest. The parishioners asked for £15,000 and 'the moment of fighting' may have seemed near; at any rate, Latham now offered Miss Buss influential names among the Brewers' Company.

The Government also moved into action. As we shall see, the reforming vigour of Lyttelton and Roby had proved too much. They were to be dismissed. An Act passed in August 1874 disbanded the Commission from the following December. Its work was taken over by the Charity Commission; and a most unlucky takeover this turned out to be from the point of view of girls' education. The Camden schools, though, were not affected. Latham, in the midst of his summer holidays, took a moment to explain to Miss Buss that he hardly thought the Government would overthrow the Schemes for Aldenham and the Camden schools against the wishes of both governing bodies.[17]

Nor did it. The new Act required the Schemes to be republished, with a further period allowed for objections. The Aldenham parishioners returned to the charge. The vicar came up to see the Lord President. The people of Bushey and the vicar of Frogmore also asked for money for their elementary schools. But at last, in May 1875, the Schemes, unchanged, received the Royal Assent.

As Latham recalled later, endowment for Camden had been 'one of the main ambitions of the Commissioners from their first appointment'.[18] Before it was achieved its progenitors were sacked and it was from other friends in the Commission – the main staff carried on under the new regime – that messages reached Miss Buss with the news.

Tapping large funds and stretching small ones

The Commissioners' good fortune in the case of Camden had been to find a source of uncommitted money. This was their ideal in regard to Section 12, a clause so patently awkward to apply 'when, as in the vast majority of instances, an Endowment is actually enjoyed by Boys' Schools'.[19] The wealthy Brewers were not the only Company to be called in aid. The Haberdashers' Company, with an income in the region of £8000 p.a., promoted four new day schools, two of them for girls.[20] The Merchant Taylors provided a girls' school in addition to their boys' school at Crosby in Lancashire. The Grocers assigned new funds to education, for boys in the first place, but taking power to convert the schools for girls if they wished to do so later. And all these Schemes went through without trouble. Company and Commissioners might not see eye to eye over free education for freemen's children – a favourite proposal but one which offended against the Taunton principle of merit – or over the Brewers' or Haberdashers' right to exclusive control of the governing body – but these things were ironed out. The money was there, often swollen far beyond the dreams of the founder. Companies quite often were not unwilling to seek advice on how it should be spent and ready to venture some of it on girls.

Apart from the companies there were other foundations where increased wealth and willing trustees gave scope to the Commission. At Newcastle-under-Lyme, Orme's Foundation was gaining large revenues from coal and ironstone, yet maintained only an elementary school. The print was hardly dry on the Endowed Schools Act when one of the trustees wrote to the Commission urging that the fund should be made the basis of a secondary school system. And this was done. The Scheme provided for first and third grade boys' schools and a school for girls. At Stamford it was not mineral royalties but the addition of the surplus funds of Browne's Hospital which brought the income up to well over £2000 p.a. Here again three schools were established: first and third grade for boys and a third grade school for girls. In Leicester two second grade schools were established, one for boys and one for girls, out of the funds of Wyggeston's Hospital newly turned over to education. In Burton-on-Trent the grammar school endowment was amalgamated with Allsopp's Charity, which had lately increased its income, and this made possible the foundation of the Allsopp's Schools for boys and girls. In Bedford the prodigious Harpur revenues, amounting to some £12,000 p.a., were reorganised so that much the greater part – ten-elevenths – now went on education, and most of that on grammar schools, including two for girls. Here the educational scope of the endowment was not only increased at the expense of almshouses and other eleemosynary objects but the Commissioners' insistence on school fees enabled them to graft more schools onto a charity which had hitherto provided free education on a truly spectacular scale. At Wakefield converted apprentice fees and doles helped to transform an endowment income of £400 p.a. into one of £3000. Three schools were projected, one of them for girls. At Warwick no fewer than thirteen small charities were amalgamated and the total endowment again supported three schools, one of them for girls.

In some cases, then, for a variety of reasons there was 'new' money to be disposed of and girls got a share of it. In other cases they were able to benefit from increased funds that were not new to education but had not before been used for secondary schools. Roan's Charity at Greenwich and Palmer's at Grays Thurrock were two where the income, now much expanded, had so far been spent on elementary education, but the trustees were ready to be more ambitious. This gave the Commissioners rare freedom of action. 'The place is insignificant', wrote Roby of Gray's Thurrock, 'but the Endowment is large . . . The School has hitherto been only an Elementary one; and the Trustees have judiciously postponed attempting to reconstitute it with their larger sums pending the action of this Commission. It may be looked on, therefore, as practically a new case, unembarrassed by what has previously happened.'[21] Girls stood to benefit, he went on to say, 'by the freedom . . . of the fund from existing claims. There can be no more obviously strong case than such a one as this for the inclusion of Girls' Schools.' They were indeed included at both Greenwich and Grays Thurrock and also on several London foundations which had hitherto supported elementary schools only: Prisca Coborn's Charity in Stepney, Lady Eleanor Holles's in Cripplegate and Sarah Bonnell's Foundation in West Ham. In all these, as Roby said of Grays Thurrock, there was an 'obviously strong case' for girls. But how strong was it where a modest endowment was firmly committed to a boys' grammar school? Forster had anticipated trouble here long ago, during the debates on the Bill. At about the same time, in 1869, Fitch had warned those who shared his feminist sympathies that 'in four cases out of five, endowed schools revenues were far too small to allow of their being divided'.[22]

Experience brought this home to the Commissioners. Having begun by instructing their Assistants 'to ascertain in each case' what was required for girls[23] they soon perceived that this would be a waste of time where the endowment was so small as to make such provision 'obviously impossible'.[24]

How small was that? Circumstances varied. But, apart from buildings, Robinson reckoned that a third grade school for some forty girls needed £100 p.a. from endowment.[25] On the credit side there would be fees as well – £2–£5 p.a. in a school of this type. On the debit side there would be running expenses, including the stipend of the headmistress, fixed probably at £40–£50 p.a., and the capitation fee she earned for each pupil, which might range from 10 shillings to £2 a head. Assistants would have to be paid as well, though their stipends were not usually fixed in the Scheme, and money might be assigned for exhibitions and for a repair-and-improvement fund. In a school of higher grade everything was higher: school fees, stipend and capitation fee; and, of course, more income from endowment was looked for. But whatever the grade the problem was the same: how to balance the books, and under conditions which no businessman would have tolerated.

For Endowed Schools Schemes were both rigid and chancy. Whatever they laid down had the force of law, so that stipend, school fees, age-range and so on could not be altered to suit the market; but assumptions had to be made about demand, that is, about the fees to be expected, which might or might not be borne out in practice. In every Scheme there was an element of guesswork and this, of course, was particularly true in the case of that unheard-of thing, a grammar school for girls.

When Latham spoke of the claim to endowment of the Camden schools he had adduced their success: '254 girls in the Upper and 286 in the Lower School'.[26] In cash terms this meant so many sets of parents willing to pay £10–15 p.a., or £4–£8 p.a. in the Lower School, to give their girls a serious education. But no one could estimate how many parents up and down the country would follow this example. The Taunton Commissioners had not tried to do so. And their view of parents as a class was so low as to give little ground for optimism. They saw rich parents as only too ready to squander money and their daughters' youth on meretricious accomplishments; the less rich slavishly following the rich; the humbler parents keeping their daughters from school on the least provocation. Parents, the Report says, 'will not pay for good teaching when they might have it . . . oppose what is not showy and attractive . . . are themselves the cause of deterioration in competent Teachers . . . their own want of cultivation hinders it in their children'.[27] What was desirable, according to one witness who favoured the advance of girls' education, was that 'the notions of the parents should be altered; and of course no legislation can do that'.[28] Yet the financial viability of endowed girls' schools depended on its being done, or at least on sufficient parents coming forward to pay fees for the new style of schooling.

Time and time again the Commissioners were told that the demand did not exist. 'This is a poor place', wrote the rector of Elland, a Yorkshire mill town, 'the manufacturers and shopkeepers are themselves quite uneducated, and while they would make a certain extra effort for their sons, in the hope that they may ultimately be of some additional assistance to themselves, would scarcely be disposed to spend £4 or £5 on the education of their daughters.'[29] Fitch found that most of the people he consulted at March, in the Fen country, felt very doubtful whether a girls' school would be a success. 'It is said that the National Schools are freely used by the lower class of tradesmen for their daughters; and that the classes above them, as soon as they can afford it, send their girls away to boarding schools.'[30] A group of Bedford residents offered the opinion that 'even if proper buildings and establishments were provided for the superior education of girls they would not be availed of by the great majority of parents having girls whose position in life required such education'.[31] While at Rishworth in Yorkshire the Wheelwright trustees asserted, 'from their long residence in and acquaintance with the neighbourhood', that any girls' school would be a failure.[32]

All these predictions were made about the time that Miss Buss's Lower School was proving itself. They were not necessarily disinterested. Yet they might be correct. Fearon, new to the West Riding, had written, 'I mistrust all the statements they make to me about the non-existence of a sufficient constituency to support a school in any place'.[33] But Assistant Commissioners had little to go on, beyond what could be picked up in the locality, and more often than not, in the case of girls, the question of demand was a question of faith. As members of the Vestry of St Martin-in-the-Fields, who saw no sign of demand for a girls' school, commented shrewdly: 'The Commissioners seem to think that the *want* exists and that if the School be supplied, the demand for it will be developed.'[34]

There was something in this. There were limits, however, to what faith could accomplish without money. Just as Robinson's Bradford Circle had come unstuck at Otley and other places with two-figure incomes, so it was impossible to graft on a girls' school where the income was low. The smallest fund which supported such a Scheme was the Kendrick Charity at Reading where the Commissioners proposed to establish third grade schools for both boys and girls on an income of only £200 p.a.

Sometimes slender resources could be stretched; for instance, if a boys' school were made co-educational.

> 'We might go much further than we do in the direction of having mixed education,' Winterbotham had pointed out in the debate on the Endowed Schools Bill. 'We have it in the primary schools, where boys and girls are educated side by side . . . It is obvious that the same building and the same teaching power in a town might very easily be made applicable to the education of girls as well as to the education of boys. This is a mode in which girls might take advantage of these endowments equally with boys, and I claim it on their behalf.'[35]

When the work of reorganisation began, the Assistant Commissioners were formally instructed 'to collect opinions as to the possibility, in Third Grade Schools at least, of introducing the plan of teaching boys and girls together'.[36] We see the fruits of this at Thornton in Yorkshire where a mixed school was established on an endowment bringing in only £120 p.a., and in a number of other places where the Scheme provided that girls might be admitted if the governors wished. Such provision was made at Rastrick, Yalding, Sowerby, Mirfield and Great Baddow – very small foundations yielding roughly £100–£200 p.a. – and also at Audley, Gillingham in Dorset and Newport in Essex, which had incomes ranging from £280 to £350 p.a. It appears too in the Giggleswick and Sedbergh Schemes, in regard to the third grade schools which were designed to serve the locality. The exact manner in which girls should be admitted – whether, for instance, in a separate department – was generally left to the discretion of the governors.

What is most marked is the social limit which the Commissioners assumed for this expedient. They proposed it only in third grade schools, that is, schools with a leaving age of fifteen, drawing their pupils from the social stratum just above that which fed the elementary schools. A number, as we see, were proposed for Yorkshire and here there was almost an indigenous tradition of mixed schooling, inasmuch as country grammar schools, as they sunk to the elementary level, had often in the past taken girls as well as boys. Fitch found this on his inspection for Taunton and he did not think much of it. The girls, in his view, gained little educationally and were often worse off than in a National School. But when such endowments came to be reorganised the presence of girl scholars seems to have created a presumption favourable to their remaining. As girls were already at the school in Thornton, 'many of them apparently of the Third Grade Class', there seemed to be no problem in making it a mixed school, Fearon was told. But opinion should be tested. 'The question is how far small tradesmen, shopkeepers and farmers will use a mixed school higher in type than an elementary school.'[37] At Dent, near Sedbergh, Fearon found seven girls on the books along with thirty-nine boys and noted, 'No harm whatever appears to arise from the admission of girls; and, with proper premises, the practice might be continued.'[38] Proper premises would have been a facer with endowment worth only £60 p.a. No Scheme was made for the grammar school at Dent and it carried on till the end of the century, undisturbed, teaching elementary subjects but also a little bit of Latin, French and Euclid to the sons and daughters of the farmers of the dales.

The Commissioners' unwillingness to consider mixed education higher up the social scale was made clear at Burnley where it spoilt their chance of doing something useful for girls. The income was £276 p.a. Their Draft Scheme envisaged a second grade boys' school with a leaving age of seventeen, and when it was published a group of Burnley ratepayers sent in a memorial drawing attention to Section 12 and asking that the grammar school 'and all its advantages may be open to Girls as well as boys'.[39] In support they urged that there were ladies still living who had been taught there, and the Scheme as it stood would 'exclude the Girls of our town from a valuable means of education formerly enjoyed'. If these views were typical the people of Burnley must have been ahead of the rest of the nation for, as we shall see, there was usually reluctance to concede a ha'p'orth of endowment to girls. In the circumstances it is rather sad to read the reply from Victoria Street. The Commissioners, committed as they were to Section 12, nonetheless decided that it would be 'inexpedient' to admit girls to Burnley Grammar School. The reason they gave was that many of the pupils 'may be expected to continue their attendance until 16 or 17 years of age'. What they offered instead was a clause to provide that something should be done for girls when there was money, either by establishing a girls' department or by means of exhibitions. They wrote in this provision and can hardly be blamed for the fact that it lay dormant for twenty-six years.

Winterbotham, the Burnley memorialists and one or two other pioneers apart, it is hard to doubt that 'the social feeling and habits of the English people' at this time, as Fitch put it, were against co-education. In 1869 when the subject had come up at a meeting of the North of England Council for Promoting the Higher Education of Women, Josephine Butler had urged its advantages, especially on the score of economy. Others, including Fitch, were more tentative. He would be glad, he said, to see 'something like the Scotch system' introduced into English Endowed Schools but he doubted if it could be done.[40] This seems to have been broadly the Commissioners' line, at any rate with schools above the third grade.

What other ways were there of stretching endowment? High expectations had been formed in the first place of money that might come to education from funds bequeathed for doles and apprentice fees, ransoms, dowries, the relief of debtors and other purposes long outmoded. Section 30 of the Act enabled such endowments to be converted for education, if the trustees were willing. Winterbotham had certainly expected that girls might benefit under this clause, as did other promoters of their claim. In June 1870 Josephine Butler quoted at a meeting of the North of England Council a letter she had received from Hobhouse warning that not too much should be expected from the readjustment of endowments where anything would be lost to boys. 'But on the side of misapplied charities he hopes, and we all hope, for a great deal.'[41] The snag, though, was needing the consent of trustees. This proviso, added in Select Committee, had considerably weakened the clause, and left the Commissioners with no better prospect than to try and nudge them in the right direction, hoping, as Lyttelton did at Wallingford, that they would consider whether a dole gift 'really confers any sensible benefit on those who receive it and on the town generally'. Conscious that their own initiative was limited, the Commissioners formally instructed their Assistants to do what they could to influence trustees, and, in advice on individual cases, usually drew attention to any local charities that looked promising.

The Kendrick boys' and girls' schools at Reading were founded entirely from a dole charity. At Kingston-on-Thames the small grammar school endowment was more than doubled by conversion of doles and this made it possible to found Tiffins Day Schools for boys and girls. At Barnet a very small grammar school endowment was supplemented by the Jesus Hospital in a Scheme which made an assignment to girls. Converted charities at Wakefield, Warwick and Stamford have already been cited as sustaining Schemes from which girls were beneficiaries. But in general the Commissioners were disappointed at the response under Section 30. Trustees did not always share their conviction that the transfer of doles to education was desirable. At Walsall, for instance, under Lyttelton's direction, Stanton spent a long time making inquiries into the prospect of converting doles from a charity so casually dispensed that he was told 'if I presented myself in the garb of a pauper I should have an equal chance with the others of receiving half a crown'.[42] But no conversion was agreed and the idea of establishing a girls' school had to be given up for the time being. Sometimes the outcome was hardly worth the effort. At Sherborne a number of charities intended for apprentice fees, bread doles and shifts for the poor were converted but produced less than £50 p.a.

The Act gave the Commissioners unprecedented powers to divide or amalgamate endowments and amalgamation was clearly one way to make the most of limited resources. This was done successfully at Keighley where the income was brought up to £336 p.a. by amalgamating Drake's and Tonson's Foundations and a girls' school was established. At Elland, on the other hand, the Commissioners' idea of combining two charities had to be abandoned since the two stood differently under the religious clauses of the Act; and this was one of the factors which contributed to nothing being done there for girls. At Beaminster it had been hoped to start a girls' school, but that was at a stage when it was also hoped to combine the foundations of Beaminster and Netherby. The Netherby headmaster was an awkward man who turned out also to have a vested interest which it would have been expensive to compensate, so the plan was given up. All things considered, the Commissioners had reason to describe the business of combining endowments as 'an operation of which the difficulty is in full proportion to its value'.[43]

In the last resort, if nothing better could be managed and there seemed to be a little money to spare the Commissioners assigned it to girls for exhibitions. £20 p.a. at Beaminster and Bideford, £40 at Shaftesbury, £50 at Lutterworth, £60 at Holbeach – but there dependent on a pension's falling in – were set aside to enable girls to proceed from elementary schools to something higher. It was a *pis aller*. As Fitch explained to trustees at Wells, the Commissioners were anxious 'not to leave girls out of sight in the arrangements for Endowed Schools, but in this case they feel that the endowment will not suffice for two schools. They do not see any better plan than . . . to apply a certain sum in providing exhibitions.'[44] Providing them was one thing. Where they could be held was another matter in the early seventies and for many years ahead. The predicament of a Lincolnshire charity some years later illustrates the problem. The governors had only filled one exhibition:

> It was held by a girl who first went to a school at Wallingford where her brother was Clerk in a Bank; then at Carshalton where her sister was married to a gardener; and lastly at the High School, Oxford, to which place her brother moved from Wallingford. On her brother leaving Oxford and going to Banbury she had to resign the Exhibition. She is now at home. The Governors think there is no chance of appointing Exhibitioners till the Girls' School at Lincoln is established.[45]

There were great practical difficulties, then, in admitting girls to a share in endowment. The Commissioners, looking back upon their first two years, draw attention to the problem arising 'when, as in the vast majority of instances, an Endowment is actually enjoyed by boys' schools, and is not more than enough for the local needs of male education'.[46] But they are not defeatist. On the contrary, they have, they say, 'gladly' taken every opportunity of extending endowment to girls.

Much the same points were made by Lyttelton in June 1872 at a meeting promoted by the National Union for Improving the Higher Education of Women. The Act was complex, he told his Albert Hall audience, and the Commissioners could not move so fast as they would like to, but he left no doubt of their sustained belief in the importance and 'righteousness' of making an endowment contribution to girls; indeed, 'he argued forcibly in favour of giving a liberal education to the women of this country, of whom many were obliged to support themselves by their own intellectual exertions'.[47]

His had become a familiar presence wherever such sentiments were publicly acknowledged. In or out of Victoria Street he was the constant ally of the pioneers; 'a friend when friends were few', as one of them said later.[48] It was Lyttelton who had presided at the public meeting held in St Pancras ('one of the very first public meetings concerning the education of girls')[49] to launch Miss Buss's Lower School; he was in the chair at the Society of Arts to inaugurate Maria Grey's National Union and now again, in the Albert Hall, to launch her brainchild, sponsored by the Union, the Girls' Public Day School Company. Through Lyttelton's influence the Union had the prestige of a Royal President, the Princess Louise, and the Company the prestige of a noble council member, his daughter, Lady Frederick Cavendish. Girls' education was something he believed in and would do everything to assist – or all but one thing: he would not take shares in Maria Grey's Girls' Public Day School Company, highly as he esteemed its object, on account of scruples which prevented him from ever becoming a shareholder.[50]

Luckily others had a different view. Fitch, who seems also to be found on every platform where girls' education is promoted, was one of the first to take shares in the Company. And in other ways the Endowed Schools Commission gave it a helping hand at the start. The scheme for the Company's first school, in Chelsea, which was to be the prototype of so many more, was sent by order of Princess Louise to Victoria Street for Canon Robinson's comments. He wrote back at length to Maria Grey about it, ending with good wishes for the success of her venture which, he said, 'will . . . supply a great want. I should be very glad if we could help you with endowments in the form of Exhibitions or otherwise.'[51]

Another enterprise in women's education – the founding of Girton – drew support from these men. Roby had been involved from the first with Emily Davies in the college at Hitchin, helping to draft its constitution, design its scheme of studies, set its entrance papers and stock its library. Now, in the midst of his official duties, he gave enormous help over the move to Girton.[52] Lyttelton and Fitch took part also in the necessary fund-raising campaign and Fitch from the first was on the governing body.

It was therefore something more than a matter of words when Lyttelton, in answer to a memorial about girls' education from a small provincial town, added to the formal acknowledgement assurance that the Commissioners were bound by the Act, 'not less than prompted by their own convictions', to do what they could to get endowment for girls.[53] And they had great need of such convictions. For lack of money was not the only thing which hindered the working of Section 12. There was considerable opposition to it.

4. Opponents

Hewers of wood and drawers of water would still be wanted, and in properly educating such to gain their living by their honest labour . . . Emanuel Hospital is fulfilling its proper function in the work of education.

Emanuel Hospital trustees, 1871[1]

No one denies that providing for the education of girls is a desirable object; but why is it to be done at the expense of the education of boys?

Unsigned pamphlet, 1873[2]

Robbing the poor

'The state of strong prejudice in the public mind' struck Maria Grey as a formidable obstacle to all the efforts made to get endowment for girls[3] and the Commissioners themselves admitted that nothing met with less support from trustees. Amongst 'disinterested persons,' said Robinson, there was a strong conviction that more should be done for girls' education out of endowment; 'but amongst those who have to manage individual endowments there is a feeling that their particular endowment ought to be exempted from the liability'.[4] Trustees 'seem to have a preference for boys,' Roby said.[5] And we shall see how they expressed it. But before that it is worth considering how girls were involved in a wider conflict arising from the operation of the Act: the struggle which accompanied middle-class encroachment on the rights of the poor in the old foundations.

By the middle of the nineteenth century, it was not necessary to recall that Eton had been founded for 'indigent' scholars to see that grammar school endowment had a tendency to move in the direction of the better-off. The years just before the Endowed Schools Act was passed showed this plainly.[6] In 1868, following the proposals of the Clarendon Commission, the Public Schools Act released Harrow and Rugby from what had become a contentious obligation to take local boys free. A few years earlier King Edward VI Free School at Berkhamsted was authorised by Chancery to take fee-payers and limit free scholars to a maximum of fifty, roughly one-third of what the founder had required. In 1867 Manchester Grammar School was enabled to meet the demand of wealthy citizens and take fee-payers. There were many such cases. Grammar schools, especially in small towns like Berkhamsted, had found themselves on the horns of a dilemma, required by the terms of the original foundation to do two things which were no longer compatible: take free scholars and teach the classics. Victorian Berkhamsted could not produce anything approaching 144 boys to come as foundationers and learn Greek and Latin. There was local demand for a commercial education, but that would have destroyed the standing of the grammar school; and there were parents outside Berkhamsted ready to pay boarding fees for classical teaching; but to take their sons in preference to foundationers would have contravened the terms of the charter. It was left to Chancery to unravel this knot, releasing the school, and others like it, to soar aloft into the public school class, but leaving the town with a good deal of bitterness and the feeling of having been robbed.

'When the King orders that there shall be a *free* grammar school for the youth of Sherborne for ever, is it lawful . . . that strangers shall be admitted . . . and that Sherbornians should be asked to pay £20 a year for admission?'[7] This was said in protest, not against Chancery, but against the Scheme the Endowed Schools Commissioners drafted for Sherborne in 1870. For their Taunton inheritance supplied them with a stronger and far more coherent ideology antipathetic to free education than anything current in the Charity Commission or the Court of Chancery which had settled such cases before the Endowed Schools Act was passed. 'A free grammar school is an anachronism', Fitch said.[8] He had seen too many in Yorkshire which were grammar schools only in name, dragged down by indiscriminate free education to something barely of National School level. The Commissioners, then, applied the Taunton principle that free education could only be admitted when it was given as the reward of merit; in effect, when foundation scholars were selected on examination. In some schools this meant the introduction of fees for the first time. In others, such as Sherborne and Giggleswick, there were fees already but the school was striving to shake itself free of local foundationers, as the great public schools had done. The new Schemes made this possible and, despite protesters who 'did not see much difference between the midnight burglar and the School Commissioner',[9] the Commissioners themselves had no doubt that they were right.

What has this to do with the claims of girls? Schemes from one angle, as we have seen, were an exercise in book-keeping: the more that was paid in, the more there was to pay out; introducing or raising fees made the admission of new claims possible. This was particularly obvious at Cambridge where the Perse School was endowed for a hundred foundationers who were required to pay only a few shillings and where the possibility of starting a girls' school was linked to a very substantial increase. Dr Perse, said one opponent of the change, had left his money to assist poor boys. Was the new proposal

> part of the progress of which they had heard so much? Because if it was he thought it would be as well if they had no progress. This was the fruit of a Liberal Parliament, elected as much as any for the protection of the rights of the poor. He thought they had gone too far at least in laying their hands on the Perse School. Then, the Commissioners propose, out of the surplus of the fees . . . to establish a girls' school.[10]

He went on to talk of 'robbery of the rights of the poor boys of Cambridge' and indeed the school had been described by Richmond, in his days as an Assistant Commissioner for Taunton, as 'of great benefit to the town and a means by which many boys, sons of comparatively illiterate parents, are advanced to the University'.[11]

The most dramatic imposition of fees was at Bedford, where the Harpur Foundation had provided free schooling on a scale unequalled anywhere in England. Bedford had come to be colonised by 'squatters' – widows and half-pay officers drawn there to claim what was described to the Taunton Commission as 'a supposed birthright to educational alms'. The Endowed Schools Commissioners debated very earnestly whether they ought to impose fees in Bedford – one might even say, whether they *dared* – for Roby seems almost to have had cold feet; but Lyttelton stood fast against contravention of what he called 'one of our General Principles';[12] and certainly, to abandon it at Bedford would have been equivalent to Edwin Chadwick's deciding to renege on the Workhouse Test. Apart from that, the arithmetic here pointed in the same direction as at Cambridge. This colossally rich endowment, the Taunton Commissioners had been informed, was strained to breaking point by free education. 'The time must soon come when some class must pay fees . . . Such an increase of means would allow of other extensions of the education . . . Chief among these would be a school for girls.'[13] The Commissioners drew up a Scheme on these lines. 'If Dukes, Lords, MPs and Gentlemen in this County want a Collage for young ladies, let them subscribe and build one', wrote one man bitterly.[14] But the Harpur Foundation was reformed nonetheless to carry two girls' schools.

The poor were 'robbed' in another way at Bedford. As we saw in the previous chapter, the Scheme assigned to education all but one eleventh of the Harpur funds, cutting down sharply on the eleemosynary purposes which had hitherto been met and confirming beyond doubt the outcome of a battle between schools and alms which had raged in Bedford for more than twenty years. Where doles were converted to education – and in some cases conversion made it possible for a girls' school to be established – there were usually objections on behalf of the poor. The girls' school at Kingston came out of a Scheme which, as the Kingston Vestry objected, proposed 'to apply for the benefit of the middle classes the entire income of Charities which were, for the most part, left for the benefit of the poor'.[15] The Working Men's Liberal Association at Reading complained that converting the Kendrick Charities to provide middle-class boys' and girls' schools was 'robbing the poor' and pleaded that 'Class', in the phrase 'Middle Class', be struck from the Scheme, since 'we think it not improbable that at some future time these schools may be claimed for children of the middle class only, to the exclusion of the poor and working classes'.[16]

The interests of the poor, too, were often invoked when it was proposed to use for secondary school purposes funds which had hitherto maintained elementary schools. The Commissioners' Scheme for a girls' school at Ambleside was denounced by their principal opponent as 'a robbery of funds left solely for the poor'.[17] The same cry arose at St Helens in Lancashire. Fearon began by explaining at a meeting the proposals to use the Cowley Foundation to provide secondary schools for both sexes. He pointed out that Section 12 bound the Commissioners to extend the benefits of endowment to girls 'so far as conveniently may be,' adding that, 'if ever there was a case in which convenience could be established, this is one. If secondary education is to be extended to girls at all this is as clear a case as could possibly be.'[18] His views were apparently well received. The local paper praised him for his tact and courtesy. Then everything changed. A movement got up to resist 'the PRESENT FOUL ATTEMPT to spoliate the Funds of the Trust and to Deprive the Children of the Poor, and the Artizan Classes, of the Present Cowley Schools.'[19] At Newcastle-under-Lyme a public meeting castigated the Commissioners' proposal to provide girls' and boys' secondary schools as 'an outrageous scheme of plunder' since they would supplant the elementary school hitherto maintained on Orme's Foundation. It was 'most infamous and dishonest, and savoured much of a den of thieves'.[20] In response to the trustees' objection 'that the great working class to whom an elementary education would be the greatest boon are ignored', and to complaints from the School Board and inhabitants, the Commissioners made a substantial assignment for elementary schools. On a Scheme which proposed that Sarah Bonnell's Charity in West Ham should in future support 'a good middle class girls' school, not an elementary school', Latham advised that 'it will be expedient to make some concession to the cry of robbing the poor';[21] and he was right: the vicar and churchwardens protested against the charity being used in this way.

It was Latham who persuaded the trustees of Roan's Charity that their function to provide elementary schools in Greenwich had been superseded by the passing of the Elementary Education Act and that they should establish for boys and girls schools of 'a somewhat higher type'. Support for this view came from Emily Davies who, as one of three members of the London School Board speaking at a public meeting in Greenwich, turned the familiar defence of 'the poor' to embrace those 'who would be thought the poorest of all – widows of professional men with small incomes, having children whose education they could less afford to pay for than many working men could for theirs . . . The "poor girl," ' she said, 'had also claims to be remembered, as one more difficult to provide education for than the poor boy.' She was very glad that the girls were noticed by the Commissioners, and hoped they would not be forgotten by the parishioners.[22]

The passing of the Elementary Education Act reinforced feeling for the interests of the poor with feeling for the interests of the ratepayers. As we saw, the vicar and parishioners of Aldenham were very anxious to avoid a School Board and urged the prior claims of their elementary schools to that surplus of the Platt endowment which the Scheme directed mainly to the North London Collegiate. The girls' endowment here was also at risk from a similar claim made by the people of Bushey while yet another came from the vicar of Frogmore who asked for help towards meeting the requirements which the Education Act imposed on his parish.

For the town of March in Cambridgeshire a School Board had already been elected and its chairman, who was also a Charity trustee, led a determined and successful struggle to get a substantial capital assignment as well as an income for the elementary schools. His opponents claimed that he was saving the rates. Whether or no, he resisted strongly the idea of establishing a grammar school for girls and did not hesitate to threaten the Commissioners that unless the elementary school money was forthcoming, 'the Trustees would pass a similar resolution to that of the School Board declaring that in their opinion a "Girls Grammar School" . . . is not required and that it . . . would not be in accordance with the Founders' desires to benefit "the poor" & etc. of the Parish of March'.[23] The upshot was that the original proposal for a girls' school in March was watered down to the mere possibility of providing one 'as soon as practicable' after three years from the date of the Scheme.

There were varied reasons, then, for championing the poor. But of all who did so none claimed better right than the trustees of the Hospital Schools; and indeed it was in 1871, in the fight against the Scheme for Emanuel Hospital, that 'robbing the poor' became a call to arms. Such was the publicity surrounding this battle, such the resources of the City Corporation in canvassing support that all over England attitudes hardened against the Act: in Bedford the trustees of the Harpur Foundation dropped their Scheme like a hot potato just at the point where it had almost been settled; in Newcastle-under-Lyme defenders of the poor 'wished they had Lord Salisbury to stand up for them' as he did for Emanuel.

The Hospital Schools, hybrids of poor relief and education, were the embodiment of every principle which was repugnant to the Taunton Commission. Their governing bodies were narrow and exclusive; they not only taught but clothed and housed children, thereby entirely relieving parents of all expense and responsibility; and worse, admissions were made through patronage, 'at the whim of trustees' and not uncommonly from the children of their servants; intellectual merit did not come into it. On this basis, at Emanuel Hospital, only sixty-four children were supported on an income of £2000 p.a.

From the Taunton point of view this was scandalous, and the Commissioners were barely installed in Victoria Street before they set about making a change. Looking broadly at the Westminster endowments they proposed Schemes whereby Emanuel Hospital, and the comparable Greycoat Hospital, would support large day schools in Westminster as well as boarding schools in the suburbs. Fees would be charged and gratuitous schooling confined to exhibitioners selected on merit.

The outcry was tremendous. Emanuel Hospital might have been endowed to shelter the weak but it was governed by the very powerful. The Lord Mayor and Aldermen did not take kindly to this challenge to their authority and, as Roby put it later, the City solicitor 'sounded the tocsin'. Circulars were sent out to governors of endowed schools and municipal bodies all over England enclosing forms for petitions to Parliament. The press joined the battle. City Members were lobbied and the Schemes were thrown out in the House of Lords where Lyttelton's defence of the principle of merit was no match for Lord Salisbury's picture of the Hospital endowed by Lady Dacre 'to feed the hungry, to clothe the naked and to educate the poor'.

Two very different views of the poor emerge. To Salisbury, talk of promotion on merit is 'a kind of jargon' and he sees the poor as 'those who [are] unable to help themselves'.[24] To the Commissioners the best of the poor can and should help themselves; what they require is an exhibitions ladder, by means of which, as Roby told the Greycoat trustees, 'some even of the poorest class may (if industrious) rise out of the primary schools into a higher region of education'.[25] On the one hand we have the trustees' picture of Emanuel Hospital properly devoted to 'hewers of wood and drawers of water'; on the other, urged in support of the Scheme, the Lord Chancellor's vision of a hierarchy rising 'from the elementary schools to the Universities'.[26] From that standpoint, as he explained, poor children meant those who wanted better education. 'Those who exerted themselves,' said Lyttelton.[27] Emanuel children were not called on to do *that*, entering on 'a quiet, soporific existence' within the Hospital, according to *The Times*, with the prospect of a small gratuity on leaving and the more remote prospect, for which they learned to pray, of meeting the Lord Mayor and Aldermen in Heaven.[28]

Times had changed, Roby told the Greycoat trustees; the spirit of independence was spreading 'and in all classes . . . there is a greater disposition to accept nothing as a favour which can be claimed as a right; and to open the roads of advancement to those who prove themselves likely to use them'.[29] In this last group the Endowed Schools Commissioners were ready to include girls and nothing makes plainer the contrast between them and the Hospital trustees. In the debate on the Emanuel Scheme, Salisbury, apparently unconscious of irony, had claimed the trustees were in advance of their time: 'for they had long seen the advantages of female education, and the Court of Aldermen were among the few – the very few – trustees of schools in this country who have not forgotten the girls'.[30] There were certainly girls at Emanuel, educated, as in every Hospital School, to make good servants.

'A girl', wrote Fitch sardonically, 'is not expected to serve God in Church or State, and is therefore not invited to the University or the grammar school; but she may, if poor, be wanted to contribute to the comfort of her "betters" as an apprentice or servant, and the charity schools are therefore open to her.'[31] Though there were one or two – notably Christ's Hospital – which gave a first-class education to boys, none of them extended it to female children.

The struggle to reorganise the Greycoat Hospital shows what the Commissioners were up against. Numbers there were much as at Emanuel: sixty-six boys and thirty girls. The Commissioners proposed that Emanuel Hospital should support a system of boys' schools and Greycoat a system of schools for girls, catering for that 'vast number of persons within reach of [Westminster], artizans, clerks, keepers of small shops, [who] stand in need of but do not find good secondary education'.[32] As at Emanuel there was great resentment that the old order should be challenged – the trustees included the the Duke of Buccleuch, the Dean of Westminster and the Archbishop of Dublin – and the same clash between what might be called the static and dynamic view of the poor, but sharpened here because girls were in question. Greycoat boys at least learnt algebra, Euclid, mensuration and Roman history as well as the three Rs; they were the sons of artisans but many of them, as Roby discovered, went on from the Hospital to clerical jobs. Greycoat girls had elementary education but worked in the Hospital's kitchen and laundry, the main object being, as the trustees explained, 'to fit them for domestic servants'. The trustees could not contemplate betraying their trust to the poor of the parish of St Margaret, Westminster, by establishing a fee-paying day school there and a fee-paying boarding school outside London in place of the free institution of the Hospital. But nor could they contemplate that in such schools girls would learn science and a modern language; that women should sit upon the governing body; that the headmistress should be given such powers as to make her 'almost irresponsible'. What the Hospital had offered poor girls was 'seclusion from the unfavourable influences of their crowded homes'[33] and a future in service; what the Commissioners wanted it to offer was a way in – free – for the cleverest poor to a secondary school and a chance at fifteen to go on from there with a leaving exhibition to 'a place for the Higher Education of women'.[34]

After their Schemes for Emanuel and Greycoat had been rejected by the House of Lords the Commissioners rewrote them, reducing the fees and increasing the proportion of free places available to orphans and poor children in St Margaret's, Westminster. In 1873, after further opposition, the Schemes went through. Had the poor been robbed? The later history of the Greycoat School contributes to both sides in the debate. It is certainly true that by the end of the century it had become predominantly middle class; but its scholarship system gave free entry to a school which sent girls to the university.

All over England the Hospital interest resisted ambitious education for girls. At Rishworth in Yorkshire the Wheelwright trustees, though willing for their boys to learn Greek and Latin, proposed that 'the course of education in the Girls' School shall be such as will fit the Scholars for their probable future positions in life'.[35] What they expected these to be is shown by the fact that the girls' school curriculum included helping with domestic chores. At Exeter, the Commissioners' proposals for reform, which involved extinguishing the free education enjoyed by twenty-five Blue Coat boys, provoked the customary defence of the poor. 'The tree of charity is to be stripped of its . . . orphans and children of impoverished parents, in order that a few "monster goosberries", a few intellectual prodigies, may be grown and nurtured upon exhibitions.'[36] But there was also indignation that some of the endowment of St John's Hospital would go to establishing a high school for girls or, as its opponents significantly termed it, 'a ladies college'. 'Who will say that Ladies Colleges and "exhibitions for Ladies' Colleges", such as the Commissioners would create out of the confiscated funds, can compare with the benefits conferred upon society by [charity schools]?' At least two men said it: the Mayor of Exeter and its Bishop, Frederick Temple. Temple, who had argued the same case strongly in the Lords during the Emanuel debate, pointed out how few of Exeter's children benefited from the Hospital School. As for girls, it could scarcely be maintained 'that the middle classes, from the shopkeepers upwards, do not need efficient schooling for their girls, as well as for their boys', nor that this was inconsistent 'with the purpose of a Foundation which aims at the good of the citizens generally'.[37] The Mayor said opposition to the girls' school was short-sighted. 'There is no want that has been so seriously felt as that of adequate education for girls of every station of life.' Many men had risen through charity schooling. But while they had been 'placed on the road to fortune' girls had been condemned to domestic service or a limited range of female occupations.[38] The Commissioners got their girls' high school at Exeter, with funds assigned from the Hospital endowment, but at Bristol they failed, defeated in the end by the absolute refusal of the Charity trustees to do anything ambitious for girls.

They were themselves ambitious in their plans for Bristol. Right at the start, the missionary zeal which led them to bite off more than they could chew in Bradford and Westminster focussed on a city so richly endowed that funds for a *system* of secondary schools really did exist there. There were three great Hospitals: Queen Elizabeth's, Colston's and Red Maids', as well as the grammar school. The total income was well over £14,000 p.a., a very different thing from the scrappy little funds on which Robinson tried to base his Bradford Circle. With such resources the Commissioners began by working out how many schools Bristol needed. This they did quite systematically, using, for boys, the Taunton estimate of sixteen places per thousand population; and for girls, since no one had ever thought of estimating, making up their own minds on twelve per thousand. They next drew up a Schedule to show how the endowments, combined together and augmented by fees (for free education would be abolished) could provide the bulk of what was needed.[39] Instead of supporting three elementary schools the Hospital funds could be stretched to sustain nine secondary schools of various grades, four of them for girls. This meticulous Schedule, a more precise exercise in bureaucratic planning than had become familiar in 1870 for elementary, let alone for secondary schools, landed on a city already up in arms and was shot to pieces.

From the moment, months before, when Fitch had first gone there as Assistant Commissioner to open up discussions on a possible Scheme, Bristol had been frantic for its Hospital Schools. The Commissioners' plans, said the *Western Daily Press*, would 'take away the breath of Old Bristolians . . . These old citizens, familiar in their boyhood as in their manhood with the quaint dresses of the children in our three great Hospital Schools, will find it difficult to believe that these schools are on the eve of dissolution'.[40] 'Breach of faith with the dead and with the living' ran one headline, in reference to a promise

Forster was supposed to have given the trustees that they had nothing
to fear from the Endowed Schools Act.[41] There was more at stake
than the children's quaint dresses. The proposal to do away with free
education was of course completely unacceptable. But by the same
token the trustees opposed any raising of the Hospitals out of their
sphere. Thus, they did not want the grammar school endowment and
Hospital endowments to form a common fund. Each should be distinct, 'to secure their development within the limits of the classes for
whom they were intended'.[42] They did not want Queen Elizabeth's
Hospital to support a second grade boys' school, as suggested; third
grade was the limit for the Hospital Schools. And above all,
they opposed absolutely the idea of setting up a high school for
girls.

In the Explanations which accompanied their Schedule the Commissioners had enlarged on the school they had in mind. They
envisaged it as something like Cheltenham Ladies' College, catering
for the sisters of the grammar school boys with English, French,
German, Latin, maths., and science, 'besides the usual studies appropriate to a girls' school of the highest class'. They toyed with the idea
of calling it the Queen's School, a name 'which associates it at once
with Queen Elizabeth's Hospital, from which it will derive its
revenue; with Queen's College in London, which it may hope to
emulate; and with the Sovereign in whose reign this great reform has
been enacted'. The trustees utterly demolished this dream. A deputation protested in London that there was no need to provide instruction 'adapted to the sisters of boys now in the Grammar School'.[43]
References to Section 12 did not move them. They would have none
of it. The Commissioners, then, included in their Draft Scheme
eventual provision for a girls' high school, proposing meanwhile to
assign £200 p.a. to girls. The trustees said there was no money for
this. The Commissioners replied that they did not believe it, listing
the resources available in Bristol. In revising their Scheme they had
by now conceded that the grammar school should be kept apart from
the Hospitals; but they proposed that both should contribute substan-
tially towards the provision of a high school. The trustees then
adopted the position from which they never budged as the affair
dragged on: the grammar school, they said, could not spare the
endowment; on the other hand, to alienate Hospital money was not 'a
proper application of funds left for the poor'. At the time they said
this they were themselves proposing to 'alienate' thousands from an

old loan charity – Peloquin's – under Section 30 of the Act, for the benefit of the grammar school. Logically, their view was indefensible. But then, they did not need logic to defend it. The conversion of funds under Section 30 was only possible with their consent.

The struggle over Bristol spanned the whole five years of the Commissioners' term of office and in the end they had to settle for much less than had been envisaged in their Schedule. It was true that the Scheme for Queen Elizabeth's and Red Maids' established three girls' schools and three for boys, while another girls' school and two for boys were established by the Scheme for Colston's. But the Hospitals survived; and it had had to be conceded that a large number of foundation scholars should be clothed, maintained and educated free. Apart from that there was the great disappointment of failing to establish, in a major city, exceptionally well endowed, a high school for girls.

With hindsight it is very easy to see that the ideas of the trustees and the Commissioners simply did not meet when it came to girls. Even as the debate was going on, the 'poor women children' for whom Red Maids' had been founded spent their Saturdays doing housework. They generally left for domestic service and the trustees saw nothing outmoded in proposing, in their own Draft Scheme for the school, that they should leave with marriage portions. Talk of 'the sisters of the Grammar School Boys', of Section 12, of 'the great disproportion . . . existing between the Endowments in Bristol applicable to boys' education and those applicable to girls' was talk in a foreign tongue; unintelligible. The trustees answered that they could not consent, 'with due regard to their obligations', to alienate funds from Red Maids' Hospital for a 'higher class'; that they failed to recognise 'either the principle or the justice' of girls having half the Peloquin money which they wished to divert to the grammar school. 'We are not as a body very favourable', they said, 'to establishing these schools for girls'.[44] And there they spoke for every Hospital in England.

The Bristol trustees did not hurry themselves to carry out the requirements of the Scheme. Ten years later the Red Maids' day school had still to be started while the Maids themselves continued to delight the eye of Old Bristolians. 'Their walking out', wrote Stanton in the eighties, 'was a solemn and picturesque affair, and the street was hushed and the traffic suspended to witness the mediaeval pageant of 80 maids in scarlet frocks and an open tippet of snow-white linen, two and two in slow procession passing across a thorough-fare.'[45]

Robbing the boys

The fierce hostility the Commissioners met in Bristol arose not only from their threat to the Hospitals but from what was seen as their threat to the grammar school. This was the darling of the Charity trustees, 'a credit to the City', and not to be impoverished by hiving off part of its endowment for girls. On the contrary, it was to be enriched by converting funds from the Peloquin Charity so that it could have buildings and equipment to stand comparison with those at Clifton.

The prestige of Bristol Grammar School had suffered from a Chancery ruling in 1860 which disallowed boarders and, two years later, from the foundation of Clifton College. In this context, the Commissioners' insistence that money be contributed towards a girls' school, regarded by themselves as no more than fulfilling 'the plain requirement of Section 12', seemed to the trustees to mark a 'strongly hostile animus' towards the school in which they took so much pride.[46]

Even those who professed some sympathy with the principle of Section 12 usually feared to 'injure', 'jeopardise' – even to 'cripple' – a particular boys' school. 'The principle of girls' education is approved of', wrote the governors of Bradford Grammar School, 'but they consider it of much more importance to have a first rate boys' school and until that is established would prefer not to *cripple* the funds.'[47] The *Mansfield Reporter*, expressing regret that provision of a girls' school was postponed, added, 'to have *crippled* the resources of the Boys' School would not have met with the approval of . . . the public; the want most felt . . . is a high class school for boys'.[48] The trustees at Borden claimed that, while ready 'at the request of the Commissioners' to devote £50 p.a. to girls, they had 'never agreed to *cripple* the ultimate success of the Boys' School'.[49] Loyalty of this kind was not diminished by the fact that no boys' school yet existed. Funds to provide one had become available and in their mind's eye the Borden trustees were already building it a chapel. From Gillingham in Dorset came a similar response. Here, too, new funds were being used and the trustees, 'whilst admitting in the abstract the desirability of providing . . . for girls', feared to jeopardise the future of the boys' school, 'the success of which they had so much at heart'.[50] For good measure, the Commissioners were assured that there was no demand for a girls' school anyway. Round Gillingham, it seemed, 'the population [was] widely scattered and the roads in winter dirty'; at Borden, it was said, 'the better class of Farmers', for whose sons a grammar school was needed, would not make use of such a school for their daughters; in Mansfield, the social mixture would be shunned, for 'those parents who may be so desirous of giving their daughters a . . . refined education will also make their selection of the persons with whom they would place them'.[51]

'None were enthusiastic; most of them reserved, some hostile', wrote Stanton of the Stourbridge governors. 'They desired, they said, before all things to promote the interests of the Grammar School, and required that those interests should be fully provided for before considering the wants of girls' education.'[52] To this end they proposed that the Scheme should make clear that the 'efficient conduct and maintenance' of the grammar school for boys took precedence over the girls' assignment; a 'dangerous concession', as Stanton told Lyttelton, since it could very easily result in wiping out the money for girls altogether.[53]

The fact was, there had probably never been a time when it was harder to set a limit to the needs of the grammar schools, or seemed less 'convenient', in the sense of Section 12, for them to lose endowment. The status of many of them was precarious. Bristol, as we saw, was overhung by Clifton College. At Mansfield, the grammar school had been in abeyance for some years and was about to reopen. The trustees spoke of buildings to be built and debts to be paid and were quite unwilling to consider any assignment to girls 'before the boys' school is in full working order'. Similarly, at Ashby-de-la-Zouch, the grammar school had been going downhill but was now to have new buildings and Fitch was asked that any obligation to girls might be postponed till it was 'fairly started in the new premises'. At Pocklington an initial disposition to 'admit of the fairness' of providing for girls disappeared when both trustees and inhabitants became involved in fighting for first grade status. That their school should be second grade, as proposed, seemed to them entirely unworthy. Could it not lay claim to four exhibitions at St John's College, Cambridge? Did it not teach Greek? Had not 'the illustrious Wilberforce' studied underneath the great elms in the playground? Between such a past and the future they envisaged for a high-class boarding school there was no room for girls. '£200 p.a. would be better used for paying the Headmaster a larger salary and for providing for Assistant Masters.'[54]

They appealed vigorously against a clause 'which gives nearly one-sixth . . . of the whole income to purposes alien to the wish of the Founder and distasteful to . . . the inhabitants generally', asking that it should be held in abeyance, 'at least while the School is being first formed'.[55] When the Commissioners conceded this they were still dissatisfied. Further appeals were sent to the Education Department and gained what amounted to indefinite deferment.

The Commissioners' experience with Berkhamsted Grammar School shows how hard it was to force a new claim on a school poised between a difficult past and the wide horizons which seemed to lie ahead. In 1864 it had been taken in hand by Dr Bartrum, a forceful headmaster who set it on the upward road for the first time since the middle of the eighteenth century. Twenty years or so before he was appointed the school had emerged from a hundred years in Chancery; a Hundred Years War, it might well have been called, between headmasters and the locality. The next big step had been that Bartrum's predecessor, perceiving that the future of a country grammar school could never be great if it were tied to the district, petitioned for reduction of the number of free scholars and for authority to take in boarders. Despite strong opposition from the town this was approved in 1865. The way was now clear for the promotion of a public school and Bartrum was just the man to direct it: an able, energetic 'building' headmaster, extremely conscious of the school's deficiencies and always ready to pop up to London to urge on the Commissioners the need for a Scheme which should make it worthy of its endowment. To him and to the governors it was an outrage that the draft when it came made an annual assignment of about one-fifth of the income to girls. To be asked to give up some £300 p.a.! It was, they pointed out, 'their bounden duty' to make the boys' school thoroughly efficient, 'and to do this will require a sum of money so large that it will be impossible to spare any income for a considerable time'.[56] Later they specified the need for 'such appliances as . . . most good schools now possess viz. Chemistry Laboratory, covered tepid swimming bath, Fives Court, Carpenters Shop and Smithy, Reading Room and Library, Museum, gymnasium'.[57] All these things, and an infirmary too, were possessed by the new Bedford Middle School, wrote Bartrum. '*We have not one of them.* We have been looking forward for years to some such additions and had hoped the Commissioners would have assisted us in attaining them.' Like the Stourbridge trustees he wanted the Scheme to guarantee that everything would be done 'to make the

School thorough, attractive and efficient before any portion of the income is abstracted to establish a girls' school'. He did not object, he said, to aiding girls eventually, when funds were sufficient, 'but I think we ought to be just to the boys before we are generous to the girls'.[58]

Dr Bartrum's sense of justice was stronger than his arithmetic. At least, as the Assistant Commissioner noticed, he did not trouble to include tuition fees on the credit side of the accounts he forwarded when pleading poverty. The argument dragged on. Early in November 1874 the Commissioners saw three deputations from Berkhamsted. And then the whole thing was overtaken by events. The following month brought the end of the Commission. But not of Dr Bartrum. Ten years later he was still fighting for the needs of the grammar school, blandly facing the Commissioners' successors with what he called his 'motto': 'Be just to the boys . . .' And it was not until 1887 that the Endowed Schools Commissioners' efforts bore late fruit in terms of money for a girls' school.

On their disbandment, in 1874, reviewing five years spent on Dr Bartrum, Bristol, Emanuel and a host of others, they expressed regret that their success with Section 12 had not been greater. It required, they said 'much firmness of purpose' to give effect here to the intentions of Parliament.[59]

5. Supporters

To the Ladies, I may say a parting word. I have exposed myself to adverse criticisms, if not obloquy, for venturing to advocate the claims of the female sex to a share in the Endowment. I accept it cheerfully, feeling confident of your moral support and sympathy, and backed in my opinion by many of the most eminent writers on Education, and distinguished advocates of the progressive enlightenment of all classes of the English Community.

Mr Carey Tyso, Wallingford, 1871[1]

Trustees and townspeople

As we know the outcome, there is something poignant in the high hopes, not to say ideals, with which the Commissioners began their work. They had no reason to fear publicity, Hobhouse told Fitch in the spring of 1870 when the Bristol case was just under way, 'on the contrary they will look to the public to support an enactment which brings them great benefits'.[2] Of the Bristol public it can only be said that they stopped short of burning Fitch in effigy. Of the rest, that by the following year Lyttelton had sunk to the weary hope that 'the time would come when they should cease to be called plunderers';[3] two years more, and their opponents taunted that the Commission was 'on its death-bed';[4] and the year after, these words came true. At the end of December 1874 the Endowed Schools Commission was disbanded, 'slain by the force of public opinion'.[5]

Allowance can be made for the histrionic language used by their opponents but there seems no doubt that the Commissioners were very unpopular. Almost any local newspaper confirms it. When Dr Thring, the headmaster of Uppingham, spoke of 'these powerful and practised red-tapists . . . matched against poor me'[6] he voiced the anxiety of all who feared to lose by reorganisation. But girls stood to gain. And while the Commissioners themselves were mainly conscious of how hard it was to drum up support for Section 12, they did get some. It can hardly be quantified – indeed, it is probably overstated – by looking, as we do, simply at cases where some measure of success was achieved. But it is possible to glimpse the kind of people who were prepared, in the early seventies, to back the advance of girls' education.

Here and there a trustee emerges who is actually enthusiastic about it. Charles Roundell was one. In the early seventies Roundell was secretary to the Cleveland Commission inquiring into university finances. Before that his radical sympathies found vent in work as private secretary to Gladstone, negotiating over the Irish Church; as secretary to the Commission of Inquiry into the handling of revolt in Jamaica; above all, as leader of the agitation among college Fellows in Oxford and Cambridge for the repeal of religious Tests.[7] Roundell came from Yorkshire. As a governor of Giggleswick he had appeared before the Taunton Commission; from 1870 he took a leading part in the making of the Giggleswick Scheme and showed much interest in the assignment of funds towards establishing a girls' school at Skipton. At the London end, in 1872 he was one of Maria Grey's supporters when she launched her Girls Public Day School Company. Roundell became the first chairman of its council and one of its first parents – his daughters attended the Company's pioneer school in Chelsea. At the same time, as a governor of Dulwich, he strongly backed the Commissioners' efforts to get a girls' high school on that foundation. 'I succeeded yesterday at Dulwich beyond expectations', he wrote to Lyttelton, explaining that the girls' school proposal had been carried.

> When therefore the Scheme again comes before you, you will find that we are prepared to establish a thoroughly equipped first-rate School for Girls. I am anxious to mention this, and especially the favour with which our Governors regard the proposal, because a unique opportunity is thus offered for establishing a School which may be a model for others, though perhaps no other Foundation can offer such pecuniary means. I shall not be afraid of asking for any sum, however large, which may be necessary for carrying out thoroughly this proposal.[8]

Roundell's chairman of governors at Giggleswick was Sir James Kay-Shuttleworth. The great educationist also served as an active member of the council of the Girls Public Day School Company, lending his prestige and experience to everything from its choice of headmistresses to its choice of linen blinds. When we find the governors of Giggleswick, therefore, proposing that their own school and neighbouring foundations should be 'equitably taxed' to provide for girls we are reminded that this is not a body consisting solely of local farmers.[9]

Roundell and Kay-Shuttleworth were widely known. Who knew Mr Carey Tyso of Wallingford? Mr Tyso was one of the trustees of Walter Biggs Charity which had at its disposal no more than one-sixtieth of the income at Dulwich. He was, however, very much interested in the problem of endowed school reform and had, as he put it, 'amassed above 1000 pages of MS. and printed matter' in this field, the result of inquiries made, all over England, of grammar school headmasters and interested persons, including Roby. Mr Tyso sent in his own Scheme for Wallingford, proposing that the charity, worth £260 p.a., should support a girls' school as well as one for boys and justifying this at length and in terms which might have come from the Commissioners themselves. His reasons were set out under seven separate heads, the most notable of which were that such a girls' school had once existed in Wallingford, that to provide one would probably double the beneficial range of the endowment, that the female population there exceeded the male, 'and consequently there are more female children of school age needing instruction than male', that women now had municipal rights and therefore *ought* to be educated and that the funds of the endowment were sufficient to provide for both sexes.[10]

It would be odd to present Mr Tyso as a typical grammar school trustee. But between his vigorous commitment to the idea of endowing a girls' school and the out-and-out resistance at Pocklington, or March, lies a whole range of degrees of acceptance. It has already been suggested that where there was uncommitted money girls had a chance. Thus at Burton-on-Trent the Allsopp trustees approved without difficulty Stanton's proposal to establish two schools and received 'very favourably' the idea that one of them should be for girls.[11] 'The proposed Girls' School gave satisfaction', Hammond reported of the trustees at Stamford.[12] The deputation which came up from Rivington to discuss a Draft Scheme with Canon Robinson appeared well pleased with the proposal for girls while the trustees at Grays Thurrock were described as 'unanimously in favour of trying the experiment' and at Bedford the Harpur trustees were even ready to boast about it. The Commissioners, they hoped, would approve their proposal.

> to establish for the first time out of the endowment a school for the higher education of girls . . . Although the attempt must be con-

sidered to a certain extent tentative the Trustees think that the experiment could not be tried under more favourable circumstances than at Bedford where there is a large population resident for the sake of the educational advantages and where the presence of the boys' schools and the proximity to London and Cambridge offer facilities which few places possess.[13]

Cambridge was a rather sophisticated place when it came to female education and the idea of starting a girls' school on the Perse Foundation got considerable support. The trustees' acceptance of this new departure was very strongly backed by the town. As the Charities Committee of the Borough Council pointed out, fathers paid a lot for their daughters' education and an endowed girls' school would compensate for the increase in fees that was proposed at the Perse. 'Considering, too, the provision now being made by the University in various ways for raising the standard of girls' education, there appears some reason for affording by exhibitions and otherwise increased opportunity enabling girls to take advantage of this provision.'[14]

In Birmingham, where trustees and town were at loggerheads on important aspects of the Scheme proposed for King Edward VI Foundation, the provision to be made for girls was not one of them. The trustees' suggestion of an upper girls' school was warmly endorsed, according to Hammond, as 'the most pressing of all additional objects' when he discussed it with a committee of the Grammar School Reform Association. The local press rejoiced in the idea.

'In no point of the education system', announced the *Birmingham Morning News*, 'is there more pressing and urgent necessity for reform than this. The Branch Schools of King Edward's Foundation have done some good work in this department; but there is still much more to be done, and no system can be said to answer the wants of the time which does not afford equal facilities for the education of both girls and boys.'[15]

If they did not aim at equal facilities, both trustees and townsfolk in a number of places were, as Fitch said of the people of Yalding, 'not unwilling to try the experiment'.[16] In Loughborough he found the Committee of Inhabitants ready to support the trustees' plan to develop the girls' school on their foundation.[17] A public meeting in the village of Northleach voted unanimously to have a girls' school and here there was support from the grammar school headmaster who, most untypically, was interested enough to speculate on ways in which the boys' and girls' schools 'would mutually keep and strengthen each other'.[18] A meeting of the inhabitants of Ilminster reacted to the prospect of establishing a girls' school, already accepted by the trustees, with the practical reflection that 'There were as many girls to be educated as boys, and would it not be as great an inducement to persons having girls to educate to come to Ilminster so as to have them educated at that school?'[19]

In some towns, though, the views of the inhabitants, expressed at public meetings, in the local press and through committees specially formed to consider the future of the grammar school, represented a progressive standpoint utterly at variance with that of the trustees. At Stourbridge, for instance, the Improvement Commissioners seem to have spoken for nonconformist and radical elements eager to see a girls' school started. Girls' education, they told the Commissioners, was 'scarcely less important' than that of boys;[20] they appealed for intervention under Section 12 and their chief spokesman, Mr Maginnis, a Unitarian minister, was encouraged by Stanton to form a committee representing these views. The trustees, on the other hand, were fiercely jealous of the interests of the boys' school and somewhat contemptuous, Stanton said, of Maginnis's 'enthusiasm for the cause'. The girls' school proposal was lost in the end for technical reasons which rendered inaccessible the small endowment on which it depended, and at that point it was wholly due to Mr Maginnis and his committee that an effort was made to salvage something for girls. 'Respectfully' they advised the Commissioners that the Scheme should make provision for a girls' school to be started if ever funds became available. A clause of this kind 'would tend to keep the subject before the Governors and might lead to some future gift of funds for the special purpose'.[21] It never did. But, like a flag marking some forgotten endeavour, an appropriate clause was planted in the Scheme.

Mansfield was another place where local opinion supported the extension of endowment to girls against the wishes of the grammar school trustees. The school had been some years in abeyance and a public meeting to discuss its future opened with a speech from the local Member in which he argued the girls' case warmly, adducing in support a range of data from de Tocqueville's views on American women to the excellence of Mansfield's water supply.[22] A Grammar School Committee was formed on the spot and one of its objects was to press for a girls' school. As against this group, with its Liberals and Dissenters, were trustees of the old stamp: ultra-Tory; unwilling to depart from the original trust 'founded for the benefit of boys' and impervious to what the Commissioners themselves called the 'clearly expressed local want' for a girls' school. Public support for this at vestry meetings and in the local press they brushed aside as 'the expression of a few only and not of many persons here'.[23] The girls' assignment was made in spite of them.

A tendency for schools to pull away from the locality, aiming where they could at high fees and boarders, was common, we have seen, and much resented. It is not surprising then to find the girls' claim caught up in the running fire of town and trustees, as it was at Hipperholme in Yorkshire. The trustees, who were predominantly Anglican, wanted to preserve a first grade boarding school. The Grammar School Inquiry Association wanted to have governors representing the locality (which had a strong Dissenting element) and a grammar school adapted to local needs, among which they included provision for girls. The idea of establishing a girls' school was scouted by the trustees as quite unnecessary, 'there being, first, no element in the District to avail itself of such a School and second, there being no funds . . . for the object'. To set aside any part of the endowment they thought 'a needless . . . limitation which may operate with great disadvantage to the working of the existing school'.[24] The reformers wanted a second grade mixed school and argued that there was a large demand for it. As opinion polarised, the girls' cause was urged as the cause of the locality, a girls' school became 'the great want of the district' and 'our girls at home left to get an education as best they may' were contrasted with 'the sons of gentlemen at a distance' whom the trustees were eager to admit as boarders.[25] 'The better education of "the daughters of England" is now admitted on all hands to be of equal importance to that of the sterner sex', wrote a correspondent to the *Halifax Courier*, no doubt sincerely; but in fact the girls' issue was also another stick to beat the trustees with.[26]

It appears in the same light at Brentwood where there was considerable resentment about the way the wardens of Brentwood School had administered their trust. The school, it was contended, had become little more than a private boarding school and should be reformed to meet the needs of the locality, which were not interpreted as solely masculine. On the contrary;

> it was the anxious wish of the committee that some arrangement should be made for the education of girls. All who were parents were no doubt anxious that their girls should have as good an education as their boys. Girls had to fight their way through the world as well

as boys and there was no reason why boys should have the advantage in matters of education. [27]

At Berkhamsted, scene of the 'Hundred Years' War', it would have been surprising if the claims of girls had not become inscribed on the banners of the townsfolk in their struggle with Dr Bartrum. The Endowed Schools Commission had hardly been appointed when the *Hertfordshire Standard* devoted some attention to the 'very serious matter' of women's education. Women had lately gained the municipal franchise and would probably soon have the national one as well.

> We must educate our Masters, says Mr. Lowe; we must educate our wives, our sisters, the mothers of our children, say we . . . and we are glad indeed to think that something will be done to improve the education of the girls as well as of the boys of Berkhamsted. The funds of the Grammar School, we strongly suspect, will be called into requisition to promote this . . . and the Executive Commission will, in all probability, provide for the girls as well as the boys, of the happy Berkhamsted family. [28]

A few months later the Berkhamsted Vestry resolved 'that the Grammar School does not meet the educational requirements of the Town' and appointed a committee to watch local interests. The suggestions made to the Endowed Schools Commissioners by its secretary, Henry Nash, resemble those urged upon Fearon at Hipperholme: any new Scheme should be designed with a view to 'the practical wants of the Town and neighbourhood'; parishioners should elect a fair proportion of governors; and 'considering the large income of the School and the limited number of boys in the parishes of Berkhamsted and Northchurch . . . provision should be made for the establishment of a Girls' School in connection with the Grammar School and under the same management'. [29]

We know how Dr Bartrum and the governors reacted when the Draft Scheme proposed an assignment to girls. But the Vestry Committee was full of approval, assuring Hammond that the town itself would strongly support an appropriation. Battle was joined, and proceeded not only by rival deputations to Victoria Street but by resolution and counter-resolution in the Berkhamsted Vestry where Dr Bartrum did what he could to block approval of the girls' clause. What makes the fight at Berkhamsted interesting is not just that Bartrum exhibits so frankly all the loyalties and limitations of the rising public school headmaster but that his intense devotion to the school is matched by an intense devotion to the town in his opponent,

Henry Nash. Here was the townsman Hobhouse might have dreamed of when he looked to the public 'to support an enactment which brings them great benefits'. Nash was a Liberal, Free Church shopkeeper who had grown up in that deplorable era when the Berkhamsted Grammar School was closed and who often said publicly how much he regretted never having had the chance to attend it. With all the fervour of a self-taught man he prized education and devoted himself to every means of bringing it to ordinary people: the British School, the Mechanics' Institute – later, the School Board. Thirty years on, and Nash was Berkhamsted's 'Grand Old Man'. But what Bartrum faced in the early seventies was a redoubtable fighter for the town, recently involved in the classic resistance to the fencing of Berkhamsted Common, and ready, it might seem, through the Endowed Schools Act to breach the exclusiveness which for so long had fenced off Berkhamsted Grammar School.

In a negative sense it was a victory for Bartrum that very little progress had been made with the Berkhamsted Scheme by 1874 when the Endowed Schools Commission was disbanded. The case was then delayed by the transfer of powers from that body to the Charity Commission. When it was resumed in 1876 Dr Bartrum was as vigorous as ever. But so was Nash. And, as we shall see, he got girls onto the endowment in the end.

The women's movement

Whether or not it was unrealistic to look to the general public for support, the Commissioners could expect backing from those who had pressed for the reform of girls' education. When the Social Science Congress met in 1869, just after the Endowed Schools Act was passed, Charles Kingsley, who was president that year of the department on education, drew attention to the needs of girls, both in his Address and in the general discussion of what might be expected from the new Act. 'I do hope that in discussing the question of endowments, we shall bear in mind that they are the appanage of girls as well as boys,' he said, inviting support for resolutions which would urge the Commissioners to share endowment equally between the sexes, where this was possible, 'and to arrange schemes of education for girls in addition to those prepared for boys, so as to carry out in a practical manner the provisions of clause 12 of the Endowed Schools Act'.[30] Three years later the Address on Education by the then president, George Woodyatt Hastings, called again for hearty support for the work of the Endowed Schools Commission which, he said, had special claims on their sympathy, 'for it was our Council which obtained from Lord Palmerston's administration the issue of the Schools Inquiry Commission, out of which grew . . . the commission which is now dealing with endowed schools'.[31] Lord Lyttelton, he said later in discussion, not only wished to make the best use of all endowments, 'but also to devote as large a portion of them as possible to improving the education of girls'.[32]

The special interest which the women's movement had in this field was underlined by the Manchester suffragist, Elizabeth Wolstenholme, who wrote while the Endowed Schools Bill was going through that no one who cared for the advance of education could afford to be indifferent to it.

> Least of all can women be so. If that measure . . . should ever become law, it will be the fault of women themselves, if they do not use it as the most powerful lever ever yet applied to raise the education of women. It will be their duty . . . to claim for girls, wherever grounds of right or of expedience can be shown, their share in any and all educational endowments, to insist that the necessities of girls shall not be forgotten.[33]

A few months later, a number of feminists resident in Ambleside took up the case of Kelsick's Foundation exactly as Miss Wolstenholme could have wished.

Kelsick's was one of the many grammar schools which had sunk to elementary school level, a fact in itself not sufficiently remarkable to bring in the Endowed Schools Commissioners promptly. However, the schoolmaster had recently died, which, as the Inhabitants informed the Commission early in January 1870, made possible a new disposition of the funds. 'We therefore take this opportunity of pressing upon your consideration the great need of a good school in Ambleside for the education of girls whose parents are both able and willing to give their daughters more varied instruction and the benefit of more personal influence than can be obtained in a National School.'[34] Whoever first read this in Victoria Street, wondering at the radical temper of the Lakes, must surely have turned next to the list of signatures and found them headed by a cluster of women: Mrs Harrison of Scale How, Miss Emily Napier of Gale Bank, Harriet Martineau, the Knoll, Mary Arnold and Frances Arnold of Fox How and Margaret Morse of Gale Lodge. After these there followed joiners, drapers, grocers, plumbers, a letter-carrier, bobbin-turner, hotel-keeper, painter, photographer, nurseryman, gardener, shoe-maker, plasterer, waller and others, all proposing that 'the interests of the community would . . . be best promoted by giving encourage-ment to the education of girls as well as boys' and trusting the Com-missioners would act accordingly. On the same day came a letter from Miss Clough, founder of the North of England Council, no less, and also an Inhabitant. She made the same points. 'The townspeople wish for a better School, and many of the most respectable inhabi-tants would be very glad if a portion of the increased revenue were devoted to the Education of Girls.'[35] She estimated that in Ambleside there were fifty boys and thirty girls who would want secondary education and suggested that 'a portion of the money be given to support a day school for girls or to help in providing a suitable building'.

The official response was prompt and sympathetic. The Inhabi-tants were told that the Endowed Schools Commissioners were 'very sensible of the importance of the subject to which the memorial relates and . . . prepared to give it the fullest consideration'. They were indeed bound by the Act, said Lyttelton, 'no less than prompted by their own convictions' to extend endowment to girls wherever possible'.[36]

Without the initiative of this group of women it seems unlikely that the Ambleside Scheme would have provided for a girls' school. Kel-sick's had been run as a school for boys, offering free elementary education. The income was less than £200 p.a. and it soon became clear that there was strong opposition to the idea of giving priority to girls. Whether or not the humbler inhabitants had been overawed by Miss Martineau, Miss Clough, the daughters of Dr Arnold and the rest, four of those who had signed the memorial turned up later on a Ratepayers' Committee pledged to resist the girls' assignment. The moving spirit here was William Donaldson, a man who had himself been to Kelsick's School though he no longer lived in Ambleside, and who raised the cry of 'robbing the poor'. If girls were to have money from Kelsick's, he argued, it should be by way of free elementary schooling for those in poor families. Better-class girls could attend the private schools. This view was certainly backed by the trustees who regarded Kelsick's as part of the provision that would have to be made in Ambleside under the Elementary Education Act.

Faced with the resistance of trustees and ratepayers the Endowed

Schools Commissioners took their stand on the Inhabitants' memorial. Kelsick's should benefit girls, they said, 'in accordance with the provisions of the 12th section of the Endowed Schools Act, 1869, and in deference to *a very numerously and influentially signed petition from the Parish*' (my italics).[37] Though they made concessions they would not yield. The boys' elementary school was to continue; but within three years of the date of the Scheme a secondary school for girls was to be built. Donaldson urged in vain that no one wanted it 'exclusive of a section of that part of our population to which our gallant devotion and unquestionable deference were at one time frankly and loyally given, on the plea that they were too gentle and refined to fight their own battles in this rough world'.[38] The women had fought this battle well. But, as we shall see, the Scheme they had promoted turned out to be a rod in pickle and they were hardly victors in the end.

Apart from this rather special Lakeland colony, what was the response of the women's movement? As Henry Winterbotham had acknowledged by his approach to it in 1869, the centre of organised experience and influence most likely to back up Section 12 was the North of England Council formed by Miss Clough to promote the higher education of women. The Council, it is true, had not shared his conviction of the need to get 'equally' into the girls' clause, but it had petitioned for the clause in general and discussed at length what steps could be taken, once the Bill was law, to make it effective. The Council's president, Josephine Butler, had launched this discussion by pointing to the need to collect information throughout the country, 'wherever endowments exist and the educational wants of girls are pressing'. The North of England Council, in her view, was 'a very proper body to undertake such work'. Although any claims must come from the locality, 'somebody will be wanted', she said, 'to show people how to claim help for girls. I think it possible we could devise some plan whereby our Council would be the means of stirring up and helping the local people to claim and to act, and also of aiding the Commissioners themselves, by giving them suggestions . . . and information'.[39] It was resolved to form a committee to collect information about endowments and suggest the best ways of applying them. Fitch, who seconded the resolution, thought that 'nothing could be more judicious'.

The committee was formed, and based on London. Mr E. C. Herbert, a barrister, 'a very clever man and a great friend of Mr Winterbotham', was appointed secretary at £100 p.a. The committee's first action was to circulate suggestions on the application of endowment to girls – suggestions which were exceedingly general and did not really face the awkward problem of money, though that, perhaps, was hardly surprising when the Council's most knowledgeable member, Fitch, had already been forced to admit that endowments were often too small to be divided. The committee seems to have established itself among those contacts in the women's movement – Miss Davies, Miss Buss, Mrs Fawcett and others – whom the Commissioners sometimes consulted on questions relating to girls' education. The more active role, described by Mrs Butler as 'stirring up and helping the local people', was also attempted. In 1870 Council members learned of the committee's efforts to make people aware 'that the Commissioners were willing to devote a portion of the endowments to the establishment of girls' schools'. Their idea was to concentrate on various places to which Assistant Commissioners had been sent – 'if possible, to be beforehand' – and try to encourage public feeling in support.

> The Secretary has corresponded with many in various parts of the country, who have shown a great wish to further this object. Miss Boucherett in Lincolnshire has been preparing the minds of people in her neighbourhood to be ready to offer suggestions when the Commissioners come. The subject is being taken up in Bristol and Cheltenham and in Yorkshire . . . In Westminster the Committee have been endeavouring to make a public expression of their sympathy with the work the Commissioners are so ready to do for girls.[40]

What in fact happened? Nothing much, if we are to go by the Commissioners' files. There is no sign of any feminist initiative in the great struggles with the Hospital interest that dominated Westminster and Bristol, for instance. And how, one wonders, did Miss Boucherett's people ever manage to offer the suggestions with which they had been primed in 1870, for the Commissioners had scarcely touched Lincolnshire by the time they were disbanded. Schemes, as we know, took years in the making, but the North of England Council had not lasted a decade when it was disbanded in 1876 and none of its constituent bodies was really geared to a waiting game. In one case, luckily, the need did not arise: the Commissioners came early to Bradford and Fearon was in touch with the committee set up there to forward the interests of girls' education. In April 1870 its views were made plain in a long memorandum which argued strongly the need for a girls' school, with women governors, and a curriculum from which, it was urged, 'merely elegant accomplishments' should be excluded; if need be the committee was prepared to raise a public subscription towards expenses.[41] But elsewhere the timing was less fortunate. In 1874 the North of England Council took note that the Commissioners had not yet come to York and that the Leeds women had been waiting for them, too, for the past four years. As their records show, the Leeds Ladies' Educational Association had long before this agreed it was essential to impress 'both on the public generally and on those in power the . . . claim of girls to a fair share in educational endowments'.[42] In 1876, as there was still no sign of action under the Endowed Schools Act, they launched their own company to start a girls' high school. Manchester had done the same the previous year. In 1871 the women's group there had been encouraged by receiving a letter from one of the Commissioners, pointing out that the Endowed Schools Commission had already done something in the battle for women's education 'and if the promoters of the movement now on foot . . . will bestir themselves and make a strong public opinion, we shall do a good deal more'.[43] But the Commissioners, in the event, did not get to Manchester before they were disbanded, and their successors proved less encouraging.

Problems of timing, then, may help to explain why the efforts of the North of England Council made so little impact in the fight for endowment. But there were other problems which, not unnaturally, in these early days it failed to anticipate. 'We must make a practical effort this year', declared Mrs Butler in 1870, 'to secure our share in the readjustment of misused, now useless charities'; and the Council fell to discussing the prospects of girls under Section 30 of the new Act whereby obsolete endowments could be converted to education. She read out an encouraging letter from Hobhouse, who had high hopes of 'misapplied charities'.[44] But at that time neither he nor the Council had glimpsed the intransigence of trustees, whose consent was needed for such conversion. Mrs Butler's plan was that Council members should try to bring pressure to bear on trustees; but sadly, as we shall see later on, when something of the sort was attempted in Leeds, over the Poors Estate, it failed entirely.

It is questionable, also, whether the feminists were not over-sanguine about the kind of work which could be done by even the most dedicated amateurs in support of Section 12. At the Council's meeting in 1870 Mrs Butler read the very detailed advice of one correspondent:

The friends of women must investigate the local endowments, must look into the original deeds or charters, and ascertain whether girls were . . . included . . . and so whether a claim can . . . be preferred for them on historical grounds . . . It will be necessary also to investigate the present state of the funds . . . and to prefer claims for girls on the ground of expediency and natural right.

Manchester was taken as an example.

We must make to the Commissioners a clear statement as to what educational endowments there are . . . whether for girls or for boys or for both; the relative proportion . . . thus provided for and the numbers of both belonging to the class for which the endowments were intended . . . and finally, we must be prepared with specific suggestions and recommendations as to the best mode of applying such endowments as may be held to be so applicable to the education of girls.[45]

What this reads like is a description of the duties of an Assistant Commissioner. Untold hours, as the files make plain, were spent by these men poring over charters, examining 'the present state of the funds' and drafting 'suggestions and recommendations'; work which called less for partisan zeal than for the discipline of the professional.

It was not as easy, then, as it sounded for feminists to take Miss Wolstenholme's advice and use Section 12 as 'the most powerful lever' ever yet applied to raise girls' education. The battle for endowment was entirely different from any other battle in which they were engaged. Female suffrage, after all, was the same issue from Bradford to Bournemouth; the fight to change the law on married women's property promised victory applicable to all. But the fight for endowment had to be conducted in a multitude of small encounters, quite unlikely to benefit any but the girls of a particular place. And the assistance the Commissioners looked for was of a kind most difficult to organise: that of friendly partisans or guerillas wherever hostilities should break out next.

The period spanned by the Endowed Schools Commission saw many gains on the women's side: there was the municipal franchise, and the right of wives to keep their earnings; notable feminists – Lydia Becker, Emily Davies and Elizabeth Garrett – were elected onto the new School Boards; a women's college was launched at Girton, and in London, an embryonic medical school. A novel of the time pushed the whole thing further: J. P. Maguire, in *The Next Generation*, actually had women cabinet ministers. In real life, though, they had not even got the vote and suffered the greater humiliation of the Contagious Diseases Acts. These two causes drew the main interest of some of the ablest. Thus Josephine Butler ended her connection with the North of England Council in 1873 and thenceforth was entirely absorbed in the Contagious Diseases campaign. Lydia Becker became identified more and more with suffrage. The link between enfranchisement and education seemed obvious enough to her, if not to others. 'Men must be wilfully blind', she wrote, 'if they suppose it will be possible to provide for girls the same intellectual training which is given to boys, and to maintain the disability which precludes women from qualifying as Parliamentary electors.'[46] Emily Shirreff, driven to despair at public indifference to the need for girls' schools, wrote that, if women cared for education, 'this one thing would be enough to make every woman an agitator for the suffrage'.[47] In general, however, those who were committed to advancing the education of girls preferred to avoid the odium which attached to involvement with the political campaign.

Miss Shirreff's sister, Maria Grey, took this view in the early seventies. The education movement, as she recalled later, 'was fighting its way against much prejudice, and to weight it with the still stronger prejudice clustered round Women's Suffrage would have done it a great injury'.[48] Her talents – and nobody saw more clearly the need for 'a systematic plan of campaign' to promote girls' schools[49] – found expression in launching the Girls' Public Day School Company. This was started in 1872 on the lines of the companies that had proved so effective in launching the new public schools, and represented a diametrically opposite approach to the supply of education from that implied in the Endowed Schools Act. While the Commissioners were bound, more or less, to gamble that supply would create demand, Maria Grey's Company would not start a school before a certain number of shares were taken locally and a certain number of pupils guaranteed. Everything had to come from the locality. To that extent it worked on the Free Trade principle so much admired by Robert Lowe, who expected nothing from reform of endowments but thought that if things were left to take their course, 'There would be schools wherever there is a demand for education, just as there are ironmongers' shops wherever there is a demand for hardware.'[50]

Fortunately, Maria Grey was not quite such a committed Free Trader and in the early seventies she exerted herself conspicuously on the subject of endowments. One of the aims of the National Union for Improving the Education of Women which, with encouragement from Lyttelton, she had inaugurated in 1871, was to restore to girls the endowments 'originally intended for their benefit'. During 1872 she did as much as anyone to keep the question of girls' endowment before readers of *The Times*. From her they learnt that Miss Buss's appeal had brought in only £47 while £60,000 had been readily donated to found a boys' school in the City.[51] A few months later, in 'painful astonishment not unmingled with bitter feelings', she drew attention to the sleight of hand which had transferred to this selfsame boys' school £5000 subscribed for girls.[52] Next, in an article to demonstrate the need for her newly formed Women's Education Union, she drew attention to the 'monstrous' inequality of grammar school endowments. The country was covered with endowed boys' schools, their annual income nearly £300,000, while the few endowed girls' schools had one-hundredth of that sum.[53] Warned by *The Times* that she was practically saying 'Let us rob Peter to pay Paul, let us mulct the men to endow the women', Maria Grey denied it. 'Surely it is not robbing the boys to restore to the girls what was originally intended for them?' The reform of endowments was sanctioned by law.

> We do not ask for equality of endowments for girls . . . but when we find it shown by the last Census that the proportion of women supporting themselves by professional work is to men in professions as 1 to 7, and their share of educational endowments is as 1 to 92, it does not appear unreasonable or extravagant to ask for some rectification of this enormous inequality at the hands of the Commissioners intrusted to carry out the Act.[54]

She knew, though, that this 'rectification' was proving exceedingly difficult. Indeed, it was against the background of difficulty in working Section 12 that her Company had been launched. Lyttelton, presiding on 7 June 1872 at the meeting which launched it, told his audience what some may already have learnt from the Endowed Schools Commissioners' Report earlier that year: that it was far from easy to allocate endowment to girls. In some senses it was true, he admitted, that the hope of endowment was a remote one. The Endowed Schools Commissioners, like Taunton before them, felt strongly that such assistance should be given, 'but the Act of Parliament they had to administer was one of considerable complication and the work was difficult. They might not be able, therefore, to do as rapidly as they wished all they had to do'.[55]

Fitch, from his experience, had more than once expressed anxiety lest too much be expected of endowments. However well organised by the Commissioners they would be inadequate, as well as suffering, in his view, from 'a want of elasticity . . . not to be found in voluntary enterprise'. It was the first time, he told a meeting of the Women's Education Union in 1873, that the people of England had become alive to the vast importance of girls' education 'and he hoped that they would bear in mind that the comparatively small sum from endowments available for this work must be supplemented by considerable local efforts'.[56] Maria Grey's Girls' Public Day School Company appeared, then, as a practical answer to a question which had occupied some of the feminists: 'Failing any State action, and whilst waiting for the development of the Endowed Schools Act to meet the case of girls . . . What could be done . . . by voluntary effort?'[57]

In regard to official effort, the women were grateful but disappointed. That is the impression given by the reports of the endowments sub-committee set up in 1871 by the Women's Education Union to keep an eye on progress under Section 12. This committee, while always acknowledging the help which it received from the Commissioners and their readiness to press to the utmost the claims of girls to share in endowment, also lamented 'the apathetic, if not the adverse state of public opinion' which often neutralised the Commissioners' sympathy.[58] In the event, as their analysis showed, girls had many fewer Schemes than boys. 'How can we hold our peace', cried Emily Shirreff, 'when day by day additions are made to the old reckoning; when the feast is still liberally prepared for boys and the crumbs grudgingly dropped to the girls?'[59] It is time to see what the crumbs amounted to.

6. What was achieved

We have no doubt that the broad and comprehensive spirit in which Lord Lyttelton and his colleagues have provided for girls' education will be productive of incalculable blessings to many thousands of the rising generation.

Journal of the Women's Education Union, 1873[1]

Output

Even a simple, unopposed case took at least a year, said the Endowed Schools Commissioners when they reported in 1872 on their progress in working the Act. A difficult case would need at least two, while if difficulties were joined to opposition, it was hard to say how much time would be required. By way of illustration they cited Bristol, where they had begun work in 1870 but did not expect to have settled the Schemes 'for at least some months to come'.[2] In the event this proved too sanguine. The Bristol Schemes were not finally settled until 1875, along with many others which had been completed by the Commissioners and forwarded to the Education Department before the end of their term of office but which received the Royal Assent only later.[3]

In view of all this it is not surprising to find that at the end of their five years' labour they had made Schemes for scarcely more than one-tenth of the three thousand endowments which came within their purview. Some of these had had to be for elementary schools. So far as secondary schooling was concerned, they could claim credit at the end of the day for one hundred and thirty schools for boys, forty-seven for girls and a mixed school, at Thornton. In addition, they had made provision in over thirty Schemes for the interest of girls by way of exhibitions or comparable benefit either at once or 'when funds admit', or, in some cases, when a pension fell in or a vested interest had been compensated.[4]

It is not easy to find a scale on which to measure their achievement. So far as Section 12 was concerned, the Commissioners themselves

would have been hard put to it, as would Emily Shirreff and the rest,
to formulate their hopes in terms of arithmetic. What had they to go
on, beyond the fact that girls could not expect to get half the
endowments? Any such idea had been thoroughly scouted during
the debates on the Endowed Schools Bill and even such a
stalwart as Emily Davies, when she said that girls had a
claim to half the grammar schools, meant a claim in equity, not in
practice.

Not half, but just above a quarter of the grammar schools which
the Commissioners established were for girls, some of them in
Schemes which were still in the pipeline – submitted for approval but
not yet approved – when the Commission was disbanded; so much
emerges from the lists of Schemes which they published with their
final Report.[5] Many of the schools, though existing in law, had no
existence in bricks and mortar till after 1874, and a few never started.
Their legal existence was the Commissioners' standard of achievement, and must be ours too, in assessing what was done, both by these
men and by their successors. In all their reports and public statements
the Endowed Schools Commissioners expressed regret that they had
not been able to do more with Section 12, in face of 'very general
reluctance' from the public.[6] Hardly any part of their plans, said
Roby, met with less support,[7] and the women's interest had, however
sadly, to acknowledge this. The Endowed Schools Commissioners,
said Maria Grey, 'have done as much for us as was possible in the
state of strong prejudice in the public mind'. They had not pursued
an abstract justice, 'but they have at least allowed our claim . . . and
given us some measure of justice as far as was practicable under the
circumstances'. It was her belief that the Commissioners had done 'as
much as the state of public feeling permitted'.[8] To another sympathiser they appeared 'rather in advance of the opinion of the
locality . . . although they might not be in advance of the requirements of the district'.[9] Lady Stanley of Alderley saw public indifference as the barrier to providing for girls from 'remodelled' endowments, 'even with the strong desire to do so on the part of the . . .
Endowed Schools Commission'.[10] And when Lyttelton's daughter,
Lady Frederick Cavendish, opened the Bradford Grammar School
for Girls – thus appropriately marking the 'fruition of one of those
objects which he had so much at heart' – the difficulties facing the
Commissioners were mentioned.[11] Not without pride, perhaps; there
is a touch of that in her own diary entry on opening this school: 'the

first of the sort . . . it has an endowment of £200 clawed from boys' education'.[12]

'Clawed' is not a bad word to describe what was involved in applying Section 12. The feminists might see it in terms of the battle which had to be fought against public prejudice. The files of the Commissioners show, in addition, the hard negotiation of competing claims, the intransigence not just of persons but of funds which nothing could have overcome but drastic action beyond anything they were ready to contemplate. These were reformers but they had their limits. They did not, for instance, press for mixed education, an obvious means of extending endowment. And while they might query the aspirations of rising public schools such as Berkhamsted, they acknowledged without question the lofty status of some that were established: Repton, for instance, and Sherborne and Uppingham and even Sedbergh – with all that this implied in terms of Schemes to extricate these schools from the local difficulties standing between them and a national future.[13] In cases of this sort the claims of girls are found to be very far down the queue. Having said that, one can only record, as the women did, their zeal and persistence in pressing Section 12. There is scarcely a case in which they succeeded where success came easily, while we may judge from their work in the West Riding how much effort must have run into the sand elsewhere, producing not a farthing for girls.

The women's interest, Maria Grey acknowledged to a Select Committee in 1873, owed them 'a very deep debt of gratitude'. Just how deep she could have judged more easily many years ahead when the Endowed Schools Act, and Section 12 with it, had been worked by their successors. From the first day of January 1875 administration of the Act was transferred to the Charity Commissioners, who carried it on until 1903 when they in turn handed it over to the Board of Education. By then it had ceased to be explosive matter. Time and the Charity Commission had defused it. That this should happen had been the intention when the Endowed Schools Commission was dismissed. A more tranquil administration was looked for. It comes as something of a shock, nonetheless, to find that, at least where girls were concerned, the new one was tranquil to the point of torpidity. In over twenty-five years the number of girls' schools for which Schemes were made no more than doubled; that is, another forty-seven were added to the forty-seven launched by the Endowed Schools Commission.[14]

Comparing such figures, it is perfectly true, ignores the fact that the making of new Schemes slowed down generally as time went on. But if the provision for girls is expressed as part of the provision for girls and boys together, there is still a significant decline. Girls' schools comprise 27 per cent of the Endowed Schools Commissioners' output and 15 per cent of the Charity Commissioners'. And this decline took place in a period when public opinion was generally agreed to have become more favourable to girls' education.

The organisation of girls' schools

The *rapport* maintained between the pioneering women and the pioneering administrators did not prevent some feminist criticism of the new girls' schools. Maria Grey wished that more of them 'gave a first grade education' and regretted that so many were third grade schools.[15] When the Commissioners published their Draft Scheme for the magnificent foundation at Dulwich she pointed out that none of the girls' schools it envisaged would be on a level with Dulwich College.[16] 'We cannot but feel deeply disappointed', declared the Women's Education Union, 'that the beneficent action of the Scheme has stopped at this point . . . We have noticed with regret that this has been generally the case in the Schemes framed by the Commission; and this only increases our anxiety that advantage should be taken of . . . a fair opportunity of making a really considerable step towards supplying the want which . . . exists.'[17]

The question of grades was a rather cloudy one so far as girls' schools were concerned. Lyttelton explained to Maria Grey that the Commissioners did not attempt to make the sharp distinctions they employed for boys,[18] an admission which in itself highlights the void from which girls' grammar schools came into being, for sharp distinctions were of the essence in the Taunton plan of reform. If the schools were put into three distinct grades, the argument ran, they would cater for the needs of different strata of the middle classes. The rising generation of shopkeepers and businessmen as well as those intended for the university could then be taught at an appropriate fee and with a curriculum suited to their prospects. But what exactly were the prospects of girls?

This sort of question, if pressed too far, might well have thrown in doubt the whole concept of grading, depending as it did on rather old-fashioned notions of boys content to follow their fathers. The

Commissioners simply settled for two kinds of girls' school: upper and lower. In the case of Dulwich, they altered their Draft Scheme to include an upper school, in deference, it seems, to the views expressed by the Women's Education Union. Spurred by Mr Roundell, the Dulwich governors approved the idea of 'Alleyn's High School'.[19] Its high fees – up to £20 p.a. – and leaving age of nineteen put it on a par with the boys' school, Dulwich College, but there was to be no Greek in the curriculum. Greek, which was the hallmark of a first grade school, the crown so fiercely contended for at Bradford, does not appear in the course designed for any of the handful of upper schools which the Commissioners proposed for girls. Its absence is yet another reminder of their isolation from the busy throng in which boys prepared for jobs or careers, or, in this case, for the university where Greek remained an entry requirement. That the universities were closed to women does not, however, seem to have weighed with Lyttelton when he decided in the first place not to have Greek on girls' school curricula. Emily Davies noticed its omission when he sought her advice about subjects to be taught. 'Is it not hard', she asked, 'to exclude Greek, which tho' rare, is not unknown in existing girls' schools?'[20] She pressed him further. 'I am sorry you object to Greek. Judging by the number of ladies who study it for mere pleasure, it would seem specially congenial to the female mind.'[21] He had not set down his reasons but more than probably they arose less from his opinion of girls than from his opinion of Greek. Lyttelton wore his own scholarship lightly but he held strong views that Greek should not be taught unless prolonged study could be given to it. 'It is because I know something of Greek – because I know something of its beauty, its value, its difficulty,' he told the Lords during the debates of 1874, 'that I protest against the degradation of the most illustrious language ever spoken on earth, by a wretched smattering of it being presented to be learnt by boys who have to leave school at [an] early age.'

In 1870 he and his colleagues had knocked together, one might say as a necessary chore, what came to be accepted as the standard course for grammar school girls for the next hundred years. They had to settle boys' curricula as well but in the case of boys there was something to go on. In the case of girls, the Taunton Commissioners had shown quite plainly what was *undesirable* – the overloaded private school extravaganza – but gave few guidelines beyond the fact that 'the main and leading elements of instruction' should be the same for children of both sexes.[22]

Lyttelton consulted Emily Davies. Schoolmistresses themselves were distracted, she told him,

> by the contradictory advice they get from educational reformers, each pressing his favourite subject. It is almost pitiful to hear them constantly asking how all the things are to be got in, each being evidently good in itself. They really need guidance, and I believe that a curriculum recommended by authority might be of great use to private schools.[23]

She did not think much, though, of the Commissioners' first suggestions.

> 'The list of subjects seem to me rather too much like the ordinary ladies' school prospectuses, in extent and vagueness. The course proposed for boys has a more thorough and practical look about it ... Is it', she asked, 'because girls are more – or less – prosy than boys that they are to be specially taught poetry? Some one modern language and one branch of Physical Science, and some branch of History would surely have a better chance of being well taught than so many languages and sciences.'[24]

Lyttelton was sorry that she did not like the list, 'about which we took much pains'. It was meant, he explained, to offer a range which the governors would choose from.

> My idea is that the subject of instruction fit for girls is still so unsettled that it is quite essential to give a large range of selection and if so it is impossible to avoid the appearance of 'flashy' multifariousness. I shall be very much obliged, however, if you will take the trouble to put the whole section into accurate language such as you would approve.[25]

He added that the special reference to poetry was a suggestion of Mr Robinson.

When the Commissioners got into their stride the curriculum they usually employed for girls had shed some of the options Miss Davies disapproved of. There remained English, history, geography, French or German, and mathematics, as well as Latin and some form of science. The weakness of the grammar schools in science was well known. In future, in all of them without exception, 'whether for boys or girls', said Lyttelton, 'we propose to require as a substantial and indispensable part of their course . . . at least one branch of Physical Science'.[26] As for Latin, the Taunton Commissioners had recom·mended it as part of the curriculum in almost any school, advising it for girls 'as a means of mental culture and strengthening of the intellect, and of mastery of grammar and language'.[27] The Endowed Schools Commissioners were of the same mind.

> 'I recommend the addition of Latin', wrote Fearon when they drew up the curriculum for Keighley, 'I think instruction in this language at least as important in second grade schools for girls as in those for boys. Even if there should be some difficulty in securing a Principal Teacher who can teach Latin, which it may be reasonably hoped will not long be the case, the proximity of Bradford, Bingley and Skipton will enable a visiting Master for Latin to be provided at little additional cost.'[28]

Girls, then, were to learn much the same as boys. No longer would the feminists have cause to lament, as Fitch had done during his Taunton inquiries, that 'everywhere the fact that the pupil is to become a woman and not a man operates upon her course of study negatively'.[29] The pioneers of female education in Bradford who had urged 'that merely elegant accomplishments be excluded from the curriculum'[30] could feel satisfied that drawing and music now came very far down the list. And music meant class singing. The trustees at Uffculme pleaded in vain for the piano, on the grounds that 'all the poorer gentry and even the richer farmers and tradesmen have pianos and harmoniums and expect their daughters to play them'.[31]

Lyttelton, however, made some concessions towards the conventional domestic side, telling Miss Davies that he put in needlework, 'for which I presume girls are more fitted than boys', and the Laws of Health, 'which are of course useful to both, but which on the whole I think girls have a special aptitude for, in themselves and in their circumstances'.[32] She was not much interested. Miss Garrett, she informed him, did not believe in teaching the laws of health 'but very much in enforcing healthy habits'.[33] Despite this advice the closing cadence of girls' school curricula was to remain: 'Domestic Economy and the Laws of Health'. Other vocational subjects were rare. Bookkeeping appears in one or two Schemes and the trustees of Red Maids' in Bristol were allowed to include telegraphy, 'or other branch of science having a bearing on skilled industry suitable for women'.[34] But these are exceptions. The Commissioners did consider providing for girls at Newcastle-under-Lyme some kind of artistic or technical training relevant to employment in the Potteries but gave up the idea when they discovered that women were only used as unskilled labour.[35]

The very fact that the subjects to be taught were listed officially shows as well as anything the gulf that divided the new girls' grammar schools from the typical ladies' establishment. To attempt to thrust female education into the strait-jacket of a Scheme was something new. Even boys' grammar schools were reined in tighter by these Schemes than they had been before, but girls' schools, like home-workers entering the factory, were being disciplined for the first time. True, it was not the private girls' schools so much censured by the Taunton Commission which were being brought into line. But the fact remains that when the Queen assented in June 1871 to Schemes establishing the first girls' grammar schools at Keighley and Grays Thurrock a prototype was laid down of great significance.

The uninspiring phrases of Endowed School Schemes paint what amounted to a Brave New World for those who sought for a measure of security such as could not be found in private education, even at its best. 'Private schools pass away', said the promoters of the Manchester High School for girls.[36] A Scheme is for a school which will not pass away. It aims to provide the means of stability which for so long eluded even Miss Buss and does so by assuring an income under cer-tain restrictive conditions. Unlike a private school headmistress, the head of an endowed school must answer to governors, whose con-stitution and powers are defined. Her own authority is also defined, her salary and the school fees settled. She is not free, as in private teaching, to raise those fees as her school becomes more popular, to sack her assistants without appeal, take in children without examina-tion or let them stay on indefinitely. On the other hand, the school does not cease because she has overreached herself or suddenly died or retired on her profits. An endowed school has what the pioneers longed for, 'elements of *permanence and development*'.[37] For its Scheme, as one headmistress said proudly, is like the charter of a university; it can be amended by legal process 'but nothing except an Act of Par-liament can destroy the existence of the school'.

The Schemes broke fresh ground in other ways, most of them running counter to what might be called the 'delicate spun glass' view of girls. Charles Kingsley, advocate of female education, was nonetheless fearful of subjecting girls to the strain of being examined. The difference between a boy and a girl, he told the Social Science Association, was like that 'between a cart horse and a race horse, between English heart of oak and delicate spun glass'.[38] Examina-tions, though, were a routine feature of all the Schemes, whether for boys or girls. Children were to be examined on entry. After that, they were to be examined every year by an independent examiner who had to make his report to the governors. Lyttelton seems to have thought originally of including in the Schemes for girls some kind of directive to avoid publicity in the conduct of examinations but only once does any such caveat appear.[39]

Girls, then, were no longer to be exempt from the operation of the law of merit. They too must have access to the educational ladder and Schemes for girls' schools provide, as for boys, for the admission of foundation scholars from the elementary schools by competition. 'All butchers and bakers and candlestick makers', wrote Charlotte Yonge snobbishly of the new high schools. Certainly that part of the girls' school ethos which rested on social exclusiveness was threatened. Endowed school fees were relatively low. At the £20 per annum end of the scale it might not seem so; but then, there were no 'extras'. And this high figure was only charged by the few top endowed schools. A leaving age of seventeen usually meant a fee of £5 or £6 a year while at a lower grade school like the Greycoat a parent could expect to pay as little as £2.

Relative cheapness was a product of endowment and also of numbers. The *size* of the new schools was yet another difference from the private school world, or rather, from the myriad of private little school worlds, close and disorganised, in one of which at least a head-mistress could admit that 'she never *counted* her pupils; she had a feeling that it was unlucky to do so'.[40] Perhaps, too, she could see at a glance how many there were. Ladies' schools averaged twenty-five pupils, Fitch had reported to the Taunton Commission, and at that time the North London Collegiate, with over two hundred, was quite exceptional. 'Persons whose opinions are entitled to respect have expressed their preference for small girls' schools and their fears of large schools such as that under Miss Buss', recorded the high school lobby in Manchester.[41] The new girls' schools were smaller than the boys', but two hundred pupils was not at all uncommon and some were meant for three or even four hundred.

Women in authority

From what part of a patrician upbringing or a lifetime devoted to Greek and cricket did Lyttelton, one wonders, get the idea that head-mistresses ought to have status and women ought to sit upon govern-ing bodies? His declared support in the 1860s for the autonomy of public school headmasters need not necessarily have transferred itself to a profession so largely rooted in the equivocal history of the governess. As Charles Roundell said, many years later, 'Women have not had the training of our Schools and Universities, or of the tradition which is part of the School and University system. They are not subject, as Head Masters are, to the public opinion of the profession.'[42] The body which began to build up that opinion so far as women were concerned was the Head Mistresses' Association launched by Miss Buss in 1874; and at the outset it not only affirmed the need for a headmistress to have full authority but recorded its gratitude 'for the position given to women as Head Mistresses and members of the governing boards in the Schemes drawn up by the Commissioners'.[43]

   The question posed by lack of educational background was a very awkward one at the start. Schemes for boys' schools usually insisted that the headmaster should be a graduate. There were no women graduates. In 1870 Emily Davies advised the Commissioners that there were as yet no qualifications for school mistresses which were worth considering. To insist on their holding a College of Preceptors or Society of Arts certificate, she said, might mean taking some who were

> quite unfit, and the governors might be obliged to appoint them, to the exclusion of some cultivated lady in whose case it would have been altogether infra dig. to think of going in for such examinations . . . The same reasons apply against attaching this qualification to the Mistress-ship. The very small numbers of women of full age who have as yet passed any examination at all, to say nothing of the quality of the examination, seems a fatal objection to make it a necessary condition at present.[44]

The Schemes, then, said nothing about qualifications but merely required that the post should be advertised to invite competition and secure the best candidate.

   Once appointed, the endowed school headmistress, like the headmaster, became responsible for 'the whole internal organisation, management and discipline of the school', which, in schools above the third grade, generally meant that it was she, not the governors, who appointed and dismissed assistant teachers. The Greycoat trustees protested strongly against what they saw as excessive independence.

The Scheme of the Commissioners is stated to be to make the Mistress . . . supreme within the walls of the school; but the result of their proposals is to make her almost irresponsible, as well as supreme. She is to have absolute and uncontrolled nomination of the assistant mistresses, to be allowed to expel any pupil at her will and pleasure.[45]

Maria Grey tried to persuade her fellow councillors of the Girls' Public Day School Company that their headmistresses ought to have authority to appoint and dismiss assistants, adducing Lyttelton's support for this view.[46] She did not succeed; and in an organisation which overlooked everything in its schools, down to the arrangements for the pupils' umbrellas, perhaps it was not to be expected that she should. But it is worth noting that this forward-looking body lagged behind the Commissioners here.

Adequate pay was a necessary adjunct of the new profession. The unkind judgement of the *Saturday Review*, 'Governesses get little because the wares they sell are worthless', was pleasantly reversed in endowed school Schemes where the headmistress's remuneration was provided for in terms of the stipend and capitation fee to which she was entitled. If her stipend was less than the headmaster's (a difference which the Commissioners justified, when they were challenged by Lydia Becker, on the grounds that headmasters were generally married and headmistresses single),[47] the fact remained that the endowed schools opened up employment of a totally new order for women. This was not lost upon those most interested. When the North of England Council met in 1874 Miss Clough drew attention to careers in the new schools and produced a table which showed the range of salaries applicable to particular cases.[48] Even at the lower end these could be substantial, provided numbers kept up well. At Bonnell's in West Ham the stipend was £50; with the addition of a capitation fee of £1–£2 for each pupil (and the school was meant for two hundred) the headmistress could expect anything between £250 and £450 p.a. At the Bedford High School a stipend of £200 plus £3–£5 capitation fee on one hundred pupils might bring as much as £700 p.a., equal to the pay of an Assistant Commissioner and more than was earned by an inspector of schools. Miss Buss found even more dazzling rewards. 'St. Paul's is the greatest prize in the profession . . . Do you see, the salary might be £2000 a year. *Ours* is second, with a hundred more pupils and therefore more work and less pay than St. Paul's.' The North London Scheme envisaged four

hundred girls; the stipend was £100 p.a., the capitation fee £3. On
this reckoning Miss Buss could have earned £1300 p.a., only £200
short of Lyttelton's salary as Chief Commissioner. It is no wonder
that she concluded, 'such prizes are not to be had elsewhere. Look at
Scotch girls' schools. At Germany also. We women owe a deep debt
to the Endowed School Commission.'[49]

Part of that debt, as she also acknowledged, was for the Commissioners' unremitting efforts to get women onto governing bodies.
'It has been made the subject of ridicule,' Lyttelton was told at his
interrogation before a Select Committee of the Commons, 'that you
have thought it right in the case of girls' schools to provide for women
governors.' He demurred at this.

> I do not think we have been so unfortunate as to be ridiculed for
> providing women governors in the case of girls' schools. I think the
> great unwillingness which I have found, with some surprise, to admit
> women to be governors has hardly been carried to the extent of
> openly denying the justice and propriety of their being part of the
> government of girls' schools.

What was often proposed, however, was that they should be an
inferior part; the Commissioners were asked to provide for the
appointment of a subordinate Ladies Committee. 'That we have
invariably refused to do, and in every case where a girls' school is part
of the Scheme we require that a certain number of ladies should be
governors.'[50]

This determination had been put to the test at an early stage by
the Greycoat trustees who reacted to the idea of women governors
much as to the thought of 'irresponsible' headmistresses, firmly maintaining that 'a body of male governors ought to be in supreme com-
mand and that females should only act under their directions'. If
women attended governors' meetings opinions would not be so freely
expressed and it would be 'absurd to have ladies concerned with the
administration of the Estates'. The Commissioners responded at considerable length, admitting that this was a new departure and might
not always work. 'But the same thing may be said of other changes in
the composition of Governing Bodies which are being introduced
under . . . this Act. And there is at least equal reason for trying the
introduction of female Governors as for trying any other new ingre-
dient.'[51] They went on to refer to the Taunton evidence which
showed how endowments common to both sexes had gravitated to the
male. 'It is difficult to suppose that such would have been the case

had women been on the Governing Bodies; nor is it easy to devise any durable remedy except to recognise their capacity to serve.' The government of an institution was moulded by the minds of the governors, they said. 'If therefore female minds ought to take an influential part in organising girls' schools they should share in the government and not be in a subordinate position.' The Commissioners' trump was that there now existed, in the new School Boards, public bodies on which women were eligible to serve.

> They do not insist on this as conclusive because the experiment is still untested. But they think the enactment of such a provision shows at least that the present Legislature considers either that the presence of women, in assemblies much more numerous and public than such a Governing Body as this, is not embarrassing; or that the mischief of such embarrassment will be overborne by the advantage of having the help of women in the Government of Schools.

The Greycoat trustees stuck to their guns. They urged upon the Education Department that women should form a subordinate committee. When the first Scheme had been rejected by the Lords and another was prepared the dispute went on. There must be women governors, the Commissioners insisted, otherwise girls' schools could not be run properly. As for the expedient of Ladies Committees;

> To make such Committees simply the servants of the male Governors will, as the Commissioners think, place both parties in a false position. If the women are to do good service they must have power, and power and responsibility must go hand in hand. The Commissioners see no middle course between requiring women governors and total silence on the matter. Of these alternatives they are clear in preferring the former'.[52]

They got their way. And it was indeed theirs and not just a case of following the line of the Taunton Commission, which had nothing to say on this subject. The leading women felt strongly about it, as was clear from the Taunton evidence given by Miss Buss and Emily Davies and even clearer from Maria Grey's insistence in 1873 to the Select Committee that women should be governors of *boys'* schools too.

Few trustees could conceive of such a thing but Lyttelton was thoroughly in agreement. In his own evidence to the Committee he said that he would like to see women made eligible to serve as governors of almost any school. 'I believe women often are highly qualified for it, and when I see the admirable part which such women as Miss

Davies and Mrs Anderson take in the highest educational questions, I cannot tell that there may not be ladies equally qualified in many parts of the country.'[53] Those who had charge, though, of large foundations maintaining several schools, where the general provision 'Women may be governors' could actually lead to their governing boys' schools, took a different view. At Bristol, for instance, when an early Draft Scheme combined the grammar school and Hospital foundations, the grammar school masters complained bitterly that there was no other classical boys' school in England 'on the governing body of which it is proposed that women shall have a place. For this arrangement no reason of any kind has ever been given; and against it objections both numerous and weighty must present themselves at once to any equitable mind'.[54] When a separate Scheme was drawn for the grammar school it still provided 'Women may be governors'. The Commissioners had to climb down eventually, faced with strong resistance from the trustees, but they refused to demote the female governors in the Scheme for Red Maids Hospital to the status of a sub-committee.

Again, at Exeter a similar clause relating to the governing body of the whole trust was objected to. A memorial from the Mayor and Councillors protested 'that the feminine pronoun should be struck out of all clauses relating to the Governing Body of the Grammar School and St. John's Hospital'.[55] Likewise, the Stourbridge trustees expressed a hope 'that the three women named as Governors would at all events have nothing to do with the Grammar School',[56] while those at Beaminster, where it was planned to have a girls' school eventually, took care to make the point 'that women may fairly be nominated to act on management of a Girls' School but not otherwise'.[57]

Fitch tried to reason with the Bath City Councillors when they proposed there should be no women governors until a girls' school was actually established. The two things were connected, he said. 'One of the objects of the Scheme is to establish a Girls' School as soon as circumstances permit, and the question is more likely to be fully and maturely considered, if the Governing Body contains some of those who will naturally feel the strongest sympathy with this object.' He added, 'It is not that bodies of male governors have any thought of doing injustice to women; but that the interest which is out of sight, almost invariably falls out of mind.'[58] But the trustees insisted that no women governors should be appointed for at least five years from the date of the Scheme, and in the last resort, the Commissioners found it hard to require such appointments where there was no prospect of setting up a girls' school immediately.

The appointment of women was not always opposed;[59] and when it was, it was not always by those like the Greycoat trustees who were out of sympathy with an extended view of girls' education. The trustees of King Edward VI School, Birmingham, were in favour of establising a high grade girls' school but greatly disliked the idea of women governors.[60]

Lyttelton put all such resistance down to prejudice. It could hardly have arisen from the fear of being outvoted, for most Schemes contemplated female governors as a very small proportion of the governing body. Five out of twenty was far too few, suggested Elinor Bonham Carter in her comments on the Greycoat Scheme.[61] She thought that half the governors should be women, but the only place where this happened was Bradford. In many places it was difficult enough to impose any kind of female presence. And difficult to find the women to serve. For the Greycoat School, Lord Salisbury sneered, the Scheme had named five women governors 'of whose efficiency, seeing that they had hitherto had no opportunity of displaying their ability, the Commissioners must have judged by intuition'.[62] The five included Maria Grey, Elinor Bonham Carter and Mrs Bruce, the wife of the Home Secretary. Where, outside London, could such women be found?

'As a girls' school will be part of the plan, you will not forget to impress on all minds the importance of having the assistance of ladies on the Governing Bodies', wrote Hobhouse to Fitch when he started his inquiries at Ilminster, 'and that not as a sub committee . . . but as possessing an equal share in the general management with their male colleagues. Enquiry should be made whether any can be found willing to serve at once: if so they can be named in the Scheme: if not, provisions must be made for assuming some into the body whenever they can be found'.[63]

They could not be found in the neighbourhood of Ilminster, according to the headmaster of the school. He suggested a sub-committee. In the Keighley area, Fearon acknowledged, he could not recommend 'with any degree of confidence, the names of four ladies who should be appointed'.[64] In a fastidious city like Bath, Fitch told the Commissioners, it would be important to select ladies of the right social standing.[65]

The Endowed Schools Commissioners were undeterred. Indeed,

from the moment they instructed their Assistants to the point where they had completed a Scheme for the Education Department's approval, the appointment of women governors was a matter over which they exercised great vigilance. It was also one on which they spoke with the same voice from their first day to the day they were dismissed. One of the letters despatched that last day, 31 December 1874, was to inform the Loughborough trustees, fluttering at the thought that ladies might be present during their future deliberations, 'that the Commissioners attach so much importance to the services of women in the administration of a girls' school, that they cannot comply with the wish you express to erase this clause altogether'.[66]

7. The changeover of 1874

We lent them a pruning-hook and they have turned it into a sword wherewith to sweep over the land.

William Torrens, 1874[1]

As Falstaff says, Rebellion lay in his way and he took it: so I suppose I must say, Confiscation lay in my way, and I took it – but not from any particular pleasure I have in it.

Lord Lyttelton, 1874[2]

When the Conservatives returned to office in February 1874 it was clearly only a matter of time before they despatched the Endowed Schools Commission. *How* this should be done they were not wholly agreed and in the end they did it so clumsily as to bring some discredit on themselves. But that it was bound to be done few doubted. The Commission's existence had now become 'a rather burning political question'.[3] Indeed the reform of endowments had been so almost from the start. For this very reason Maria Grey was careful in 1871 not to give it too much prominence when it came to drafting the aims of her Women's Education Union.[4] However it might have seemed at the beginning – and the Endowed Schools Bill, as we saw, was presented as more than a party measure – it had become one with a vengeance as soon as attempts were made to apply it. Then the Tory press in Bristol exclaimed against despotic powers conferred by 'an obsequious or sleepy Parliament', and in Exeter opened fire on 'Liberal apologists of confiscation', while in London the Tory peers defended Emanuel Hospital so fiercely that the Government was forced to retreat. 'It took all Gladstone's strength to maintain the law', Hobhouse said later. The City, he recalled, Liberal for long periods in the past, turned straight Tory out of resentment at interference with its 'property', and cries of 'Robbery' from this quarter swayed the election of 1874.[5]

This was reminiscence. What struck him at the time was that the Act was premature, scarcely understood and not properly discussed during its passage to the Statute Book. 'The consequence was that when set to work, even in the most moderate fashion, it came by surprise on nine-tenths of society and excited resentment against its agents.'[6] That Hobhouse saw the Commissioners as moderate would have astounded many people. He himself had never been forgiven for the opinion he expressed years before on the subject of founders' wishes: 'those words "distilled as it were, from flint" . . . which fell from the mouth of a "Charity" Commissioner'.[7] Lyttelton was tarred with the same brush. 'This', as one opponent lamented, 'was the class of men with such communistic views which had been let loose on the country.'[8] The *Bristol Times and Mirror* was more realistic but scarcely more flattering. Lyttelton appears as 'at once arbitrary and frank', exercising power 'with a high and hard hand' with the help of subordinates, 'the Fearons and the Fitches', equally offhand and imperious. On this occasion the Commissioners' friend, Bishop Temple, is cast for good measure as 'the High-Priest of that advanced free-thinking democratic party'.[9] The words of their opponents, then, show the Commissioners as variously prejudiced, treacherous, rough, destructive, stealthy, insidious and unjust as they press ahead with their task of spoliation; but they are never moderate.

That they should have tried to be was a fallacy, in Lyttelton's opinion, arising from failure to comprehend the true rigour of the Act. 'I am told we have neglected the great principle of compromise. Compromise! Where, I should like to know in the Act of 1869, is there any indication of compromise? What I find there is not compromise but thoroughness.'[10] The Commissioners were accused of being sweeping; was it possible, he demanded, that there could be a more sweeping Act?[11] To the charge that it had never been intended that such 'very stringent and drastic' powers should be exerted to their full extent the Commissioners answered that they had not been exerted 'to anything like their full extent'. However, they affirmed that so powerful a law showed Parliament's sense of the 'accumulated evils which have gathered round this mass of Endowment . . . Now that it has been passed we cannot believe that it ought not to be administered in the spirit which dictated its provisions.'[12] In any future revision of the law, Lyttelton said bitterly in 1873, Parliament 'should say what it meant and mean what it said'. He hoped that it would not entrust Commissioners with the largest possible powers 'and then turn round and call them to account for having acted upon them'.[13]

The calling to account began in 1871 over the Scheme for Emanuel

Hospital. This, from the standpoint of Victoria Street, must be seen as the end of an age of innocence. If the Commissioners, as Hobhouse put it, were 'missionaries sent to lighten the heathen' the heathen they chose were the City Aldermen and the missionaries were practically roasted alive. But through this as through subsequent roastings they clung with the ardour of fundamentalists to the Report of the Taunton Commission which was their Bible, an authority, said Lyttelton 'which to them was without appeal'.[14] The rejection of their Scheme by the House of Lords was rejection of the Taunton principle of merit and even more, perhaps, the resistance of England's most powerful governing body to the new, open view of trusteeship. But the Commissioners, as Roby said later, were not 'cowed by turmoil or obloquy' to surrender their principles.[15] Far from that, the next year they published them.

In 1872 in a formal Report to the Committee of Council on Education[16] the Commissioners summarised their progress to date, enlarging upon the difficulties met with in seeking to popularise governing bodies, to grade the schools, to get endowment for girls, to abolish gratuitous education and settle denominational questions – in short, to do what was enjoined upon them by an Act intended to give effect to the recommendations of the Taunton Commission. In this 'Apologia pro Vita Sua' as an opponent derisively called it, there is, perhaps, a touch of defensiveness but absolutely no sign of retreat. Indeed, they are bold enough to issue a warning that if the Endowed Schools Act is to work it must be kept out of politics. 'Its fabrics are . . . of too . . . delicate a texture to stand the strain of political contest.'

The Commissioners at this time were entering upon the third and last year of their appointment. Their work was very far from done and they were now given a twelve months' extension by Order in Council as the Act had envisaged. But 1873 was a precarious year. Beyond it no further extension could be granted except by another Act of Parliament and for nearly half of it a Select Committee, appointed to assuage their enemies' resentment, sat in judgement on them. Its proceedings make clear that Anglican interests were foremost among those deeply affronted by their operations.

The Endowed Schools Act made specific provision against religious exclusiveness. In effect this meant Anglican exclusiveness. By custom and by Chancery practice the grammar schools had always been an Anglican preserve, a cause of resentment in Dissenting areas and one which the Taunton Commissioners had noted as practically scandalous in Birmingham, where half the population was Nonconformist but Nonconformists had always been excluded from the governing body of King Edward VI School.[17] Under the new Act it was forbidden to disqualify someone from becoming a governor by reason of his religious opinions or from becoming a master in a school by reason of his not having taken holy orders. But there was a loophole. Section 19 allowed restriction where it could be shown that the school's founder had expressly provided for religious teaching in accordance with the dogmas of a particular denomination. Through this aperture the governing bodies of the old grammar schools attempted to rush and many got stuck there. Fury broke loose at the Commissioners' strict construction of Section 19. 'The Church of England was to be robbed', one clergyman assured a diocesan conference which met in Lincoln in 1872. He urged that diocesan committees be formed which could act together as one mighty committee,

> by means of which they might put a stop to the violent delusions of 'the triumvirate'. Those men would then die a natural death, and they might be buried very decently, but without a single groan being heard for them or a single tear shed; and then such a stone might be put on their graves that they would never be able to rise again.[18]

His bishop eschewed such violent imagery but even he, the unworldly Wordsworth, spoke of it as an 'intolerable grievance' that the future of the schools should be decreed by three men, 'however respectable they may be . . . If no other result should follow from our deliberations today than the maintenance of the Christian character of the Endowed Schools of the Diocese, this Conference will not have met in vain.'[19]

The Irish Church had just been disestablished; godless School Boards rose throughout the land; Dissenters were admitted to Oxford and Cambridge. In the eyes of some, the Commissioners' appointment was only one of many 'hate-inspired onslaughts' of the Liberals on the Church of England. In such coin, according to this argument, Gladstone had bought Secularist and Radical support. 'The Church was to be harassed, humiliated, robbed. If there was no chance yet of the grand final *coup* of disestablishment and disendowment, there were many ways of inflicting insults, indignities and wrongs.' The Commissioners had not shrunk from expressing views as to the place of religion in schools, 'if admitted to any place at all', shocking to churchmen, both clerical and lay.

The clerical profession has been discredited. Holy Orders have been made a positive disqualification for offices of great moral trust . . . to my mind it is absolutely monstrous that this great national wrong . . . which . . . I am bound to believe, threatens a very large portion of the coming generation with the darkness of heathenism . . . should have been inflicted upon the people of England.[20]

The voice of the Women's Education Union, praising the Commissioners for wishing to enlarge the 'old clerico-feudal idea of education', is scarcely audible for cries of 'Antichrist' from one quarter; and from another, Nonconformist lamentations that the Commissioners show Anglican bias in the composition of governing bodies. The Act had been spoilt in its administration, said Edward Miall. 'The egg was fresh enough . . . and had in it the germ of life; but it had been addled.'[21]

In 1873, then, a Select Committee was appointed to investigate. 'M. and I had some excellent fun – going to hear Papa examined as an Endowed School Commissioner', wrote Lady Frederick Cavendish. 'He has been in high enjoyment at the prospect – announcing that he would "make sport for the Philistines" and so he did !' The hearing is recorded as if it were some tremendous romp at Hagley, Lyttelton 'in his best vein . . . wonderfully brilliant', here glimpsed making 'a famous dash into the Conservative ranks', there 'letting fly especially at the notion that "founders wills" were to be reckoned all-prevailing'; now 'triumphantly' clearing the Commission of the charge of being too hard upon Church schools and now 'delightful' on religious teaching. 'But can't go into it all', she writes. 'He kept everybody amused and good-humoured.'[22]

It was widely understood, though, that he and his colleagues were on trial. 'The Commission . . . must be taken to be *in extremis*. It is on its death-bed', cried Beresford Hope, full of Tory indignation that at such a time the House should have been expected to consider a new Scheme for Emanuel Hospital. The new Scheme passed, but almost simultaneously the Lords inflicted a savage wound by rejecting the Commissioners' Scheme for Birmingham whereby King Edward VI Foundation would have ceased to be exclusively Anglican. The *Telegraph* spoke of an organised attack upon the Commissioners on behalf of the Church; the *Globe* saluted 'Lord Lyttelton's Defeat'.

Looking back on the Commissioners' evidence on the crucial question of Section 19 it seems possible already to distinguish who is, and who is not, likely to survive. All three consider the clause unwork-able in its present form; but while Robinson would change it – and actually suggests the amendment which later makes it more favourable to the Anglicans – Lyttelton and Roby would strike it out. 'I think that such restrictions . . . cannot be defended,' Lyttelton said.[23] To him, as to Roby, Section 19 was simply one aspect of the dead hand and a founder should no more reach from his grave to determine the school's religious character than anything else. 'Could a liberal educa-tion exist without religious teaching?' Roby was asked. He agreed that it ought to include instruction 'in a man's duty towards God and . . . his neighbour. I do not think that it is essential to . . . be acquainted with the precise details in which one sect of Christians differs from another.'[24] His general approach recalls that desire 'to assert the civil influence for education' which had landed Kay-Shuttleworth in difficulty thirty years before. Insistence that instruc-tion should be Anglican, he said, 'has a constant tendency to hold out a flag of strife to the people of the place; whereas I should like to point to that which is most likely to conciliate rival parties, namely to the life and teaching of our common Lord'.[25] Not even this need have damned him. But just as in his office he could not resist pencilling humorous comments on files, so, on the third day of his long interro-gation, he dared to give a not wholly serious answer. Gathorne Hardy, a doctrinaire Churchman, pressed him on the power which the Commissioners bestowed on governors to regulate religious instruction. Did not this mean that they could, if they chose, teach 'a diametrically opposite religion' to what was taught formerly? Roby admitted it.

> 'If they became Mahomedans they could teach the Koran?'
> 'Yes, if they became Mahomedans they probably would.'[26]

By this single answer, it was later suggested, Roby 'sealed the doom of himself and the Commission'.[27]

But not immediately. In spite of a proposal from one of its most forceful Conservatives, Hicks-Beach, that there should be a change of personnel, the Committee did no worse than rebuke 'some' Com-missioners for causing alarm by their published opinions. The life of the Commission, they recommended, should be prolonged for another three years. As for the denominational problem, the Committee took up Robinson's suggestion that the scope of Section 19 should be enlarged – in effect, making it more favourable to the Anglicans – and this became part of an Amending Bill.[28] A further Conservative and Anglican triumph was gained at the eleventh hour by Lord Salisbury who saw to it that the Commissioners' powers were extended not for three years as the Bill provided but for one only. As Lyttelton put it: 'The noble Marquess and his Friends expected to come into power soon, and it was not unreasonable that they should say "We shall not allow our political opponents to deal for the next three or four years with these important subjects . . . We shall limit the operation of the Commission to one year and then perhaps we may have our turn." '[29]

Their turn came in February 1874. But the Conservatives, back in office and quite determined to get rid of the Commission, could not make up their minds how to do it. There followed months of uncertainty. The Endowed Schools Commissioners, whose work for the past year had been delayed and interrupted by the demands of the Select Committee, who had had to put off difficult decisions because of the doubt which hung over their future, struggled on now in what seems to have been an almost punitive isolation. Richmond, Lord President of the Council, and Sandon, Vice-President for Education, carefully avoided them.

> 'Never once, from the day they took office to the time when I had a private note . . . informing me that the Commission was to be abolished, was there any direct Communication from the heads of the Education Department to the heads of the Commission,' Lyttelton said later. 'Sometimes, when from want of information they could not help themselves, they sent their Secretary to see ours, or instructed him to write a note; but that is all.'[30]

For over four months they worked in the dark, moving warily. As Latham told Miss Buss, 'With the present Ministry in power the great thing . . . is to send up unopposed Schemes.'[31] In the case of Bristol, for instance, where they were battling to persuade the trustees to make a more liberal assignment to girls from the Peloquin Charity, they decided to back down rather than allow 'so important a case to be brought at issue before a new and unfriendly Government burdened with the open opposition of the Trustees'.[32]

The Government, meanwhile, faced with what Salisbury had once described as 'the extreme inconvenience of breaking up a piece of administrative machinery which would occupy some time in the repairing',[33] threshed about with different plans. Roby must go. They might, wrote Northcote to the Lord President, 'quietly transfer [him] to another sphere, and put in a man in whom our friends have confidence'.[34] A few days later, though, he changed his mind and came to the conclusion that nothing could be done 'in the way of quietly removing Roby'. 'I wish you could make Lyttelton the victim instead of his subordinate. Indeed I would rather we sacrificed the whole Commission as a body than that we picked out the one man.'[35] Roby, to whom he had spoken privately, thought it hard, said North-cote, to be made the scapegoat for the policy of the Commission though he did not deny that he agreed with it. As to the future of Endowed Schools work, Northcote's idea was 'to place the whole business in the hands . . . of the Education Department'. But Patric Cumin from that Department thought that there were objections to this and set them out in a long memorandum.[36] He advised transfer to the Charity Commission.

As late as late June nothing had been settled. Then, at the very end of the Session, in a flurry and a rush came the Government Bill. '[It] is not quite complete or I would send you a copy', ran the curt note to Lyttelton beforehand. In this first and only communication the Lord President explained that it was intended to hand the work over to the Charity Commission. 'I am sorry to say that this arrangement will if carried out bring your Commission to a close.'[37] And that was that.

It was monstrous behaviour, said Sir Thomas Acland during the debates. The Duke of Richmond, Lord President of the Council, 'who called himself Minister of Education,' had been more offhand with the Commissioners than he would ever have been with his tenants. 'If it had been a case of cattle disease or South Down sheep . . . the noble Duke would have spared no pains to communicate with the parties, to get all the information in his power, and to produce an impression on the minds of those with whom he had to act that he had not been behind in courtesy.'[38] The Commissioners' friends spoke up to defend them. What had they done to deserve to be dismissed? They had discharged invidious duties 'in a manly, courageous and faithful manner' and therefore naturally became unpopular. 'Theirs was like the labour of Hercules in cleaning out the Augean stables, and they had stirred up the spite and animosity of the worms and the vermin which had fattened upon the accumulated corruption of ages.'[39] Since when, asked Acland, was it Government practice to desert a Commission because it was unpopular? Had the Whigs deserted the Poor Law Commission? Had Peel, under pressure from the Deans and Chapters, thrown over the Ecclesiastical Commissioners? Was Lingen abandoned by the Government of the day?[40] With many persons, suggested Harcourt, the Commissioners of Inland Revenue might be unpopular 'but were they on that account to be dismissed?'[41]

Both sides linked the proposed dismissal with the changes which the Bill envisaged on the denominational question. A Dissenter taunted that the Commissioners 'could not be trusted to job sufficiently for the Church party'.[42] Sir Stafford Northcote, more urbanely, went so far as to admit that the work should be carried on by men who were 'in cordial relation with the Government'.[43] And the Government's intention, it seemed, was to open up Section 19 so wide as to sweep into the Anglican net almost every grammar school in England.

A great clan fury seized the Liberals. Sandon, one said, had achieved what they despaired of: 'He has re-united the Liberal Party.'[44] Under pressure, Ministers now failed not only to justify their amendments but even to show that they understood them. Sandon wrote nervously to the Prime Minister that they risked 'infinite damage' politically from part of the Bill which would only be admired by 'the smaller and most bigoted clergy'.[45] And indeed the Government's majority sank between the vote on the Second Reading and the vote on an amendment proposed by Fawcett that 'it is inexpedient to sanction a measure which will allow any one religious body to control schools that were thrown open to the whole nation by the policy of the last Parliament'. Shortly afterwards the clauses were withdrawn, albeit with a pledge from Disraeli that they would be brought forward again next Session. 'A very strange parliamentary transaction', the Women's Education Union called it. Gathorne Hardy and the Anglican interest were left lamenting the rump of a Bill which had been promoted on their behalf and now survived only to abolish the Commission.

'Commissioners thrown to the dogs as a make-weight!' Lady Frederick noted in her diary.[46] It could certainly no longer be pretended that they were unfit to apply new policy since the substance of the law would remain unchanged. In the Upper House the debate once more assumed the character with which it had opened before it ran aground on Section 19 – as the impeachment, in a sense, of Lyttelton, Roby and the ghost of Hobhouse. It was more than two years since Hobhouse had left the Endowed Schools Commission to take up his legal appointment in India but the views he and Lyttelton had expressed, even before they became Commissioners, were brought up now as part of the indictment. Like any outraged trustee or *Saturday Review*-er the Duke of Richmond began by harking back to their speeches at the Society of Arts five years earlier on 'founders' wishes'. To these opinions, he suggested, 'is very much to be attributed the evils complained of in the working of the Commission'.[47] The Government case against Lyttelton, in short, was that he had admitted such opinions; that, when given power to carry them out, he had carried them out; that he had not changed them; and that many people in the country did not like it. As was to be expected, he answered the charge, for the last time, by restating those opinions.[48]

> I have been supposed to mean all sorts of follies: that a trust should be respected as long as given trustees are alive; that it is right to respect it for exactly 50 years; whereas all I have ever said is to deny the perpetual right, or what would be equivalent to it . . . My Lords, people may call me what they like, as they have done – revolutionary, impious, sacrilegious, I know not what – I cannot depart from what I have maintained – that this supposed right of perpetual bequest has no foundation in right reason, in the principle of law, or in any other sound ground.

From this it followed, 'As I could not work on the principle of absolute deference to the will of dead founders, so I could not on that of absolute deference to the wish of living trustees.' On such vital points, Lyttelton said, Ministers' views were so different from his own 'that I do not believe we could have gone on together'. He made no secret of the wretched existence forced on the Commission since the previous year when its future had been cut to twelve months by Lord Salisbury. 'Nothing is more painful than a lingering death inflicted by benevolent men.'

> We were of course then, as we are now, wholly at their mercy; and he told us how they had, for a time, as it were, held the Commission between their finger and thumb, hesitating whether or not, then and there, to pinch us out of existence. They resolved, however, not to do so, but to leave us – as I believe it was expressed by one of the right rev. Bench – 'to live for a year with a halter round our necks, and be hanged at the end of it' – precisely what has happened.

On his own prospects he touched very lightly.

> *Moribundus vos saluto;* but I am certainly not about to make any Jeremiad on the subject. I like £1500 a year as well as anyone else: I have more cause to like it than most people. But the official work I do not like at all, nor this particular work.

It had had to be done, though, in the uncompromising spirit of the Act. The Commissioners

> had definite objects before them, and it was their duty to try if they could attain them . . . And if, in so doing – as we fully expected – we have been as a forlorn hope and fallen victims to our own exertions, I am content that it should be so.

As for their future reputation

> I might venture to indulge in some hopefulness. However ill a savour our doings may have in the nostrils of some of Her Majesty's Ministers, of many newspaper writers, and of many Governing Bodies in the country, I venture to believe that there will be hereafter a change in this respect; and that we may even be reckoned among those just persons, I do not say who need no repentance, but of whom it is said that – 'the actions of the just smell sweet and blossom in the dust'.

The demise of the Endowed Schools Commission was received by different people according to their lights. Not everyone was jubilant. The postmaster at Oakham added to the end of a routine enquiry addressed to Victoria Street:

> I greatly sympathise with the Endowed Schools Commissioners and I think they have been very harshly used by the present Government. They have been doing an excellent work and on the whole doing it well and as they necessarily became unpopular with Trustees whose abuses they wished to correct, the House of Commons ought to have manfully stood by them and not offered them up as a sacrifice.[49]

'Doth not this make amends?' scribbled Lyttelton.

Those concerned with girls' education felt forebodings of what they stood to lose. In evidence before the Select Committee Maria Grey had acknowledged the debt which they owed to the Endowed Schools Commission and as its future grew more doubtful the *Journal of the Women's Education Union* urged readers to use any influence they possessed in getting its terms of power prolonged. 'To women this is especially important, since the Commissioners have considered their claims in a way they have never been considered before.'[50] And when the worst came, 'We do not hesitate to say that the loss of Lord Lyttelton is a serious blow to the cause of women's education . . . he has been a friend, and an open friend, to those who are striving to secure girls their fair share in the endowments of the country.'[51] Two years later they were mourning his death.

In the grip of the depressive illness which had seized him inter-
mittently for years Lyttelton committed suicide in April 1876. How
much the harassment of his official work affected his condition one
can only guess. If Henry Solly's view was correct, 'his whole life was
one long conflict in which conscience was incessantly victorious but
under the strain of which a remarkably strong constitution suffered
terribly'.[52] On that reckoning the most punishing aspect of his years
on the Endowed Schools Commission would not have been the
grind – though he hated that – nor even perhaps the unpopularity –
he seems to have been generally indifferent to praise – so much as the
inevitable and never-ending clash upon the vital subject of bequests
between himself and fellow Christians. Archdeacon Denison plays
upon it lightly. 'I love you very much all ways but E. Schools way and
that way I hate you exceedingly', he wrote.[53] 'It is not a pleasant
thing,' Lyttelton admitted, 'to have to express an opinion which in
the judgement of the vast majority of the people of this country is not
only wrong, but impious and sacrilegious.'[54]

Those who paid tribute to him were confronted, in one sense, with
a surfeit of achievement: his accomplishments as scholar and sports-
man; his work for the Church, for working men, for county, for
parish, for the schools, for the poor – devotion, as Gladstone said,
rare outside England 'and rarely even in this country . . . carried so
far'.[55] Yet an after-taste of failure, inseparable perhaps from the
manner of his death, lingered in the contemplation of talents which
had left so little mark upon the nation. Gladstone's memoir pays
more respect to his friend and relative's sense of duty than to his work
as Under-Secretary for the Colonies or upon the Endowed Schools
Commission, whereby 'he was a paid servant of the Crown for a very
limited period'. Some sought explanations in his mental state. To the
great distress of Lyttelton's family and the indignation of his doctor
The Standard suggested that 'if with great powers he took so comparatively small a position, a sufficient explanation is given in the
evidence of his medical attendant'.[56] Another report alluded to his
apathy 'in larger circles of usefulness', while a friend argued that his
high integrity debarred him from a political career.[57]

It is instructive to turn from all this to the *Journal of the Women's
Education Union*. No shadow of doubt or qualification, nothing but a
sense of 'irreparable loss' pervades the homage of Maria Grey.[58]
Lyttelton, she says, had befriended their cause at a time when it was
simply an object of ridicule. She recalls his part in the Taunton

Inquiry, from which all else had flowed, and the efforts made by the Endowed Schools Commissioners under his direction to redress the 'enormous injustice' done to girls. 'An even greater service was the recognition of the fitness of women to have a voice in the education of the country' by insistence on their membership of governing bodies. It is difficult, she says, to express how much 'his strong and cordial support' meant to her when she was struggling to found the Women's Education Union and the Girls' Public Day School Company. Outside his own circle the shadow of his death must fall heaviest on the Union.

She was probably right. As the man in charge of the Endowed Schools Commission Lyttelton had been uniquely placed – more perhaps than could have been realised in 1869 or till others took over – to forward the education of girls. He did so, it seems, at least partly from that spirit which rose up in him against the dead hand, but it is not essential to fathom him entirely to see that from the standpoint of the women's movement he was the right person in the right place. 'A friend when friends were few', wrote Maria Grey, as she predicted that 'a younger generation . . . may forget what they owe to him, but we, whom he helped through the heat and burden of the day, can never forget'.[59]

A degree of continuity survived the changes of 1874. Lyttelton had gone; and Henry Roby withdrew to business life in Manchester where he and his wife were especially active among the promoters of the High School for Girls. But Canon Robinson was appointed as one of two new Charity Commissioners to be concerned with Endowed Schools work. Robinson, though committed to reform, had never been tarred with the same brush as his colleagues. 'If there was a man in the highest degree fitted for the work it was Canon Robinson,' declared one Member in the final debates, expressing regret that he 'was to be extinguished in the manner proposed by the Bill'. He was not extinguished. The appointment of Lord Clinton as the other Charity Commissioner responsible for Endowed Schools work was 'quite unexceptionable' according to Lyttelton. What else could be said? He was aged forty and had done nothing even distantly related to his new task beyond having served as a member of the University Commission. Robinson and Clinton were to have assistance from Henry Longley, a Charity Commissioner recently recruited from Poor Law work.

At a lower level, all the Assistant Commissioners were transferred to the Endowed Schools Department of the Charity Commission. For two years this remained in Victoria Street because there was no room for it in the main office. Probably outsiders noticed little change. 'I am still acting as Assistant Commissioner in charge of the case', wrote Fearon reassuringly in correspondence with trustees at Bentham. Many years later he looked back on the period immediately following the transfer as peaceful.[60] It was certainly different from the trumpet-and-drum days. The law was unaltered, the work went on, but the new men would not have recognised themselves as 'missionaries sent to lighten the heathen', 'a forlorn hope told off to die in the ditch', 'victors . . . knocked to pieces in the contest' or any of the warlike metamorphoses conjured up by Hobhouse, a civil servant, when he thought of applying the Endowed Schools Act.[61]

8. The long haul

We know nothing very definite at present respecting future arrangements and policy. But I am not without hope that the work of reorganisation and improvement will go on without substantial alteration.

J. G. Fitch, 5 August 1874[1]

It was well known that . . . the traditions of the one body, short-lived though it had been, and the traditions of the new authority were so different that the whole mode of administering the reformed endowments would in all probability be changed.

Journal of the Women's Education Union, 15 April 1876

It seems unlikely that in 1874 anyone had more cause to speculate as to the future working of the Act than those Taunton men, the Assistant Commissioners, who were now to have new masters, and the women's interest which owed so much to the warm commitment of the old ones. Would there be a drastic change or not? The extent of one change was barely foreseen, and that was the total difference in time-scale between the work of the two Commissions. When the Endowed Schools Commissioners were censured for having made so little headway with their task Lyttelton had warned that it was unrealistic to expect it to be finished in another five years, especially as in future only two Commissioners were to be engaged on the work full time. In the end it took nearly thirty; or to be precise, the Charity Commissioners carried it on until 1903, the 'temporary' nature of their powers marked quaintly by the need for annual renewal under the Expiring Laws Continuance Act. In that year, which saw the death of Fitch, long since retired, and the retirement of Fearon, sole survivor of Taunton days and now become a Charity Commissioner, the work was passed to the Board of Education. A new generation of Assistant Commissioners had succeeded the original well before this and that most keenly interested body, the Women's Education Union, had been disbanded twenty years back. The Act itself, which might have been regarded as a fairly new tool in 1875, was now almost obsolete, for no one any longer thought that an effective secondary school system could be created out of endowments. A much more efficient tool had been forged in the Education Act of 1902. Rates were the answer. It was a new world.

Some of its newness, as might have been expected, had impinged already on the Charity Commissioners. They had long encountered the power of the rates in the competition which the lesser grammar schools suffered from the operation of the School Boards and they had a foretaste of 1902 in the Welsh Intermediate Education Act. The reason why they had not finished making first Schemes at the opening of the twentieth century was partly that, like their predecessors, they found the work infinitely time-consuming, and partly that they had less and less time for it. From the late eighties they were preoccupied not just in making new Schemes but in modifying old ones to enable the grammar schools to take advantage of grants from the newly formed County Councils. Co-operation with the County Councils under the Technical Instruction Act becomes a common theme in the Commissioners' reports and they increasingly anticipate a future in which the administrative ambiguities of secondary education shall have been resolved.

As time went on, then, there was a tendency to look upon the Endowed Schools Act as a sailing vessel in the age of steam which, if no longer a likely winner, has done as well as could be expected. This is the vein in which the Charity Commissioners seem to celebrate Section 12 in their report of 1895 which marks the quarter-century since the Act was passed. This epoch, they suggest, will come to be regarded by future generations as comparable in the endowment of girls' schools 'to that which is marked, for the Education of Boys and Men by the Reformation'.[2] The Bryce Commissioners, reporting the same year, found this worth repeating and pointed out that some eighty endowed schools now gave secondary education to girls compared with only twelve found by the Taunton Commission. It was perhaps to be regretted, they said, that more had not been done in this direction. 'This, however, is a defect for which the backward state of public opinion and not the Charity Commission is to blame.'[3]

If there was any incongruity between this statement and their reference just beforehand to 'the great change' in public opinion in regard to girls' education the Bryce Commissioners did not examine it. Nor did they look far enough to discover that Schemes for over half of the eighty schools had been made by the Endowed Schools Commissioners in the first five years of the Act; and that, if their successors had done as well – that is, if the Charity Commission had produced an equivalent *proportion* of girls' schools to boys' – the total would have come to many more than eighty.

The feminists, in short, had been right in fearing that girls stood to lose under the new regime. But Fitch was right, too, in his expectation that the work would go on much as before. It certainly suffered the old constraints. It threw up one or two public servants who stand comparison with the earlier men, and there were classic victories for girls, notably over Christ's Hospital and Leeds. If the Charity Commissioners are to be arraigned for having in a manner let down the girls' cause it is only fair that their positive achievements should first be considered.

Old constraints

'You cannot have more of a cat than its skin', wrote a shrewd critic of the Cirencester Scheme, 'and I think that for all practical purposes the "upper girl" clauses might wait till a convulsion of nature gives us enlarged funds.'[4] Money remained crucial. There was still no easy way to get it for girls except, as before, through the liberality of the great companies with accumulated income beyond what they needed for their own members. To a committee in 1886 Richmond described the Skinners' generosity. 'They asked us simply "Where can we best act on behalf of girls' education?" They were willing to receive suggestions of any kind from us.'[5] The Skinners endowed a girls' school in Hackney; the Leathersellers offered a site for one in Lewisham; the Brewers' Company provided endowment for Dame Alice Owen's School in Clerkenwell.

Other accessions of 'uncommitted' money gave girls a chance. The most notable, perhaps, came from the Hulme Trust Estates in Manchester which provided £500 p.a. for the Manchester High School for Girls and a similar income plus £6000 capital to initiate a girls' school in Oldham. The conversion of non-educational funds under Section 30, though apparently less common as time went on, remained a useful source. The trustees of Municipal Charities at Ipswich endowed a boys' and a girls' school in this way. The warden and assistants of Rochester Bridge endowed the Maidstone Grammar School for Girls. £200 a year for girls' education was assigned from the endowment of Nottingham High School which had been increased by the conversion of part of Sir Thomas White's Loan Charity. At Hastings and at Yardley, where Schemes were made which included

contingent provision for girls, doles and apprentice fees were
converted, and at Lewisham they added to the girls' school endowment.

The Lewisham school had its origins, unusually, in a recent
bequest to found a grammar school for girls. In such a case, at least,
the application of funds to girls' secondary education was incontro-
vertible, as it was at Salisbury where the Godolphin School for '12
young orphan gentlewomen' received its new Scheme in 1886. But
such cases had little bearing on the main problem which continued
to be how to forward the claims of girls where the ground was already
staked.

In this period the rights of the poor had a new champion in Jesse
Collings whose campaign to get allotments for labourers put him in
the forefront of resistance to any assault on rural charities. He as
much as anyone was responsible for the attention paid in 1886 by the
Select Committee on the Endowed Schools Acts to such grievances as
the abolition of free education in endowed elementary schools and
the diversion of endowments from particular localities. His activities
gave new meaning to the old cry of 'robbing the poor'. How this
could affect girls was made clear at Yardley.[6] A Scheme converting
doles to education had gone through easily in 1878. It was to endow
elementary schools, but with the proviso that when surplus funds
amounted to £2000 the governors would apply for a Scheme to
establish grammar schools as well. This point came in 1886. The
Commissioners' inquiries seemed to suggest that there was a good
chance of getting a girls' school. But by 1887 local attitudes had
changed. A petition from 'cottagers and poor inhabitants' objected to
endowing a middle-class school. A public meeting in Yardley resolved
that steps be taken to provide allotments and that Jesse Collings be
approached for help in securing a Scheme which should benefit the
poor. Collings wrote to Fearon with the suggestion of starting an
industrial agricultural school. Negotiations dragged on into the
nineties when Austen Chamberlain took a hand. 'Public and parliamentary opinion,' he told the Commissioners, 'was materially changed
and he believed he had a good enough case to defeat a secondary
education scheme.' Almshouses and recreation grounds, allotments
and industrial scholarships were canvassed. A Scheme was made at
last in 1897, but not for a girls' school.

With St Olave's, Southwark, it took fifteen years to resolve the
opposition between the girls' interest and the claims of the poor. This

large foundation maintained a grammar school but also a free elementary school for boys. In 1875 when a new Scheme was thought of, the governors had all but made up their minds to close the elementary school – the London School Board now existed to make such provision – and were ready to set aside income for girls. Then on both counts they began to dither and proceedings came to a halt. When they were resumed four years later, Murray, the Assistant Commissioner, advised that if the elementary school were closed there would be enough money to start a girls' school.[7] But the parish was up in arms at the thought of losing free elementary education. The governors themselves blew hot and cold and were still doing so in 1886 when they gave evidence to the Select Committee. They would be glad, said the warden of St Olave's, to extend education to girls. But he spoke with feeling of the elementary school which gave the boys of Tooley Street their chance. 'If our elementary school is done away with we shall cut off from the very poor all the great advantages of the grammar school.' As it was, 'the ladder is complete [and] any boy of ability can go from our elementary school to the university'.[8] He viewed the opportunity offered by scholarships with the same scepticism as Jesse Collings. In any scholarship competition middle-class children would sweep the board, and so to close the free elementary school would be to take away the birthright of the poor.

The Committee heard equally impassioned evidence from Mr Bayley, the Vestry Clerk, who was foremost in the battle for a girls' school. He had already sent the Charity Commissioners a long memorandum, quoting Section 12 and arraigning the governors of St Olave's for having ceased even the modest payments to local charity schools for girls which they once made. 'The future welfare of the nation demands the higher education of women.'[9] Bayley was hissed, though, at a local meeting for having told the Select Committee that the parish favoured closing the elementary school and the Commissioners' Scheme with this provision was thrown back nervously for amendment by the Education Department. The governors turned once more to arithmetic to see where expenditure could be trimmed in the interests of the school's survival and came to the conclusion that the girls' assignment could be cut down by three-quarters. This item, they argued, 'would appear to be one that would most readily admit of reduction'.[10] The Charity Commissioners, though unwilling to cut provision for girls so drastically, did in fact reduce it a great deal in the Scheme which found approval in 1890, and under which the elementary school was to continue and to have new buildings; even if, to local indignation, it was not to be continued *free*.

In Southwark the entrenched position of the poor masked that obstacle to girls' advancement which throughout remained commonest of all: namely, the entrenched position of boys. The Highgate governors, like those at Berkhamsted, wanted boarding-houses and laboratories and a swimming-pool and gymnasium.[11] Trustees complained to the Charity Commission, as they had to their predecessors, that no money could be spared for girls, at least without damaging the prospects of the boys' school, and the result was almost always a watering-down of the girls' provision. At Kirkham the Commissioners ended by accepting that the £200 p.a. they had proposed should be postponed for a three-year period 'or such further period . . . as may be allowed'.[12] At Rochester they allowed the assignment of £100 p.a. to be deferred for five years.[13] At Handsworth they accepted that provision for girls could only be from the residue of income.[14]

A striking demonstration of loyalty to boys came from Blandford in Dorset where the Commissioners were beaten down in their attempt to make a girls' school out of a boys' school that was actually defunct. For an old foundation it had shallow roots, having been transferred to Blandford in the previous century from Milton Abbas, since, as the local story ran, 'the boys used to bag Lord Milton's fruit'. The girls' school idea was put forward by Fitch when he went to Blandford in 1870 and found pupil numbers very much run down.[15] For the same reason, five years later when the Charity Commissioners took up the case it seemed to Robinson ideal for conversion. The trustees promised to sound out the locality and according to Fearon the grammar school master was 'decidedly in favour' of the change. But, as often happened, when it came to the point more conservative attitudes prevailed. In 1877 the master retired; the school was closed, but Blandford people petitioned that it should be reopened for boys, and that was the beginning of a ten-year struggle.

The Charity Commissioners rested their case on the fact that while there were a number of grammar schools within reach of Blandford the whole of Dorset contained no comparable school for girls. This, as one of them explained, 'coupled with the increasing desire on all hands for an improvement in girls' education [was] sufficient answer to the allegation that a girls' school in Blandford [was] unnecessary'.[16] There were few signs, though, of increasing desire for girls' education in the Blandford district. The Commissioners sought and obtained support from one or two of the local gentry; they were backed by the education committee of the Salisbury diocesan synod and by Mr T. Holford Bastard, a pioneer whose main commitment was to the cause of co-education. But apart from this their only encouragement came from one parent who wanted a girls' school, and indeed felt obliged for lack of one to send his girls to Miss Buss in London, but who begged that his letter be kept private 'or it will bring down a storm of vilification upon me'.[17] At a very hostile public meeting in 1884 the three County Members pledged themselves to resist the change. One of them had already protested to the head of the Charity Commission about 'a crotchet which one of your colleagues has started for turning Blandford School, now closed, into a Girls' School',[18] and the whole thing became the subject of inquiry in 1886 by the Select Committee investigating the Endowed Schools Acts.

Witnesses from Blandford told the Committee how people had driven many miles to sign petitions against the Scheme. 'The evidence in favour of the boys' school comes in clouds all round,' said the Mayor.[19] As for its decline in recent years, he dismissed this as only reflecting a temporary shortage of professional families. Now there were a number and he had no doubt that sixty boys at least would be forthcoming. He was not interested in neighbouring grammar schools. People did not want their sons to have to travel. If, said the rector, they could not have a grammar school, he would sooner see even a technical boys' school established at Blandford than a school for girls. An absolute dislike of 'the whole high pressure system' of a girls' high school comes across strongly; the example of Weymouth, where 'they have a B.A. or M.A. or whatever it is from Girton' as head-mistress, is cited with distaste.[20] The mother of three daughters had told the Mayor she would never use a girls' school if it were established.

It never was. The Charity Commissioners put their Scheme to the Education Department and that Department turned it down. The Blandford trustees were able to consider plans for reopening the school for boys. When they next confronted an Assistant Commissioner one of them asked if the Girls' School Scheme, 'a copy of which he held in his hand', might be considered dead. On being told, yes, he marked the occasion by 'its quiet but significant rending in pieces'.[21]

It was not Blandford, then, that Richmond had in mind when he professed to the Select Committee: 'I think that more and more of the public have come to see that girls ought to have . . . their fair share'.[22]

Nor can it have been any of the Hospital Schools. The Charity Commissioners had just as much trouble in this area as their predecessors. Why should the Blue Coat School be reorganised, asked 'An Old Boy' in the *Gloucester Mercury*, in order that 'some gentlemen with *philanthropic* minds may carry out a crotchet of their own called "the higher education of women" '? Of far more use, he thought, would be an institution 'where *poor* girls would be taught modesty, civility, cleanliness, knitting, sewing, darning, mending, making and cooking. This sort of education would qualify them to be good wives and mothers in the labouring classes.'[23] 'As regards Girls', wrote the Sub-Dean of Lincoln, 'I feel that loyalty to the Founder must force a Trustee, however unwillingly, into *active opposition* to any Scheme which . . . comes to Christ's Hospital for funds.'[24] His double objection was only too familiar: that it was improper that a different sex and also a different social class should benefit. At Rishworth, where the girls on the Wheelwright Foundation received a much inferior schooling to the boys, the trustees responded to the Charity Commissioners as to their predecessors ten years before, that the education needed by local girls 'is a good plain practical education with a knowledge of domestic economy, needlework and housework'. To provide any more 'would from the circumstances of the case be inexpedient and . . . disappointing'.[25] But the Hospital battle to end all others during the Charity Commissioners' reign was with Christ's Hospital; not the one in Lincoln but the great Christ's Hospital, beloved of kings, with its schools in London and Hertford and £48,000 to spend on them annually.

Like Emanuel, that other Goliath, Christ's Hospital possessed every feature likely to make it difficult to handle. Its government was controlled by the Lord Mayor and Aldermen; its President was a Royal Duke. Little could be done without challenging the patronage of five hundred donation governors, breaking with traditions which went back to the Renaissance and moving the principal school, in London, from its hopelessly congested site.[26] It was, as was often claimed, *sui generis*, not least in the fact that its school for girls was the oldest endowed girls' school in England. A row of girls and a row of boys knelt before King Edward in the 'Foundation Picture', where the artist, supposedly Holbein, neatly showed fifteen of each. By the nineteenth century the sex distribution – seventeen girls to 1200 boys – would have posed something of a problem aesthetically. The Taunton Commissioners found it almost more unjust than if girls had been left out altogether, while the Hospital governors made quite clear that they would have been glad enough to get rid of them if it had been possible. In 1867 they went so far as to take advice on whether the provision for girls could be dropped and found it could not. For once, it seemed, the dead hand actually favoured girls: the terms of one of the old trusts forbade it. In this respect, then, as in almost every other, Christ's Hospital presented a target for reform.

The Endowed Schools Commissioners had fired on it, naturally. The Royal Duke had risen at a Mansion House banquet and declared, to cheers, that he intended to maintain 'the noble institution in the proud position which it now holds in the City of London';[27] and that was more or less how matters stood at the time the Charity Commissioners took over. In the fifteen years which elapsed before they succeeded in making a Scheme they wrestled with a number of complex issues, of which the girls' claim was only one, but from start to finish it remained a stumbling-block. The City of London was a long way from Rishworth and the Royal Duke a very different proposition from the mill-owners of that working town but when it came to girls' education there was not a pin to choose between them. Christ's Hospital, for all its Grecians and the shades of Coleridge and Lamb, was in this respect not *sui generis* but simply of the genus 'Hospital School'.

In 1875 its Committee of Almoners went so far as to recommend raising the intake of girls to fifty, these to have 'a course of sound and useful instruction' consisting of the usual elementary subjects. They thought that in the mornings the older girls should help with 'sweeping, cleaning and the like' and that

> one or two afternoons each week might be occupied by such Girls as are old enough to do it, in making or repairing their Clothes etc. Some of the Girls should also assist in the lighter laundry work . . . and should be taught cooking . . . All the above-mentioned duties should be made a part of the regular Girls' school course.[28]

Under pressure they later decided that the number of girls should rise to one hundred, in which proposal 'the Governors feel that they are really complying with the Statute', and taking girls, '*so far as conveniently may be*'. Their Hertford girls' school would hold no more. 'And moreover, the travelling of Girls four times a year unprotected to great distances, necessarily contracts the area from which they can be brought, consistently with female delicacy.'[29] The Charity Commissioners in 1880 envisaged provision for four hundred girls,

organised in two schools, the higher of which was to be first grade
with a leaving age of nineteen. The progress of their Draft was checked
by the need for an inquiry to determine whether certain parts of the
hospital revenues were exempt from the scope of the Endowed
Schools Act. When a new Draft was published in 1885 the proposal
was to take five hundred girls and the governors reacted strongly.
They did not object, they said, to benefiting girls.

> They have indeed shown already their loyalty in this matter to the
> Act of 1869 by increasing their Girls' School at Hertford to a com-
> plement of 90 but they do strongly object to the present proposal.
> The registers of the Hospital . . . and its other records show the very
> small number and slender amount of the Endowments specifically
> given or bequeathed in favour of girls . . . the girls . . . were always
> much fewer in numbers than the boys, and donors . . . deliberately
> intended the far larger share of their gifts to be applied in favour of
> boys.

Girls, however, had not been disregarded, for donors felt then,

> as many feel now, that the taking of the whole charge of a boy out of
> a family leaves in the hands of the parent what the saved expense of
> the boy represents, to help in the education of the girls and other
> children.

The Commissioners' proposal that future presentations should be
shared equally between boys and girls not surprisingly provoked
resistance. A boy's presentation was worth more, said the governors,
and was more sought after. They also objected to the idea of appointing a women's committee to oversee the girls' school, and indeed to
the whole idea of a *multitudinous boarding school for Girls* for moral, social
and physiological reasons 'on which [they] feel it unnecessary to
dwell'.[30]
     It would be tedious to rehearse the fencing by which the final
numbers were decided. The Charity Commissioners fought all the
way. What they got by the Scheme of 1890 was a school for 350 girls
and one for 850 boys. In future, admissions were largely to be made
on competition from the elementary schools, while a much reduced
number of presentations was to be shared between boys and girls in
the ratio of two to one. The *Daily News* thought the Commissioners
and the public, 'in whose interests they have acted', were to be congratulated on the victory.

New men

In 1874 the links between the Taunton Commission and the administration of the Endowed Schools Act had been quite deliberately
broken. But even had they not been, time would have broken them
as it did, by degrees, with the Assistant Commissioners transferred
wholesale to the Charity Commission. Of the five Taunton men originally appointed, only Stanton held the post till retirement. J. L.
Hammond died prematurely; Elton, an 'occasional' Assistant Commissioner, seems not to have continued after 1874; Fearon was promoted in 1886 to be Secretary of the Charity Commission while Fitch,
the most outstanding, in 1877 reverted to work in the inspectorate.
'The Assistant Commissioners "go in for the girls",' Emily Davies had
said long ago. Did their successors? Was there among them anyone
who believed, like Fitch, that 'intellect is of no sex'? The answer lies
where one might least expect it: the liveliest comments on the later
files, those which hold most sense of the future come from that devotee
of the past, Arthur Leach, historian of medieval schools.

In later years Leach attributed the interest which inspired his
research to the investigations he had had to make in the course of his
work for the Charity Commission. It is certainly easy to see the author
of *English Schools at the Reformation* in the close of his report on Walsall,
for instance:

> If it is desired to make the name of the foundation correspond to its
> true origin, the name of the schools should be altered from the fancy
> title of 'Queen Mary's Schools' to the 'Walsall Guild Grammar
> School' as, long before the reign of Mary, the Grammar School was
> in existence, maintained out of the revenues of the Guild of St. John
> Baptist.[31]

Leach had been appointed in 1884, with Winchester and New
College and All Souls behind him. He brought no scholarly support
to Section 12, finding 'more gallantry than historical accuracy' in the
claim that 'children' in grammar school charters had once been
intended to cover girls;[32] but there are many signs of a lively independence in his approach to official work. One of the Commissioners has
to rebuke him for having, off his own bat, asked the Duke of Rutland
to subsidise Lady Manners School at Bakewell.[33] More seriously, he
is 'severely reprimanded' by the Chief Commissioner in 1892 for
having, in spite of many cautions against it, published material
acquired through his work.[34] Leach's routine inspection reports

throw up a number of spirited comments which look more to the future than the past. The 'horrible exhibition of raw-flesh-coloured arms' exposed on a cold day by the inadequate costume of the Girls' Charity School in Sheffield draws from him the view that, as they make their own clothes, 'they really might be dressed in a decently modern garb'.[35] He cannot take seriously the attitude at Walsall of those who wish to separate the boys' and girls' schools by a high wall; his advice on siting ignores contiguity, 'which I do not think matters'.[36]

One of his tasks was the inspection of Schemes in operation and then he did what he could for girls: discovering, at Wigton, that a recent bequest made it possible to start a girls' school; pressing, at Walsall, that the time had arrived when funds would stretch to provision for girls;[37] at Loughborough simply drawing attention to the low salaries paid to women teachers by governors who also behaved 'very shabbily' towards the girls in the matter of playing fields. At Loughborough, too, he remarked on the fact that Latin was being taught as an extra though 'all those who learn it are going to be teachers and can least afford the extra fee'.[38]

More than once he opposed the duplication of boys' schools, urging the release of resources for girls. At Grantham this kind of duplication came about because the council had established a secondary school in its new Technical Institute though a boys' grammar school already existed. Leach, at a conference in 1901, 'on several occasions . . . pressed the . . . Technical Committee to express agreement with his view that in place of their present Day Secondary School a good High School for Girls should be established'.[39] Duplication at Macclesfield and Walsall arose because earlier Endowed School Schemes had served to confirm an existing pattern of upper and lower schools for boys. At Macclesfield Leach wanted to abolish the Modern School and transfer its buildings to the school for girls, then in hired premises.[40] At Walsall he canvassed the merging of the boys' schools alongside a proposal to establish one for girls and engaged in a five-year battle to force the plan through.[41] If it came to assessing what individual Assistant Commissioners achieved under Section 12 Leach would stand high. But what really pulls him out of the ruck is his capacity to speculate upon the wider implications of his work. In 1889 Leach provided the Commissioners with a report on Brunts' Charity in Mansfield in which he carefully examined a question which was topical then, and indeed still is: what ought to be the nature of a technical school and what kind of education should it give to girls?

Mansfield had an Elizabethan grammar school which had been reformed by the Endowed Schools Commissioners and now contributed to a girls' school. One of Leach's first actions in the town seems to have been to persuade the governors to raise this contribution from £100 to £150 a year. But his main concern was to raise the sights of Brunts' trustees beyond elementary schooling to the concept of a modern technical school.[42]

What courses and facilities should it offer? In 1889 working precedents were few. Such as they were Leach sought them out: the celebrated Alan Glen School in Glasgow, the Trade School at Keighley, the Technical School in Bradford. For the time being he is thoroughly absorbed in purpose-built laboratories, in the relationship which ought to exist between industry and school and the need for pupils to *experiment* in science, turning upon this novel area the single-mindedness of the muniment room. But it is when he reflects on girls that he shows Fitch's lack of inhibition. Chemistry and physics, designing and woodwork, geometry, mechanics and all the other subjects, 'except the heavier work in iron', ought to be for girls and boys alike. The trustees saw the girls as servants and dressmakers but there was no reason why they should not acquire the same knowledge of science as the boys, says Leach, 'and even of machinery'. Indeed, considering the number of girls employed in all the textile industries,

> there is a very good reason for teaching them a knowledge of mechanics, machine drawing, and designing, while the raising of female labour to a higher level of efficiency might also tend to obliterate the distinction, disastrous alike to both sexes, between the rate of wages paid to women and to men.

It is deplorable, he says,

> to go into pottery works and see the men employed as potters and designers and painters, doing the lighter and more delicate work, while the women, from want of education, are employed in the heavier work of throwing the wheel, and fetching and carrying materials and finished articles. So, too, in the lace, cotton, and other factories the women mind the machines and do heavy work on them, while the men design the patterns and supervise the workers.

While women worked in factories it was absurd to educate poor girls on the assumption that they were all to be cooks or ladies' maids 'while rich girls are all to be educated as if they were bound to be artists in music, painting or sculpture'.

Leach did not get all he hoped for at Brunts' but his recommendations enliven the humdrum records of Assistant Commissioners. At Commissioner level there is no one like him; but there is Sir George Young. If Leach's attitudes are sometimes reminiscent of Joshua Fitch, Young has something of the fighting spirit which evokes the early days of Hobhouse and Roby. It was a quality he kept into old age. The 1920s saw him still active, especially on behalf of Reading University. 'When it was announced that, after many years of effort, Reading was to have a university charter, this man of eighty-five', its Vice-Chancellor recalled, 'was the first of an audience of 1000 people to leap to his feet, with uplifted arm.'[43]

If any Charity Commissioner could enter into Hobhouse's imagery of dying in the ditch or mounting the wall it would have been Young. 'To make such schools . . . is worth a fight', he writes of Rishworth during the long struggle with the Wheelwright trustees. And at Blandford, directing operations, he tartly dismisses the tepid reaction of an acquaintance with the words, 'Sir Talbot Baker's *croak* proceeds from timidity'.

Timidity can hardly have been known to Young. Before he became a Charity Commissioner on the death of Robinson in 1882 he had already made his mark, not only by forays into Liberal politics and impressive service on various Commissions, but as a swimmer, climber and explorer. Possibly the move to the Charity Commission may be judged as a stepping aside from the large issues of his earlier years. For he had been one of that dazzling company of academic radicals from Oxford and Cambridge, authors of *Essays on Reform*, vigorous in the Tests agitation, whom in the sixties Morley had seen as 'the . . . governing generation of thirty years hence'.[44] Hardly any, in the event, ended in the forefront of Liberal politics. Young failed three times to get into Parliament and the lines of his career were settled after the murder in 1882 of his closest political friend, Lord Frederick Cavendish, whom he had agreed to join as secretary in Ireland. As a civil servant his talents carried him in the end to the post of Chief Commissioner but his main work was done in the endowed schools department where he dealt a few shrewd blows for girls.

One of them, oddly, was against Charles Roundell, that staunch friend of girls' education who nonetheless sustained the opposition in what an interested official nicknamed 'the great "Latin" or "no-Latin" case' concerning Skipton Middle School for Girls. Roundell, not only a local trustee but chairman of the Girls' Public Day School Company, adduced the Company's experience to argue, first, that the Skipton headmistress should not be given power of dismissing staff (women, he said, were more liable than men to be swayed by 'personal feeling and, jealousy') and, further, that since many girls would leave at fifteen it would be a waste of time teaching them Latin.[45]

The Charity Commissioners answered that they did not think the powers in question were 'too great to be conferred upon well-qualified persons of the female sex'.[46] But it was upon the question of Latin, where the Education Department seemed half inclined to follow Roundell, that Young threw the book at him. The Taunton Report had shown up the deficiencies of girls' schools, he said, and much of the great improvement since then was due to their following the methods of boys' schools, notably in the teaching of Latin. Young enlarged on its peculiar virtues as a mental discipline, a linguistic reservoir and a guarantor of standards. 'To provide that some Latin shall be taught . . . is to take security that the teaching of language shall not degenerate into the mere inculcation of the art to chatter in a foreign speech. It is to secure that the principal teacher, at all events, shall have had a training, in this respect, suitable for her position.'[47] Latin was retained in the Skipton Scheme.

To press the claims of girls' education it was necessary now as it had always been not only to consider them important – and Young was active in the movement to admit women to degrees – but to be o ugh, and he was known as tough throughout his years in the public service. He did not always win. Where girls were concerned the Blandford case was a conspicuous failure; but his tenacity over Leeds achieved a victory of special interest.

The Endowed Schools Commissioners, many years before, had made little progress here and gave up the case, owing, Young suggested, to strong opposition from the then headmaster. A girls' high school had been started by enthusiasts but without endowment and its efforts to get some so far had been worse than useless. Young turned to Leeds in 1884. Something should be done for girls, he told Stanton. It was even true that the founder's will, which spoke of 'young scholars, youths and children', did not actually exclude them.[48] But Stanton found the trustees wary, and not above trying to intimidate him by harking back to a supposed assurance which they ascribed to the late Canon Robinson that no new Scheme would be forced upon the Grammar School. On girls, he said, they were 'studiedly reticent and would make no statement committing themselves', despite the fact that they had once undertaken to consider an assignment to girls out of dole funds. The vicar spoke for all in that 'he failed to see that Girls' education in Leeds needed such assistance'.[49]

Young thought otherwise. The Grammar School's income was nearly £4500 a year. The Board took a strong view, he wrote to Stanton, of giving girls something out of this endowment and had agreed on £500 a year. When they heard of this the trustees said tartly that their funds were not unlimited, 'as appears to be supposed', and barely covered the needs of the Grammar School. Nevertheless the clause went in and Young dismissed their plea that it be made conditional for, as Stanton said, the time when they were likely to feel able to afford the £500 'would be a very distant one'.

As might have been expected, publication of the Scheme brought hard pressure. One of the Leeds Members called to see Young and was very belligerent. According to him, 'it was some Extreme Radicals who had professed to think Girls were neglected'.[50] The Commissioners stood firm, inviting the trustees to show why they could not find £500 for girls. When no explanation was forthcoming they put the Scheme forward in the usual way for approval by the Education Department.

The consequence of this was to shift the pressure away from Young and the Charity Commission and onto those who at this stage were their masters. And the consequence of that was that in no time at all Young had to justify the stand he had taken. In no case, he told the Education Department, had the Charity Commissioners felt it 'more peremptorily incumbent' upon them to make provision under Section 12 than they did here.[51] The pressure kept up. The Grammar School headmaster and another Member tackled the Vice-President, Sir William Hart Dyke, and this brought Cumin, the Permanent Secretary, back to Young, looking for some concession. But the concession Young proposed, whereby in certain circumstances the Commissioners might accept £400 instead of £500, cut no ice at all with the Trustees. Cumin was told by a deputation that £250 was all they could afford.

He went back to Young. The stage had now been reached, after four years of negotiation, where the girls' assignment was the only point outstanding. 'My Lords would be glad', ran Cumin's letter, 'of [the Commissioners'] further observations.' But would they, actually? It seemed to Young doubtful. He despatched Stanton to find out unofficially whether it was any good giving more reasons. 'Our reasons do not seem to weigh with the Education Department while somebody on the other side remains in an attitude of general opposition.'[52]

He had judged correctly. Stanton informed him that the Department would go no further unless the Commissioners agreed to limit the assignment made to girls to £250 a year. In its present form, opposed by all the Leeds Members, there was no chance that the Scheme would go through. Apart from that, the Education Department 'expected a fight in respect of Christ's Hospital and did not want to multiply their battles'.[53]

The Charity Commissioners would not yield. They absolutely refused to accept that no more money was available for girls. Deadlock had been reached and the Scheme was put aside. For four years, apart from desultory inquiries, the occasional Question or deputation, Leeds was disregarded. Then in 1894, mainly at the instance of the Leeds School Board, the Scheme was taken out again and dusted down and the trustees were informed to their surprise that the Education Department proposed to approve it.

They responded in character. To revive the Scheme now, they said, was untimely because of the appointment of the Bryce Commission, inquiring into secondary education. Apart from that, things had changed in Leeds; there were now two excellent board schools there giving higher grade education to girls. As for their own funds, anything to spare would be needed to supply gymnasia and swimming-baths and to subsidise reduction of fees if they were forced to this by competition from the board schools.[54]

It was true that the Grammar School had been declining. The Bryce Commission's Report when it came compared Leeds unfavourably with Bradford and Manchester. It was now one of the very few foundations in the West Riding still unreorganised; governed, in fact, by a Chancery Scheme dating from 1855. In 1897 the trustees gave in. They approached the Education Department and said they were willing to accept the Scheme. As for the girls' clause, they would very much rather that it should be expunged altogether. 'If, however, no Scheme would be approved which failed to make any provision for that purpose', they suggested, instead of an annual payment, that £12,000 should be assigned from capital at such time as a girls' school was established.[55] This was acceptable but for one thing: it was Young who put the sting in the tail by his insistence that the allocation should actually date from the date of the Scheme so that, till such time as the capital was used, it would gather interest for the benefit of girls.

9. The Charity Commission spirit

It is well known that the Charity Commissioners have excited no feeling of hostility throughout the country; on the contrary they have displayed singular prudence and common sense.

Patric Cumin, 1874[1]

If Young's vitality recalls the old days a glance once more at the relative achievements of the Charity Commissioners and their predecessors in this field of girls' education makes quite clear that the old days had gone. Lyttelton and his colleagues were responsible for Schemes establishing 178 grammar schools, of which 47 were for girls and one was mixed. The Charity Commissioners were responsible for Schemes establishing 335 grammar schools, of which 47 were for girls and 6 were mixed. If the mixed schools are divided equally between the sexes, then girls' schools comprise 27 per cent of the output of the Endowed Schools Commissioners and 15 per cent of their successors'.[2] This is a significant difference and one to which other noticeable differences, such as time-scale and total work-load, are irrelevant.[3]

No one, one imagines, would have been more surprised at such an outcome than the Charity Commissioners. In 1886 the Select Committee appointed to inquire into the Endowed Schools Acts heard that a great deal had been done for girls. 'I may say at once that we have been able to act upon that section very largely,' said Richmond, while Young, who was in charge of endowed schools work, spoke of the necessities of female education as 'specially commended to us by this clause'.[4] They could certainly claim to have favoured it, he said, 'as indeed under the terms of the Act we are bound to do'. More than once in their annual reports the Charity Commissioners draw attention to the growth of provision under Section 12 and show concern that what had been accomplished, 'however satisfactory in itself', was far from meeting the requirements of the case. They were certainly not conscious of weakened commitment yet these are the results, achieved over a period when public opinion was widely agreed to have become more favourable towards girls' education.

'Many long-applauded sneers . . . levelled against it seem apparently to have lost their force,' the feminists noted in the mid-seventies, Emily Shirreff observing with pleasure the absence of those 'button-sewing, soup-making, general man-pleasing mission of woman upon earth' arguments which had once bedevilled discussion on the subject.[5] It was, of course, still possible to meet them. In the early nineties Town Councillors in Walsall debated this question in a style which suggests that the Taunton Report had never been written.

> Councillor Baker objected to girls of 14 bəing taught at school piano playing, fiddling, painting, natural science, when at 16 they would have a beau (laughter).
> *The Mayor:* As well as the fiddle.
> *Councillor Baker:* And at 20 they'll be thinking of getting married.
> *Councillor Clare:* Wish to be perhaps (laughter).[6]

Whether Walsall was more representative of public opinion in the later years than Tadcaster, say, where the inhabitants wanted a girls' school to commemorate the Jubilee, there is no telling. We can only note that the Commissioners themselves, in spite of Blandford and Leeds and Christ's Hospital, were in no doubt that they met less resistance to the application of Section 12. Richmond said as much to the Select Committee. He thought the public had grown more willing 'to give girls what I may call their share in these endowments'.[7] Familiar himself with endowed schools work from his early days as Assistant Secretary, under Roby, to his present post of Charity Commissioner, he had seen 'a very remarkable change'. He could not now, he said, describe public feeling in the terms used by the Endowed Schools Commissioners when they spoke of the determined opposition which met their efforts to do something for girls. The evidence of Fearon and Young bears him out. Whether, said Richmond, the change were due

> to the fact that the schools which have been established for girls under Schemes of ours have . . . been remarkably successful . . . or whether it be due to the great public work . . . carried out by the Girls Public Day School Company . . . the fact, I think, is quite indisputable, that not only do we find, whenever we make a proposal in favour of an extension of an endowment to girls, provided it can be done without . . . endangering the work which the endowment may have hitherto been devoted to, that it is not objected to, but, on the contrary, we very often are urged in that direction.[8]

Then why did they not achieve more for girls? It cannot have been that the 'easiest' cases in this respect had already been settled by the time the Charity Commissioners took over for their predecessors did not work in that way. Nor are there obvious external factors operating after 1874 to account for their disappointing performance. True, in some districts in the eighties and nineties the Charity Commissioners had to contend with the effects of the agricultural depression. The fall in rents hit some old Schemes badly and more than once appears as a reason why marginal claims have not been met. Some of these claims affected girls: pension money, on becoming available, was sometimes absorbed into general funds instead of going to girls as the Scheme required; exhibitions might remain unpaid. It must be said, though, that the Charity Commissioners in their reports and public utterances never link this particular problem with the prospects of girls, nor in fact present it as cramping the making of *new* Schemes at all.

We are left then with the most conspicuous difference between the two Commissions: the difference of commitment. Nothing in that radical measure, the Endowed Schools Act of 1869, was more radical than Section 12; nowhere is it likelier that falling commitment would show than in the tricky field of girls' education. Those who cared most for it feared what would happen; and in the end the figures proved them right.

Straws in the wind

Despite the fact that one of the Commissioners and all the Assistant Commissioners continued under the new administration there are small signs, straws in the wind, of a changed spirit after 1874. The trustees of Ashby-de-la-Zouch, for instance, felt it sufficiently to make clear to Stanton that they expected the Charity Commissioners to draft a Scheme which made no provision for girls.[9] This had been a main cause of dispute between themselves and the Endowed Schools Commission and their expectations proved perfectly correct. The case of Hipperholme too has interest because it was continued by Robinson and Fearon, and Fearon in his earlier investigations had so plainly inclined to the 'progressives' as to be accused by their opponents of prejudice. 'We notice one important omission', wrote a group of residents in 1877, comparing the Scheme which had just been published with the Draft of the Endowed Schools Commission, 'viz. that you have struck out the whole of "Part 4" . . . relating to the "Education of Girls".' They went on to explain: 'We should much prefer that you would either include these clauses . . . or some others giving the Governors the power to include girls if they think proper, whenever the funds of the trust admit of it.'[10] They were not included. Fearon's comment was that the addition 'would hardly be desirable [since] there is no present prospect of any funds being available for . . . Girls'. Yet all that had been asked for was a general phrase.

> You have we believe given such power to other schools in the country, under similar trusts, and we should very much like our daughters at some future time to be able to partake of the benefits arising from such a school, and we are quite sure that such an addition would be welcomed by all who are interested in the school here.

It would be straining the evidence too far to say that Hipperholme typifies the changed mood in which the Endowed Schools Acts were now administered. There could be a hundred other cases in which no difference was perceptible at all. In one sensitive area, however, it was conspicuous: the feminists noted that the Charity Commissioners were not in the habit of putting women onto governing bodies.

At the time of transfer they had feared the worst; now, in April 1876, the Women's Education Union lamented 'that our fears are likely to be most seriously realised'. The Charity Commissioners, they observed, not only had no women governors in boys' schools, 'but strange as it may seem, in all those schemes which have been published, and which relate to girls' schools, has the provision made by the late Commissioners for securing that women should be represented on the Boards, been carefully excluded'.[11] It was perfectly true that the absence of any specific provision did not strictly bar women from serving but it seemed obvious that this was the intent, especially as 'When we analyse the recent schemes further, we seem to get a still clearer insight into the spirit which has ruled their framers. We find that provision is made by which the governors may appoint a ladies' Committee.' A weak enough provision in all respects. 'It is enacted merely that governors *may* (not even *shall*) appoint a Ladies Committee', the Union noted in a memorial now submitted to the Charity Commission. Lyttelton was among those who signed it, and indeed its arguments had been his own.

These Ladies Committees, even if appointed, will not in the very slightest degree make amends for the entire absence of any representation of female interests in the governing body. The Ladies Committee can, in fact, do nothing but what they are told, and will have no voice in regulating the school routine, appointing the teachers, and, above all, apportioning the endowments. In endowments which are to be shared between the sexes this is obviously a very important matter.[12]

The Union's memorial named five cases of recent Schemes relating to girls' schools which made no provision for women governors. 'Past experience gives too good reason to fear that if the girls' schools have no women to . . . defend them . . . their interests will be systematically and most unjustly sacrificed.' The Schemes named provided for a Ladies Committee. There were in fact others which could have been cited which lacked even this modest provision: Tideswell, Tiverton and Upholland; above all, Birmingham.

The overturning of the Endowed Schools Commissioners' Scheme for King Edward VI Foundation in 1873 had been a Tory triumph, aimed at preserving the school as Anglican and at preventing its governing body being controlled by what *The Times* called 'the wire-pullers of Birmingham vestries'. For the trustees it had meant a reprieve, not only upon such major issues but on another aspect of their constitution. Willing as they were to start a girls' school they did not want to have women governors; nor, it seemed, did anyone in the locality. 'On the contrary', Hammond had noted, 'the feeling is rather against them in Birmingham, where at the late School Board elections no female candidate ventured to come forward.'[13] Despite all this the Endowed Schools Commissioners insisted on putting into their Scheme 'Women may be governors'.

When it was revived in 1875 by the Charity Commission these words had gone. In all the hullabaloo aroused by the new Scheme's proposals for the governing body hardly anyone noticed that. Yet it had the effect that a great foundation, providing one of the leading girls' schools as well as four other grammar schools for girls, had no women governors until 1910.

Pressure from the Women's Education Union did little to modify official policy. At the end of June 1876 a high-powered deputation led by Lord Aberdare and including James Stansfield and the Dean of Lincoln as well as Maria Grey, Miss Buss and other feminists called upon the Charity Commission to reiterate the arguments already expressed in their memorial on women governors. They urged the experience of women on School Boards, the need to secure the interest of girls on mixed endowments and the ineffectual, if not harmful, results likely to arise from using Ladies Committees. Miss Buss envisaged collision with headmistresses who would naturally 'acknowledge no authority but that legally provided in the Schemes', that is, the governors; while Mrs Grey's view was that women had better have no influence at all 'than that they should exercise it in this irresponsible and undignified manner'. The Charity Commissioners' reaction to all this seems to have been courteous but noncommittal. Canon Robinson, whom the deputation noted as the only representative of the late Commission, pointed out that in several cases the Endowed Schools Commissioners had been obliged through the opposition of trustees to give up placing women on governing bodies 'under pain of losing all benefit . . . for girls'. And in a letter following up the deputation the Commissioners spoke of the practical difficulty surrounding the appointment of women governors. It would be their 'desire and aim' to give women influence in the management of girls' schools but they felt 'unable to pledge themselves to any course in particular cases'.[14]

As their minutes show, they deferred to the Union only by deciding 'as a general rule' that in Schemes providing for girls' education there should be a clause enabling women to be governors.[15] Some of their later Schemes include this provision; some do not. When Sir George Young came to explain their practice to the Bryce Commission in the 1890s he said that they usually appointed women governors but sometimes preferred a Ladies' Committee. 'Both have their advocates. I have not been able to form any decided opinion as to which is the better way.'[16]

It is in the realm of 'decided opinion' that commitment lies. The enormous importance which Lyttelton attached to this particular question would have made it impossible for him to say as Young did to the Bryce Commission on Secondary Education 'I would leave it entirely open'; or 'we have not . . . favoured placing restrictions upon the choice of those to whom the choice is committed'. It was their sense of receding commitment which drove the Women's Union in 1876 to plead for great efforts to open the eyes of the Charity Commission in regard to women governors. 'Without this, we fear that the battle which the old Endowed Schools Commissioners fought will have to be begun all over again.'[17]

A judicial body

In July 1876 when William Latham, the Assistant Commissioner, was concerned to offer guidance to Miss Buss he advised her to think very carefully before seeking rulings from the Charity Commissioners, in that the lawyer's verdict they would offer might not be what she wanted to hear. 'In exercising this function', he explained, 'they are strictly a judicial body, doing what used to be done by . . . Chancery . . . they are bound by precedents and by strict rules of interpretation and expediency in such matters is to them a naught.'[18]

This was a précis of the quasi-judicial role which had been created in 1853 when the Commissioners were first appointed to administer the Charitable Trusts Act and which had not in any sense been extinguished by the obligations laid on them later under Endowed Schools legislation. After the changeover of 1874 their work was organised in two departments, but experience of the one did not fit them for the other and it could be said that they were no more likely to shake off *cy près* overnight than the Endowed Schools Commissioners had been to forget the lessons learned from Taunton. After two years the Endowed Schools Department moved from Victoria Street to Gwydyr House. It was now part of the principal office and Endowed Schools policy was settled at a Board attended by all the Charity Commissioners and concerned also with Charitable Trusts work. What had been the climate of decision-making when Lyttelton, Hobhouse, Robinson and Roby sat round a table one can only guess; no minutes of their Board meetings survive. But generally the meetings of the Charity Commission began with the routine endorsement of Orders which had been made to appoint trustees, or extend time for the completion of sales, or redeem rent charges, or publish notices under the Agricultural Holdings Act and similar things. A tedious prologue of forty or fifty such items preceded the stage where matters were discussed 'and the opinion of the Board taken thereon'. Many of these matters were specific and technical and concerned the Charitable Trusts Acts. The overlap with Endowed Schools work can be clearly seen and it may well have been convenient, as more than one Commissioner argued, to have the two sections taken together. What is less clear is whether policy making of a dynamic kind could thrive in these conditions.

Concern with the form now rather than the spirit seems to be suggested by such an answer as the Charity Commission gave in 1891 when asked by the Girls' Public Day School Company whether there were or *were likely to be* Schemes to establish girls' schools in Gloucester. The Company wanted this information to see if it were worthwhile starting one themselves and the Commissioners replied, quite truthfully, that a Scheme existed to establish two. They did not say that their inspector had advised them, earlier that year, that a fall in income resulting from the agricultural depression made it now 'financially impossible' to start the upper school; nor that this was the latest in a series of obstacles which had prevented its being started, though there was good evidence of local demand. In short, they did not give an educational answer; and their answer helped to convince the Company that it was not worth bothering with Gloucester.[19]

Of more consequence, in that it involved the death of a girls' school already in existence, was the case of Queen Elizabeth's, Barnet. The Scheme made here in 1873 had been a particularly good example of the possibilities offered by the Act of converting alms funds to education where trustees were willing to agree. A capital sum and a substantial income was appropriated from the Jesus Hospital to set the grammar school on its feet and assign £100 p.a. to girls. Four years later, provision was made for further endowment from the Jesus Hospital and in 1883, by means of a third Scheme, another instalment from the same source enabled a girls' school to be started. Nonetheless, it was started on a shoestring, in rented premises crammed to overflowing, with iron huts to accommodate the surplus. In 1890 another Scheme was made to convert funds from the Jesus Hospital. These were used to buy the premises. Numbers went on rising and in 1891 the hospital trustees expressed their willingness to subscribe a further £1000 towards the cost of building permanent classrooms. At this point Longley, the Chief Commissioner, put his foot down.

The hospital, he said to Richmond, had been founded for six almspeople and although its income had greatly increased only six almspeople benefited still.

> Until it is shown that there is no need in the place for an extension of the benefits of the Hospital as an almshouse or for the application of the income to some eleemosynary purpose akin to an Almshouse there seems scarcely to be a prima facie case for a diversion of the income to educational purposes.

A great deal had already gone to education.

I am disposed to say that the Board must look to a *cy près* application of any surplus income and that the present proposal cannot be encouraged. [20]

If Richmond ever thought back to Taunton days the words *cy près* must have filled him with gloom. The Endowed Schools Act had cut free from *cy près* with only the proviso that trustees must consent where alms were converted to education. Here the trustees were more than willing. It seemed that the Hospital did not need its surplus; that there were three other sets of almshouses in Barnet, which in fact also had everything it needed by way of recreation ground and public hospital. Nevertheless the Chief Commissioner refused to sanction anything more than a loan.

Whether or not this decision was crucial it ushered in a time of stress for the girls' school where funds were so tight that in 1892 the loss of twelve pupils meant a deficit. The governors were driven to ask the Commissioners for permission to raise the fees, and got it after Richmond had pleaded with Longley: 'It is very hard to refuse what is asked as the finance is very close and the School most carefully managed.' [21] The only other way to economise, it seemed, would have been to cut down the mistresses' salaries 'already lately reduced by £40 a year'. Further cuts, the governors argued, 'would very seriously affect the character of the Education given. At the present moment when such efforts are being made to improve the Secondary Education of this country, it would be very unfortunate if we had to retire from the good position we have gained in the public examinations'. [22]

The fees were raised. But the school's position did not improve. The £1000 which the Jesus Hospital had been allowed to lend but not to give had not actually proved sufficient to cover the cost of the extra classrooms and the governors had had to borrow more from a bank. To pay off the bank loan, stock had been sold but this now had to be replaced out of income. Worse, in 1894 it was discovered that the governors had fallen well behind with the payment of interest on their Hospital loan. £23 a year had been agreed.

What was to be done? To put it no higher, Longley should have felt himself in a cleft stick. Two responsibilities were in conflict. The Commissioners, under the Charitable Trusts Acts, had a duty to the Jesus Hospital; the Endowed Schools Acts imposed upon them a duty to the Barnet Grammar School for Girls. It would be pleasant but unrealistic to imagine that he paused before drafting the letter which now went out to remind the governors that the interest payments on which they had defaulted constituted a first charge on their income and one enforceable under Section 9 of the Charitable Trusts Act 1855, though the Commissioners, it was said, 'would deprecate . . . the taking of such action'.[23] When they got this letter the governors were alarmed and wrote to Richmond asking to see him. In a formal answer signed by their clerk they asked if the Commissioners had changed their views, 'in accordance with which they have authorised and encouraged the employment of the surplus funds of Charities towards the promotion of Secondary Education in the town of Barnet'.[24]

It seemed that they had. Longley told the governors' deputation when it came that enough of the Hospital money had gone to education and very little 'to the extension of the eleemosynary benefits which its founder had directly in view'. For good measure he added that such funds 'would obviously be looked to in the first instance in the consideration of the question now so prominently before the public of making some state provision for old age pensions and . . . at this particular juncture it would be especially undesirable to curtail these funds in the direction now proposed'.[25] So that was that. The governors pleaded that they did not want to close the school and that local opinion was against it but in less than two weeks they announced it was to close.

These exchanges make interesting reading alongside the evidence which Longley had given in 1886 to the Select Committee. The Charity Commissioners, he ventured to affirm, had been able to profit from the mistakes, 'if mistakes they were', of their predecessors, 'and to ascertain perhaps more fully . . . the direction which public opinion is taking'.[26] But public opinion was ignored at Barnet. Longley acted there as a Charity Commissioner, that is, a kind of superior trustee, guarding the funds of the Jesus Hospital to the tune of £23 a year. Educational considerations did not come into it. They were not his business. Or rather, though he had to work the Charitable Trusts Acts *and* the Endowed Schools Acts, he spoke most readily in the idiom of the former. It should not be forgotten, he told the Committee, 'when our action is contrasted, perhaps favourably to ourselves with the action of the Endowed Schools Commissioners, that they were the pioneers who led the van of the movement'. Longley was certainly well behind the van.

Could anything else have been expected of a man who had begun his career with the Poor Law? It is more than that. The Charity

Commissioners were immured in the peculiar isolation attending an administrative Board without a minister. They were constitutionally starved of the vitality which might have come through political leadership. It is true that, like their predecessors, they had a connection with the minister responsible for education, but, in their case, this was very formal; as different as could be from the close relationship which the Endowed Schools Commissioners maintained with W. E. Forster as the minister concerned. Forster, as Roby told the Bryce Commission, took a lively interest in Endowed Schools work and there had been 'a great deal of what might be called underground communication' between his Department and Victoria Street. From this the Commissioners gained 'a force of initiative' which Roby thought they could hardly have had if they had been 'disjoined from the executive'.[27] He might have said, too, that in their brief existence they had been fuelled by tremendous zeal. Zeal is not the first requisite of judges and the Charity Commissioners' detachment did not matter while their main work was quasi-judicial. But when they took over the Endowed Schools Acts they ventured, whether they knew it or not, into educational policy-making. Then it did matter.

Local initiative

The Charity Commissioners, who in 1894 spent a little of their time, as we have seen, chasing debts for the Jesus Hospital, might have better spent it checking one of the schedules which they submitted to the Bryce Commission. For this inquiry into secondary schooling they had been asked to give details of endowments which were subject to the Endowed Schools Acts and did so in January 1895, breaking down the provision made for girls with a schedule which listed the girls' schools established and another which showed the provision made for girls in Schemes which did not establish a girls' school.[28] By running through this last one, Schedule E, the Bryce Commissioners would have gathered, for instance, that £200 p.a. from Nottingham High School, £100 from Alderman Newton's, Leicester, and other sums elsewhere were assigned to girls; that in certain cases, when a pension lapsed, girls were to benefit and that in others there was power to admit girls to the school. Taken with the schedule of established girls' schools, Schedule E bore witness to the efforts made by both Commissions under Section 12.

Unfortunately it was quite misleading. Whoever drew it up had applied the principle underlying the Commissioners' answer to the Girls' Public Day School Company. The details were correct; that is, they came from the Schemes; but in only eight out of fifty-nine cases had any attempt been made to put them into practice and in only six had girls actually benefited. Whatever the Scheme said, the governors at Nottingham had been hanging on to their £200; the school at Great Baddow with power to admit girls had been closed by the Commissioners themselves, five years previously, while for Yardley they had prepared an amending Scheme which was to repeal the relevant clause; at Bury St Edmunds when the pension lapsed it had been absorbed into general funds. And so on. Most of the clauses were worthless and in most cases proof of their worthlessness was lying in the Commissioners' files, usually in inspection reports, when they submitted Schedule E.[29]

More than likely they were simply too busy to pay proper attention to it. The impression forms of burden after burden laid upon them: the City Parochial Charities Act, the Welsh Intermediate Education Act, the Technical Instruction Act – and Schemes, like the Forth Bridge, always to be touched up. That some requirements were ignored was no secret. In 1886 a witness from Bristol complained to the Select Committee that the trustees of Red Maids' and Colston's had taken no steps to provide the new girls' schools envisaged in Schemes approved eleven years earlier. The Commissioners constantly pressed for extra staff to allow them to inspect the working of Schemes. When nothing came of it, in 1888 they began to use their Assistant Commissioners.[30] Leach was sent to Walsall and berated the governors because they had done nothing to provide the girls' school which, by the Scheme of 1873, they were bound to provide 'so soon as funds admit'. The income had increased to £1400 p.a. The time for the girls' school had arrived, he told them, 'if it had not indeed arrived before'.[31]

It was hardly possible, however, to organise a comprehensive system of inspection by using only such time as could be spared by the existing Assistant Commissioners. There were large gaps. The decade following Leach's visit to Leicester, for instance, was employed by the trustees of Alderman Newton's in unobtrusively promoting their school from the elementary to the secondary level at the expense of the allocation they were supposed to make to girls. How this would have come to light is not clear had not a local grammar school headmaster written in 1900 to complain that, as a result of this school's competition, his own establishment was 'bleeding to death'.[32] With or without inspection, then, the Charity Commissioners could not exercise strict control over the working of Schemes. Clauses might be put in to benefit girls but whether they actually amounted to anything depended more on local than on central initiative.

Berkhamsted is a case in point. It will be remembered that the grammar school headmaster, Dr Bartrum, and his governors had strongly resisted provision for girls. Nonetheless, the Scheme of 1877 provided that £250 p.a. be assigned to them when the foundation's income was 'sufficient'. Who was to judge this sufficiency? Mindful of Dr Bartrum's commitment to 'the increase and importance of his school' the Commissioners had at least taken the precaution of pegging him down to one hundred boarders. In general, though, it was left to the governors to propose a girls' school when the time was ripe, a provision tantamount, it might seem, to burying the idea altogether. Yet it was not buried. In 1884 the governors did approach the Commission with the proposition that a girls' school be started. Richmond went so far as to cite this case before the Committee of 1886 as an instance of the great change in public opinion. In point of fact what it really showed was a great change in the governing body. Following the Scheme of 1877 the grammar school governors now included three representatives of Berkhamsted Vestry, and one of them was Henry Nash. After years of lobbying for girls from the outside he was enabled to lobby from within. We see him picking his moment now and then in governors' meetings where the building of fives courts and then the paying for them was debated.[33] 'All that women require', he wrote later, 'is equal advantages with men.' It was on his motion that in 1884 the governors at last made their formal approach to the Charity Commission for a Scheme for girls. They were still divided. They were not even willing to put aside more than £100 p.a. And ten years had not changed Dr Bartrum. There was 'no crying need' for a girls' school, he said, facing the Commissioners again with his priorities – staff room, laboratory, carpenter's shop – and, word for word, with his favourite motto: 'Be just to the boys before you are generous to the girls.'[34] One newly made governor resigned in protest at the 'madness' of incurring this additional expenditure. All the same, a small girls' school was started.

It would not have been without Henry Nash. No 'bring up' system in Gwydyr House would have turned the Commissioners' attention to Berkhamsted to see if funds had become 'sufficient'. Indeed, they could not always be relied on to act when trouble was pushed right under their noses, as it was at Nottingham.

In 1882 a Scheme had been approved for Nottingham High School which made a substantial assignment to girls. In 1893 the school was inspected and the Assistant Commissioner reported that this clause had been ignored. It was, he said, 'a serious violation of the Scheme. Not a penny has been put aside out of the £200 a year appropriated . . . for the education of girls. The Governors allege want of means, but with an income . . . over £4000 the plea is hardly valid'.[35] It took six months for the Charity Commissioners to write to the trustees of Nottingham High School drawing attention to this dereliction and another nine months for the trustees to answer. When they did they dealt with a different matter and totally ignored the reference to girls. Thus fifteen months had passed from the inspection report; girls had lost another £200 and no effective action had been taken. Once again local initiative was crucial. Mr G. B. Rothera, solicitor, and one of the governors, now wrote to the Commission to ask if the girls' clause were mandatory or not.[36] Despite a reminder from him four weeks later the Commissioners seem to have sat upon this letter for all but five months before sending a copy to the clerk of the governors; and Rothera himself got nothing from them, beyond being also referred to the clerk. The peculiar futility of this rejoinder did not deter him, fortunately, from battling on to persuade his fellow governors that they were bound to honour the girls' clause.[37] He was unsuccessful. They were not to be shaken. In their correspondence with the Charity Commission the question of the girls' clause was simply ignored. For almost a year between 1895 and 1896 the governors' apathy was only equalled by that of the Commissioners, if this may be judged by their inactivity. In June 1896 Rothera once more moved a resolution that the £200 'be henceforth set apart' for girls' education. It was lost by six votes to three and Rothera resigned.

He sent a copy of his resignation letter to the Charity Commission. Its argument was plain: that Section 59 of the Nottingham Scheme seemed to him to constitute 'an absolute trust for the Higher Education of girls' and its non-observance was a breach of trust, as well as 'an injustice to those beneficiaries for whom the . . . provision is directed to be made'. In view of the emphatic decision of his colleagues he no longer felt able to remain a governor, 'so making myself responsible for a policy which I feel to be at once illegal and unjust'.[38]

Now, four years after the inspection report, the Commissioners were roused to act with some urgency. They asked the governors to send in accounts, reaffirmed that the clause must be honoured and sent down another Assistant Commissioner to bargain about the payment of arrears. Eventually, after a long discussion about the best use of the money for girls, a Scheme was approved in 1900.

Rothera and Nash exerted themselves to put pressure on fellow governors. In Watford Dr Brett exerted himself to put pressure on the Charity Commission. There was no other means of getting the grammar schools Watford had been promised. In 1875 the Endowed Schools Commissioners in one of their most imaginative Schemes had redistributed the surplus funds of the Platt Foundation, hitherto devoted to supporting the grammar school at Aldenham. From this source they found endowment for Miss Buss and also for boys' and girls' schools in Watford which had no old foundation of its own.[39] The Camden schools got their money straight away but the establishment of schools in Watford depended on the making of a Watford Scheme. Sooner or later the Charity Commissioners would probably have got round to making one but, left alone, it is hard to say when.

Dr Brett would not leave them alone. With the confidence of one who had fought successfully to provide the town with a public library, Watford's Medical Officer of Health now devoted his exceptional vigour to providing it with secondary education. 'When are we to have our 3rd grade school in Watford?'[40] This blunt enquiry came to the Commissioners with added impact from the fact of Brett's being one of the trustees of a Charity School which was also engaging their attention. His idea was that the charity endowment and the Platt money should be rolled up together to provide the much-needed grammar schools. Now, in October 1879, his letter was followed almost immediately by a petition from professional men, and that was followed, ten days later, by a deputation led by Brett. Five months passed. Then the Charity Commissioners wrote to enquire of the Brewers' Company when the Platt money would be available. The Brewers were evasive and the Charity Commissioners were obliged to fend off a request from Henry Cowper, the Watford Member, to lead another Brett-inspired deputation. In March 1881 Brett came himself, 'anxious to know if nothing could be done to hasten the Brewers'. In April he sent the Commissioners a cutting from a local paper containing a letter which he had written to the Watford Board of Health. The grammar school, of course, was not a health matter but was 'of the very greatest importance to Watford . . . and as you are the chief corporation of Watford you can act with greater effect than any private individual'.[41] In May he organised a public meeting with Lord Clarendon in the chair and again took care to supply the Commissioners with newspaper cuttings reporting the event. A Scheme to establish the Watford Endowed Schools was approved at last in 1882.

The County Councils

Dr Brett's own career hardly exemplifies his expressed opinion that public corporations could act with more effect than any private individual for he acted very effectively indeed. Further, his appeal to the Watford Board of Health on the grammar school question tells its own story: that in 1881 there was no local authority charged with an interest in secondary schools. By the end of the decade this had changed. In 1888 County Councils were created, not, it is true, to deal with secondary schools, but very soon involved with them by the back door through the curious medium of the 'Whiskey Money'.[42]

'There is something almost comic', wrote Mrs Armitage, one of the Lady Assistant Commissioners making her report to the Bryce Commission, 'in the accident which put it in the power of the County Council to provide technical instruction and the educational ladder but not secondary education.'[43] Yet the Whiskey Money, voted to the greater good of technical instruction, did find its way by various channels to irrigate the wider field of secondary education. Building grants were not confined to laboratories, senior and junior scholarships were given and annual subsidies from County Councils enabled a number of endowed schools to survive. The Charity Commissioners, as we know, were kept busy amending Schemes to allow for Councils to be represented on the governing bodies of the schools in question and were themselves extremely conscious of the 'quickening effect' of such intervention.[44]

Girls reaped the benefit as well as boys, though by no means to the same extent. By far the larger share of grants went to boys' schools, while as for scholarships, the difficulty was to find enough girls' schools where they could be held. In some counties, as a result, no attempt was made to give scholarships to girls; elsewhere there arose the curious situation which Mrs Armitage deplored in Devon of a

Council's spending money on a scholarship ladder 'while the children on the shelf to which it is supposed to climb are educationally starving'. In this context a number of Councils began to concern themselves with girls' education, sometimes using their financial leverage to ensure that a grammar school provided for both sexes. Burnley was such a case. The governors there had power under the Scheme of 1873 to start a girls' department but had never done so. Then, in the nineties, Burnley Grammar School looked like being undercut by the School Board which was planning to establish a higher grade school. After much debate the Grammar School was rescued with the aid of funds from the County Borough Council but in future it was to provide for girls.[45] Great Baddow was another case: the grammar school there had failed and was closed in 1889. Ten years later the hope of reopening it depended entirely on getting support from the Essex Technical Instruction Committee. But the Committee would not look at the idea if it were reopened solely for boys. They reasoned that as there was a boys' school at Chelmsford this endowment would, 'in the interest of the District, be best applied for the purpose of the establishment of a good Public Secondary School for Girls'.[46] Another failed grammar school, Sherrier's at Lutterworth, reopened as a mixed school in 1898 after great discussions with the County Council,[47] while Lady Manners School at Bakewell also reopened as a school for both sexes after long years in abeyance, subsidised now by funds from the County, which had pressed hard for the admission of girls.[48]

Ironically, this change, so often resisted in earlier years on grounds of finance, seemed now to hold prospects of financial salvation. As the Charity Commissioners observed, 'the rural grammar schools will find increasing difficulty in maintaining themselves in a respectable state of efficiency unless they open their doors to girls as well as boys'.[49] In Lincolnshire, where the agricultural depression had hit a number of small schools badly, the Charity Commissioners in 1899 were in touch with Lindsey County Council on the subject of the admission of girls. Lindsey's view was plain. To take in girls was often 'the best if not the only method of resuscitating a Grammar School which for want of a sufficient number of boys resident in the neighbourhood, for want of a sufficient endowment or otherwise has ceased to be capable of being carried on successfully as a school for boys only'.[50] But more than that. Lindsey had by now 'arrived at the conclusion that it was obligatory on them to make provision for the

secondary education of girls in the County' and thought that 'a determined effort' should be made to encourage their admission to existing
schools. The Council was ready to offer grants towards the cost of
providing lavatories, dividing playgrounds or other alterations, for
they faced the problem defined by Mrs Armitage: they were making
ladders which led to nowhere. Girls took up 44 per cent of
scholarships, they said, and where were they to send them?
Two of the three schools they considered suitable lay outside
their area and, besides, they had to spend a fortune on railway
fares.[51]

What gave particular edge to all this was the open conflict now
developing between the County Council and the governors at Louth.
Provision which the Louth Scheme made for girls had been neglected
year after year and Lindsey Council now wanted to know what the
Charity Commissioners were going to do about it. Rather awkwardly
it emerged that they lacked the power and the will to do anything.

The Scheme made in 1878 was quite explicit: a girls' school was to
be built at Louth three years after the date of the Scheme or at such
other time as the Commissioners approved, and £200 p.a. was
assigned to it. The Commissioners first saw that nothing had been
done in 1884 when the grammar school governors asked to be
allowed to increase the number of exhibitions, and then again in 1888
after the school had been inspected.[52] They took no action, sufficiently content to note in their return to the Bryce Commission in
1895 that the girls' school at Louth had not yet been established. Now
they were faced with Lindsey County Council insisting that the clause
take effect immediately and with governors who wanted it suspended
since they had no money to start a girls' school.

There is no sign that the Commissioners saw themselves confronted
in a sense with a moment of truth. They pleaded the state of the
grammar school's finances and its crowded site, to which the Clerk of
the Council answered that this was no explanation. If the governors,
he said, were to rearrange the staff 'and dispense with the services of
some of the . . . Masters and otherwise effect economies which could
readily be done the funds appropriated for Girls would then be
available'. Subsidies from Lindsey could not be expected till the
governors had put their own house in order, 'and unless they do
something themselves in the direction required by the Scheme I am
authorised to say that the Chairman will take steps to get the sanction

of the County Council for compelling the governors to carry out the Scheme so as to provide for the education of girls as thereby contemplated'.[53] Two months later Lindsey Education Committee asked in the same spirit 'whether the Charity Commissioners are prepared to require the Governors to definitely set aside £200 p.a. for the education of girls in accordance with the provisions of the Scheme'. It was, they said, 'the obvious duty of the Governors to carry out their obligations . . . a duty that has been neglected for now some 17 years'.[54]

The Commissioners began to take the question seriously, though not yet seriously enough. They prepared the draft of an amending Scheme reducing the stipend of future headmasters and empowering the governors to hire or purchase a building suitable for girls. This cut no ice. The Committee found there 'no indication of any determination on the part of the Charity Commissioners to see that the provisions of the existing scheme with regard to the education of girls shall be promptly carried out'. Was it, they asked, the Commissioners' intention to enforce these provisions, 'as, in the absence of some assurance on the point, it will be necessary for the Committee to reconsider their position with regard to the School'.[55] What was here implied they stated explicitly on a deputation to Sir George Young. Unless the governors could assure them that they would try to implement the Scheme 'the County Council grant of £50 p.a. would be cut off and when once cut off would not probably be again assented to'.[56] Some of their members were strongly opposed to making grants to grammar schools anyway, 'particularly a Grammar School so well endowed as Louth'.

Nine months passed with very little to show for it. The Charity Commissioners were certainly unwilling to press the governors to take any action which would tend to downgrade the school. The governors were unwilling to do more than tinker with ideas of a girls' school fund. In April 1901 the County Council lost patience and decided to withdraw their grant, adding in their explanation to the Commissioners the humiliating rider that this course had been adopted 'because it would seem that the Commissioners have also been powerless to secure the observance of the scheme made by them'.[57]

Of course they were powerless. Lindsey had stumbled on a fundamental problem in the thirty-year attempt to convert the old grammar schools into effective secondary provision: there were no sanctions. The Charity Commission, like the Endowed Schools Commissioners before them, absolutely lacked the power of the purse. At Louth a girls' school was now established by a Scheme made in 1902. The manner of its making shows how very very far, during the reign of the Charity Commissioners, initiative had moved away from the centre. It was time the County Councils took over.

10. The women's movement in the later years

These schools . . . carried forward the work of the original pioneers and made the education of girls a reality. After the first, it was not at all an exciting movement; the slow beating down of ancient prejudice, the perpetual struggle with recurring difficulties, and the gradual widening out of a new idea is a process not capable of dramatic development.

Ray Strachey, *The Cause*, 1928

That the point had come where the girls' cause was championed not by an Anne Clough or Maria Grey but by an elected local authority was a milestone, surely, a sound barrier broken, hinting at fulfilment of the feminist aim that secondary education for girls should be part of normal provision in the land. 'The existence of girls had, as it were, been discovered.' This comment made by the historian of 'the cause' on the educational scene of 1870 is just as relevant to 1900, particularly if we discard the idea that the battles waged on behalf of girls had been more or less won at the earlier date and that all that remained in the next three decades was 'the necessary but undramatic task of expansion'.[1] Naturally, what Mrs Strachey had in mind was the achievements of the pioneers: Miss Buss in Camden, Miss Beale at Cheltenham; Emily Davies founding Girton and her earlier masterstrokes – getting girls admitted to the Cambridge Locals and getting them considered by the Taunton Commission. Here, we are told, was the thin end of the wedge, and though opposition and hardship lay ahead, the thicker end was bound to follow. That may be, though whether we could now take such a bland view of the later years seems doubtful. What is quite certain is that progress in the area represented by the Endowed Schools Act cannot be described in this way.

It was, we must remember, an important area, considered from the quantitative standpoint alone. The brilliant and more frequently cited initiative of Maria Grey's Girls' Public Day School Company launched over thirty schools between the early seventies and 1900; the Endowed Schools Act launched over ninety. In that sense we have to acknowledge that the main contribution of the Victorians to the secondary education of girls was made not by pioneers but by government. It cannot, though, be seen as an expanding contribution. Here, because the Endowed Schools Commissioners were sacked in favour of the Charity Commission, we might say the thick end of the wedge came first; though, paradoxically, this did not mean that there was less drama in the later stages. Less was achieved and there was less publicity, but drama in this field, as we have seen, came not from one particular confrontation, equivalent, say, to pushing through the first of the Acts on married women's property, but from small confrontations started up from scratch, here, there and everywhere over the whole period. In the nature of things in this kind of struggle there was as much drama at Blandford in the eighties as there had been in Bristol ten years earlier, and as much in the long fight over Christ's Hospital which did not end until 1890 as in the early clash over Emanuel. There was no lack of drama from start to finish but the women's movement was not much involved in it.

Whether it could have been, and whether, if it had, more would have been accomplished in the later years are points to consider. Before that, though, we must turn to an aspect of endowed schools work which did undoubtedly exemplify the thesis of expansion and consolidation and in which women were very much involved: that is, the success of the endowed girls' grammar schools once they were started.

The new girls' schools

The inspection of the grammar schools for girls, 'a class of institutions', as the Commissioners put it, 'called into existence for the first time by the operation of the Endowed Schools Acts',[2] revealed in many cases the decided success of what had quite recently been regarded as a very hazardous undertaking.

'How is the school regarded in the neighbourhood?' was one of the questions the Assistant Commissioner had to answer after an inspection. 'Very favourably indeed', wrote R. E. Mitcheson of James Allen's School in Dulwich.[3] 'Apparently favourably', wrote Leach of the new girls' school at Ashby-de-la-Zouch, 'by the rapidity with which it is filling.'[4] Of the Wyggeston Girls' School at Leicester he stated, 'The school is full to overflowing.'[5] 'The Governors think, and rightly', it was said of Lewisham, 'that the school has had a wonderful measure of success for the short time it has been opened.'[6] The governors of the Maynard High School in Exeter appealed to the numbers seeking admission as evidence of its popularity,[7] while all five girls' schools established in Birmingham on King Edward VI Foundation were admitting more in the 1890s than they were designed to accommodate.[8]

Many pairs of new schools had come into being as a result of the Endowed Schools Acts and mostly both the boys' and the girls' school prospered. The governors of Tiffins Schools at Kingston claimed that they could double their intake if only there were room.[9] The Coborn Schools in Stepney, the Endowed Schools in Watford, the Simon Langton Schools in Canterbury all made a good start. Sometimes the governors had been specially nervous about the girls' school. What if it didn't fill? One of the earliest Schemes to be made had endowed the Orme Schools at Newcastle-under-Lyme. Less than ten years later Stanton reported that the girls' school, which had been seen as an experiment, 'acquiesced in locally with many misgivings', was most successful. 'A short time since, for 17 vacancies, there were 42 applications.'[10] While the level of success of the new 'pairs' varied, in only one instance, Wallingford, did the girls' school do markedly less well than the boys'.

Sometimes it did better, as at St Helen's where Durnford said the boys' school was worked at a loss whereas the girls' school had always paid,[11] or at Newcastle-on-Tyne where the reports on Allan's Girls' School were 'more favourable all round' than those on the boys'.[12] The Allsopp Boys' School at Burton-on-Trent was seriously threatened by the Higher Grade School but 'the numbers and success' of the Allsopp Girls' School had been little contemplated, Stanton wrote, when it was first established.[13] In other cases, where the boys' grammar school was an old one and a girls' school had been added to the foundation, similar comparisons could be made. When Leach went to Mansfield in 1889 he found the two Queen Elizabeth Grammar Schools in very different shape. The boys' school, reopened in 1875, had a poor reputation; the girls' school, 'in spite of a ten years' later start, inferior hired buildings, with no recreation ground, and no boarders, and higher fees', was a great success.[14] A few months later, making an inspection of the grammar schools in Loughborough, he found the same thing. The boys' was second rate while the girls' was 'most creditable to the Headmistress and the Governors. It . . . is already nearly as large as the Boys' Grammar School, and contains actually more from the town of Loughborough.'[15] In the early nineties, then, the Commissioners could feel confident, 'from their experience in similar cases', that a girls' school in Walsall would not only succeed but 'would indirectly assist the growth of the Boys' school'.[16] Leach had met stubborn resistance here and gained some pleasure from being proved right. In no time at all, once the girls' school was started, the governors at Walsall were applying to extend it, a fact he took the trouble to bring to Young's notice since it 'so amply justified the forcing of the scheme through in spite of the opposition'.[17]

There can be no doubt that a major factor in the success of these new schools was the calibre of the women responsible for them. Pioneer headmistresses have had a good press and the Commissioners' files do not detract from the sense of exceptional vigour and purpose conveyed by more hagiographical literature. It was the 'tact, energy, and intelligence' of Miss Crossland which made the Queen Elizabeth's Girls' School in Mansfield much more successful than the Boys', thought Leach.[18] James Allen's School prospered in the 1890s under its 'energetic and capable' headmistress,[19] while Miss Rigg, first head of Mary Datchelor, had 'gained for it a great reputation'.[20] These women faced considerable problems, though the one most often urged against girls' schools in the first place – lack of demand – seems much less prominent than the crowding of inadequate buildings. At Tiverton it was possible to boast that the girls' school was the only one in the locality 'expressly erected for the purpose',[21] but just as often schools began in rented houses and overflowed into corrugated huts. At Ashby Miss Hogg had trebled the numbers but it seemed to the Assistant Commissioner unlikely 'that so successful a teacher and organiser . . . will continue unless some improvement is effected'.[22] Three years after the Warwick school opened the governors applied to enlarge the buildings, influenced, said Stanton, 'by a desire to so improve Miss M. J. Fisher's position as to permanently secure her services'.[23] In some schools, however, headmistresses came up against a tendency of the governing body to favour the boys on the same foundation. At Ipswich the report made in 1892 shows the Boys' Grammar School had been enlarged and four new classrooms were planned for the Middle School but the girls were cramped in old buildings next the brewery where they had to put up with the smell of hops and rough behaviour in the streets. The governors said they had no funds for new premises.[24] 'I do not see why the allowance to the Boys' School should be so much larger in proportion than that to the Girls' School', wrote R. E. Mitcheson of Dame Alice Owen's in 1899,[25] while Leach thought it shabby that the girls at Loughborough had no playing field when the boys had three or four.[26]

'The ignorance and indifference of the Governors, none of whom have come into the School during her 15 months in office', was one of the things which the Wallingford headmistress blamed for her school's decline in 1891.[27] The other was private school competition, to which, as more than one report suggests, girls' grammar schools were more susceptible than boys'. Girls' education, after all, had been virtually private before this time; social objections had been among the commonest encountered in the working of Section 12 and the new headmistresses had to walk warily. A site in the middle of the town, as at Ipswich, or as in Leicester, where the Wyggeston Girls' School stood on the thoroughfare of Humberston Gate, could be a social liability. On the other hand, a good site and buildings might not counterbalance middle-class fears of social mixture in the school itself. Schemes laid down that a proportion of free places should be offered to children from the elementary schools and this scholarship ladder was always cited whenever the cry was raised of 'robbing the poor'. It did not appeal much to the better-off. Many parents in Tiverton, for instance, objected to the presence of scholarship girls.[28] In Wakefield it was alleged in the eighties that girls from elementary schools were at a disadvantage because of a 'caste feeling' in the grammar school.[29] In 1883 an Assistant Commissioner made a special inspection of Bonnell's School, West Ham, because the School Board complained that it had grown so snobbish that girls were not taking up the scholarships there. Miss Rowden, the headmistress, emphatically denied it. 'The names of the free scholars were unknown to the rest', as indeed to herself unless she looked up her records. In any case, 'the difference of social status among the paying scholars was so great that it was easy for a free scholar to pass muster'; in proof of which the Assistant Commissioner was informed of one, a prize-winner to boot, who 'might be seen any day after school hours selling apples in a small fruiterer's shop with a Virgil in one hand'.[30]

This vision notwithstanding, there was a marked tendency as time went on for the lower grade girls' schools – those, like Bonnell's, where the Scheme laid down a leaving age of fifteen and fees under £5 – to raise their sights. The Commissioners' approval was sought for girls to stay on to seventeen or later and for higher fees at Dame Alice

Owen's and Mary Datchelor's, at Roan's school in Greenwich, the Greycoat in Westminster, the Greycoat boarding school at Caversham and Red Maids', Bristol – for even the Hospitals had so far forgotten their third grade orthodoxy as to seek to rise in the world. The poorer classes tended to be left behind. The fruiterer's daughter was more and more likely to be succeeded among the fee-payers by daughters of 'poor professional people . . . clergy, doctors, teachers, clerks of all kinds'.[31] This tendency affected boys' schools too and was in part a response to the market and increased demand from the middle classes.[32] But the girls' schools were not only being pushed from below, borne aloft by rising demand, they were being drawn up from above by the influence of Girton and Newnham and the other new colleges for women of which their headmistresses were often alumnae.

Things had changed since Emily Davies had advised Lyttelton in 1870 that there were no qualifications for women worth paying any attention to. The inspection reports paid attention to them: thus, the Wallingford headmistress ignored by her governors (1891) was a B.A. London; Miss Bebbington of Tiffins (1889) had the history tripos, Miss Hamm of Simon Langton (1896) had been to Newnham, as had Miss Creek of the High School, Birmingham, who was also a London graduate; Miss Hall, headmistress of the Maynard School, Exeter (1888), had gained first class honours in the Cambridge Women's Examination but had declined a scholarship to Newnham because she wished to study at the Sorbonne.

It was maddening to well-qualified women to find themselves restricted by Schemes which aimed to terminate a girl's education just when it might lead on to something better. First grade schools were not affected, of course. With high fees and a leaving age of nineteen Miss Hall at Exeter could give free rein to what was termed an 'almost excessive ambition to make her school a phenomenal success',[33] but Miss Easton, the first headmistress at Rochester, was chafing against the leaving age of seventeen within twelve months of her appointment. Only by special permission of the governors could an occasional pupil stay longer. Ten years passed before she got her way. The school by then had distinguished itself in the Cambridge Higher Locals and won a Girton scholarship and Miss Easton herself had made a reasoned statement which convinced Sir George Young that a leaving age of nineteen was appropriate. There was, she said, no local college where girls could go after leaving school. Many became pupil teachers just to stay on. Girls could not be admitted to Oxford or Cambridge or Holloway College before eighteen, and nineteen was the upper age limit for the £60 scholarship Kent County Council now offered for the higher education of women.[34]

Grammar school headmistresses setting standards from their own experience of higher education might well have started teaching themselves under Miss Beale, or at the North London, or in schools of the Girls Public Day School Company and this, too, had its effect. The ambitious Miss Hall had been second mistress at the Company school in Norwich, Miss Easton had taught at the Sheffield High School while Miss Hickey came from the one at Ipswich to be head of the Gloucester Grammar School for Girls. This had been established as a 'lower' school but 'while keeping within the letter' of the Scheme Miss Hickey worked it up. There was certainly demand, for the 'upper' school planned for girls had not been built, while she, on appointment, 'plainly stated that her experience was derived from service under the girls' public day school company and her aim would be to conduct this school on similar lines'. The Assistant Commissioner noted that 'the result has been the lifting of the school above the type contemplated. The Social difficulty has been brought into some prominence and there have been complaints from Governors and parents that the poorer classes suffer.'[35] Miss Rutty came to Allsopp's School, Burton-on-Trent, from the prestigious Girls' Grammar School at Bradford and soon made it clear that she had set her sights well beyond the boundaries imposed by the Scheme.

> 'Since I think it necessary to raise the standard of work', she explained to one of the governors, 'I should suggest that in the list of subjects *Elements of Algebra and Geometry* should be changed to *Mathematics* so that we may take this subject as far as we please. I should also much like to add Greek, for, although it is at present impossible to take this . . . it may at some future time be desirable to do so, seeing it is required for the London degree, and for the Girton entrance examination.'[36]

She hoped to raise the leaving age and the fees and also to change the name of the school which, to her chagrin, many local people tended to link with Messrs Allsopp, the brewers. 'I myself incline to the title of "The Girls' Grammar School" as ranking us at once with the *Grammar School*,' she said, 'and avoiding all confusion with the Higher Grade School.' Miss Rutty hoped for boarding accommodation and also exhibitions so that pupils could continue 'either at the Skinner

Street Training College, or at one of the colleges at Oxford and Cambridge'. When she adds, 'a dining room is very essential', we may feel we are back with Dr Bartrum; as of course we are, in spirit. This is the kind of vitality and drive which put the public schools on the map.

It is essentially parochial, however. The energy of all the new headmistresses, even when they combined together in the Head Mistresses' Association, was not a driving force towards extending the frontiers of the endowed school system for girls. We may well suppose that the fruits of Section 12 could not have fallen into better hands but the women did nothing much to shake the tree. It looks as if, after 1874, the sense that girls' endowments were an *urgency* was lost, not only in Victoria Street but in the women's movement too.

Turning from endowment

Emily Shirreff in 1874 observed among supporters of women's education some who thought it time 'to drop the question of inequalities of endowment for boys and girls, and to smooth over all that might savour of bitterness with regard to the neglect which women . . . suffered, in this land of "freedom and equal justice to all" '.[37] It is not likely she was thinking of her sister but it certainly seems that Maria Grey's interest in the endowment question waned once the Endowed Schools Commission was disbanded. While Lyttelton and his colleagues were in charge she had, as we saw, done vigorous battle in *The Times* on the subject of endowments. At the end of November 1874 she made what seems to have been her last appearance in its correspondence columns in this connection, enlarging once more on the gross inequality of endowment between the sexes, the opposition faced by the Endowed Schools Commissioners in their efforts to redress the balance (which, she had no doubt, accounted largely for the unpopularity under which they had succumbed) and ending with what reads like a valediction: 'I can only trust that what I have said may be enough to draw the most serious attention of those who have any direct influence on the application of endowments and of the general public, the pressure of whose indirect influence would be more powerful still.'[38]

Her Education Union had done what it could to rally support to the Endowed Schools Commissioners in the uncertain days before their demise. When the crisis came and it was apparent that their powers would be transferred to the Charity Commission the Union petitioned against the Bill. The departure of Lyttelton they recognised as 'a serious blow' to women's education,[39] while their endowments sub-committee dwelt in its report on 'all these hopeful projects' (the Schemes designed to benefit girls) which must now remain for a time in abeyance.[40] Whatever happened, there was a resolve that girls' endowments would not be forgotten, 'if efforts on the part of the Union will prevent it'.[41]

In some respects, certainly, they were not forgotten. The Union, as we saw, protested strongly against the Charity Commissioners' practice of establishing a Ladies Committee instead of women governors in girls' schools. Its sub-committee continued to report on the output of Schemes which benefited girls and its *Journal* to comment on individual cases. Yet it is hard to resist the impression that after the Charity Commissioners took over, the Union lost much of its interest in endowments. In 1875 the New Year opens with a warning to readers of the *Journal* 'not to expend too much energy in attempting to secure even their rights from the old endowments of the country. Their time and strength may be better employed. It may be tempting to secure these loaves and fishes but greater results may be obtained by an expenditure of far less effort and with infinitely more personal gratification in other ways'.[42] If the efforts of all those who formed the Girls Public Day School Company, the article continued, had gone instead into trying for 'slices of existing endowments' was it likely that in two and a half years they would have been able to point to four schools and plans for many more waiting to be started? Again, in October 1875, the way in which 'the liberal schemes of the late Endowed Schools Commissioners' had been thwarted by local opposition was contrasted with the success following the energetic work of the Company, 'proof of how much may be done without endowments'. Those interested were once more warned against concentrating all their efforts on endowments 'and . . . doing nothing else'.[43]

Understandably, as time went on, the Union took pride in the part it played in helping to create public interest in girls' schools. Endowments were not entirely forgotten. In 1880 the *Journal* was still hoping 'that we shall be successful in not a few cases in restoring gradually to girls their lost privileges', or even – and the alternative is interesting – in raising new funds to secure the same end 'without depriving the boys of what they have enjoyed often so long, though . . . wrongfully'. But readers were reminded that endowments were not large and that their value was often exaggerated.[44]

As to what was actually being done with them, the *Journal*'s readers were kept informed by the reports of the endowments sub-committee, and these were not cheering. In 1877 they learned that 'very little has been done towards establishing schools for girls by the Endowed Schools Department of the Charity Commission during the past year. Enquiries have been made how far the schools for which Schemes have been framed and passed have been actually set on foot. The result is not very encouraging'.[45] Two years later it seems that the girls' claim 'has not received much more consideration in the year under review than we were able to record last year';[46] while in 1880 'no new Schemes containing provision for Girls' Schools were framed by the Commissioners during the past year and very little progress has been made in those already published'.[47]

The Women's Education Union ceased to exist in 1882, leaving its remarkable offspring, the Company, to carry on the work of getting schools started, which it did without regard to endowments, beyond ensuring, so far as possible, that they did not incur the disadvantage of being sited close to endowed schools. What other source of interest and pressure remained? The North of England Council started by Miss Clough, which, in its early days had long debated how to get the most out of Section 12, had been disbanded by 1876. As it declined a new lobby arose. Miss Buss, who understood the need for her profession to formulate standards and speak collectively, launched the Head Mistresses' Association in 1874. It was prompt to acknowledge the work that had been done by the Endowed Schools Commission to establish the position of women heads;[48] many of its members were in charge of schools created under the Endowed Schools Act. But, not surprisingly, they were more concerned with running those schools than with extending the system. A resolution that 'endowments left for *children* should be applied in a fair proportion to girls as well as . . . boys' was passed in 1896.[49] But the Association never tried to monitor the working of Section 12 in the style of the endowments sub-committee of the Women's Education Union. Indeed, when a member pointed out in the nineties 'what great work was to be done in watching the application of endowments and grants to girls, and . . . how in some counties, especially Shropshire and Essex, many valuable endowments . . . available for girls were being lost to them through neglect', the response was that 'members of the Association were far too busy to take up such work'.[50]

What they did take up was the claim of girls' schools to grants for technical education. In December 1890 at a special meeting they discussed 'the almost total omission of any provision of technical instruction especially adapted to the needs of girls' in London's proposals for spending the 'Whiskey Money.' They had sent observers to a conference arranged by the National Association for Promoting Technical Instruction at which the County Councils reported their plans. Startled to find that girls were being ignored, the headmistresses pledged themselves to work in their localities and try to stimulate governing bodies to apply for grants. Since a grant now would constitute a claim for coming years the matter was felt to be particularly urgent. At subsequent meetings they heard reports on how the matter stood under different authorities and drafted a memorial to the County Councils listing the objects for which aid was needed. In other words, they had an eye to the future and by this time endowments, as a main preoccupation, had come to seem rather a thing of the past.

A shift of emphasis away from education marked the women's movement in these later years. In Cambridge, it is true, Miss Davies continued to break lances with the Senate but from a distance what mainly appeared was that a *modus vivendi* had been found for small groups of women at the ancient universities. London admitted them in 1878 and the newer universities followed suit. The days when their presence in medical lectures created pandemonium were distant now; in 1877 the Royal Free Hospital opened its doors to women students. It was permissible, surely, to feel that in education the barriers were down; all the more by contrast with that other area where such a promising start had been made in the late sixties.

The fight for the suffrage had appeared no less hopeful at that time than the fight for education. There followed, though, a quarter-century of Bills, Resolutions, Private Members' ballots, meetings, Petitions and disappointment. When Lydia Becker died in 1890 things were no better than twenty years before when she had first emerged as leader; in fact, they were worse, for a third Reform Act had given votes to the majority of men, making the discrepancy even greater. It was suffrage, then, which filled the horizons of forward-looking women as time went on. Maria Grey, who in 1872 had 'cleared the ground' for her Union by asserting 'that this is not a woman's rights movement in the political sense of the Term',[51] brought herself five years later to recant. It had seemed unwise, she said, to drive two coaches, 'and as I was anxious to drive, or at least to be a passenger in the education coach, I thought it better to leave the suffrage coach without me'.[52] Now she wished whatever influence she had 'to be thrown into the Women's Suffrage scale. I would like to say why . . . I have felt more and more that we should never get justice in education without the suffrage, and, on the other hand, the suffrage movement has helped that for education.'

In such a context, and with the need to consolidate impressive educational gains elsewhere, the fight for endowment under Section 12 slips from the women's view; and those few instances where they involve themselves seem to indicate that such intervention was of little consequence.

Ambleside, Leeds and Manchester

Ambleside was the most curious of all. Here in 1870, as we saw, a number of distinguished women, headed by Anne Clough, had urged upon the Endowed Schools Commissioners the need to establish a school for girls on Kelsick's Foundation, and this had been done, despite considerable opposition in the town. That is, by the Scheme made in 1873 an upper department was to be added to Kelsick's boys' elementary school and a grammar school for girls built three years later. This three-year breathing space had been welcomed by William Donaldson, the Scheme's chief opponent, since he anticipated, not without reason, 'great changes in the composition and principles of conduct of the Endowed Schools Commission'.[53] The changes came, but in this instance did not bring the change of heart Donaldson had hoped for.

When the Charity Commissioners in 1880 tumbled to the fact that nothing had been done to implement the Ambleside Scheme they were not disposed to forget about the girls' school. On the contrary, the Assistant Commissioner got in touch with the women's group, such as it now was. Miss Martineau was dead and Miss Clough had gone to be in charge of Newnham. Over the years the women had done nothing to press the trustees to implement the Scheme because, he learned, 'it was generally believed that the Governors were financially embarrassed'.[54] Margaret Morse, who was now their spokeswoman, told him that she had consulted Miss Clough and those who had signed the original petition and that they still hoped the girls' school would go forward.[55] In spite of protests, then, from the governors, who had no doubt that this proposal was 'utterly opposed to the feeling of the inhabitants', a new Scheme for a girls' school was drafted.

It provoked great indignation. Local opinion now, as earlier, favoured spending the Kelsick money on elementary schools and, if there was some over, on a grammar school for boys. The Commissioners found themselves in a dilemma. They were 'somewhat embarrassed', as they told Miss Morse, 'by the divergence between the views of the Governors . . . and those of yourself and your friends, as well as by *the absence of any expression of opinion in support of the liberal provision made by the Scheme for the higher education of girls*'[56] (my italics). They had made such provision, 'relying expressly upon the assurances which they had received from yourself and others interested in promoting the higher education of girls', and had prepared the amended Scheme to assign £300 p.a. to a girls' school. 'The difficulty of securing these benefits must be greatly enhanced', they concluded, 'if the effort now made for that purpose fails to receive some local support.'

Here, surely, was a situation which could not have been conceived of by Miss Clough years ago when the North of England Council talked about stirring up local interest. The administrators were out on a limb, and that limb was Section 12, and they had ventured onto it with every encouragement, ten years back, from those who, as Miss Morse now admitted, were 'a very small minority in Ambleside'.[57] Small encouragement came from them now. Miss Clough's present view was that it would be difficult, 'indeed useless, to oppose the wishes of the people – they are set on improving the boys'.[58] And so, Miss Morse said, the women's interest had been 'led to the conviction that it would be wiser to wait even a little longer, allowing the upper department for the boys to be carried out first, if only a certain proportion of the fund can be secured for . . . girls in the future'. These were hardly fighting words and probably by now there seemed little room for fighting. 'My own personal opinion', she wrote later, 'is that Ambleside is too small a place for a school to answer . . . having only a population of 2000.'[59] The best thing might be to offer scholarships tenable at any girls' school which prepared for the Local examinations. As the Assistant Commissioner noted, she had 'very much receded from the position which she originally took up'.[60]

So the Charity Commissioners had the torch thrust upon them. It was they, not the women, who battled on against unremitting local opposition to get a Scheme which would establish a fund to endow a girls' school at Ambleside. It was Miss Morse, 'representing' the girls, who joined William Donaldson and the trustees in a memorial to the Education Department which put forward a watered-down version. It was the Commissioners who resisted pressure from a deputation to the Vice-President, citing obligations under Section 12 as the grounds on which they were 'unwilling to sacrifice' the prospect of establishing a girls' school. They got their Scheme through. A decade later the Ambleside girls' school appears in the return which they submitted to the Bryce Commission but, as Leach discovered that selfsame year, not a single brick had actually been laid.[61]

Whether or not there was a grain of truth in the angry verdict of the Kelsick trustees that Miss Clough 'wished to make everyone a lady',[62] the feminists misjudged things at Ambleside and considering their peripheral role in this small, traditional community, it does not seem surprising. Ambleside, possibly, can be regarded as a kind of freak. Leeds and Manchester cannot. What we see there in the battle for endowment is the failure of indigenous feminism.

Leeds had been involved since the 1860s with the movement to extend girls' education. It was one of the four cities where the North of England Council had started its experiment of lectures for women and interest in this area had already been channelled by the Leeds Schoolmistresses' Association and the Ladies' Educational Association before the Endowed Schools Act was passed. Representatives of these two bodies had taken part in the Council's discussions on how the Act might benefit girls and on what steps could be taken locally to improve their chances of endowment. Girls, the Leeds pioneers were aware, needed endowment even more than boys, 'for the necessity of giving boys the best education that can be invented is so fully recognised that if no such endowments existed they would still be ensured a good education – the full price would be cheerfully paid'. This was not yet the case with girls.

> The wise and thoughtful few know that girls also have a right to wholesome and sufficient mental food . . . and that they will amply repay its supply by increased mental and moral strength and beauty; but the . . . purse-bearing part of the public are not sufficiently convinced of this to induce them to pay the full price if they are not assisted by endowments.[63]

A function of endowments, they well understood, was 'to cherish through early days of adversity a good system whose merits are not

yet sufficiently recognised to cause people to provide it for themselves'. In Leeds they were, perhaps, especially aware of the uncer-
tainties of voluntary effort, for in the early seventies the number of
students attending their lectures for women declined and the Ladies'
Educational Association found itself out of pocket on expenses.
Nothing happened, though, in these years about endowment. At the
North of England Council in 1874 Miss Wilson, representing Leeds,
complained that 'they had been waiting for the Commissioners for
four years'. Though she did not know it, a Scheme for Leeds had in
fact been discussed in 1870; but the changes proposed by the Endowed
Schools Commissioners, including the need to make provision for
girls, met so little response from the Grammar School trustees and the
headmaster, Dr Henderson, that the case was set aside until Young,
as we saw, in 1884 began the marathon contest which lasted until the
end of the century.

Long before this the feminists in Leeds decided not to wait for
endowment but to start a girls' high school on their own. In 1876
they formed a company to do this, joined by a number of interested
men, including the Grammar School headmaster, Dr Henderson, and
the vicar of Leeds, Dr Gott. In the circumstances they could have
done no better. The school made a good start. Its early success speaks
for their vision and organisation and makes what happened next
seem the more surprising. It had not been long opened before they
discovered that endowment from the Leeds Poors Estate, a dole fund,
was to be transferred to education; more specifically, to finance
exhibitions for boys attending the Grammar School. It seemed
unbelievable. In all their discussions in the North of England Council
on how girls might benefit from dole conversion the Leeds pioneers
could never have envisaged £700 p.a. being made over to aid a
grammar school with an annual income of £4000. And the worst
thing was that when they got wind of it, time had almost run out, the
Scheme was almost made. It had already passed from the Charity
Commissioners, who had published it with due formality, and was
now with the Education Department which had recently done the
same. Less than a month remained for objections.

How the well-organised women of Leeds could have been so much
in the dark is a mystery. But they were not the only ones. The Leeds
School Board, the Poor Law Guardians, the Lord Mayor and Aldermen were all among those who woke up rather late in the day. The
trustees of the Poors Estate were trustees of the Grammar School and

may have handled things so quietly in the city that no one thought of looking out for the Notices which were published in the local press. So far as the Charity Commissioners were concerned, because the trustees consented to the transfer it went through very smoothly – too smoothly, perhaps. They seem to have negotiated it direct, without the aid of an Assistant Commissioner, with the headmaster of the Grammar School.

Granted that the huge disadvantage they were under reflects on the women's essential powerlessness, what happened next reflects on their judgment.[64] On the day that they heard the news the Ladies' Educational Association hurriedly posted a memorial of protest, pressing on the Education Department the claim of girls to share in funds which had been expended in doles to both sexes. But wishing, it seems, to play the game fairly, they felt they should notify the Charity trustees of what they had done and consulted the chairman. This was Dr Gott, the vicar of Leeds, a member of the group which had promoted the girls' school but a man most strongly committed to the Scheme. If they were hesitant he was not. First, he dissuaded them from raising the matter, as they meant to, at the imminent meeting of the Leeds Educational Council, 'in deference to the feeling that the matter should not be made absolutely public before the letter of the Memorialists had been acknowledged by the Trustees'; then, when the Council met, Dr Gott and the Grammar School head-master, Dr Henderson, buttonholed the Ladies' representative after-wards and asked that the memorial should be withdrawn. They put it to her that

> the Scheme was a good one, the result of the Expenditure of much time and labour and that opposition now might prove fatal to it as an Educational fund. They further said that they would use their influence in any future disposition of increased funds that the Higher Education of Girls should be provided for.

The grounds of this appeal were well chosen. The women did not wish to seem sectarian or hostile.

> As Mrs Lupton felt that the aim of the Memorialists was to enlarge the Educational advantages of girls by pressing the justice of their Claim and not to obstruct those of boys she consented to ask that a meeting of the Memorialists should be called to consider the question of withdrawing the Memorial.

At this meeting letters from Dr Gott and Dr Henderson were read and the memorialists considered their predicament. As they later put it to the trustees, they felt 'great unwillingness to render futile your efforts in the cause of Education as they are told they will if they do not withdraw'. On the other hand they felt very strongly the justice of the girls' claim, and their responsibility, 'if they were to abandon such claim without . . . an assurance so far as the present Trustees can give it that when [any] surplus arises, the Claims of Girls to participate in the benefits of the Trust shall be duly recognised'. The trustees replied that they were unable to bind their successors but that 'when the Committee are in a position to do so they will be glad to give the subject of Girls' Scholarships their full consideration'.[65] And with no better prospect the women wrote and withdrew their memorial.

In retrospect it is a sad little story. They had a good case, the strength of it attested by the support it received from other groups. Their memorial was followed by others from the School Board, the Poor Law Guardians, the Mayor, Aldermen and Burgesses of Leeds, and the Inhabitants, all making the point that since the Poors Estate applied to men and women it was unjust that girls should be excluded from the benefits of the converted fund. In a case like this a hundred memorials could not have diverted a penny to girls since the trustees had an absolute veto and would never have budged. Dr Gott made this clear in a letter to the Education Department. But if the women had stuck to their guns determined opposition might have blocked the Scheme, which was a discreditable one in its way.

They were outmanoeuvred. Before that, though, their position had effectively been undermined by the fact that in regard to the Poors Estate they had no standing with the Charity Commission. There is nothing to show that provision for girls ever entered into the negotiations between the Commissioners and the headmaster which so expeditiously settled this Scheme. Trustees had the whip hand, it is true, where charitable funds were transferred to education, but this had not prevented the Endowed Schools Commissioners from bringing all the pressure they could to bear on the trustees of the Peloquin loan fund in Bristol to get more generous provision for girls. If we turn to Manchester, another city where the women's interest was well organised and strong, we see again how little this amounted to in the battle for endowment where there was no positive interest in London.

Manchester had some claim to be regarded as the cradle of the women's movement. The drive for women's suffrage started there, under the leadership of Lydia Becker, who in 1870 launched the

G*

Women's Suffrage Journal, and Jacob Bright, who for four years running promoted a women's suffrage Bill. Manchester Members voted for the suffrage and Manchester's Councillors petitioned for it. Manchester elected Miss Becker to the School Board and if everyone did not share her view that women teachers should be paid the same as men, there were many influential people in the city keenly interested in girls' education. The Bishop of Manchester supported the movement to start a high school and had indeed been active in launching the Girls Public Day School Company; the Dean was chairman of the High School Committee; C. P. Scott, of the *Manchester Guardian*, Bryce, when he was working for the Taunton Commission, Mrs Gaskell's daughter and Roby's wife were among those most deeply concerned. This is what an early headmistress had in mind when she spoke of the High School's having been created not by a great teacher, like Miss Buss or Miss Beale, but by the citizen body itself, a product of Manchester's remarkable vitality in the 1870s.[66]

Behind it was the Manchester Association for Promoting the Education of Women which began, as in Leeds, by organising lectures and then turned its energies to starting a school. The Endowed Schools Commissioners had not yet reached Lancashire but in 1871 the Manchester group were much encouraged by a letter from one of them looking forward to help in 'the battle . . . for Women's Educational Rights' from those prepared to 'bestir themselves and make a strong public opinion'.[67] Informed of Schemes made for girls' schools elsewhere and eager that Manchester should not 'wake up suddenly . . . to find itself behind all other parts of Great Britain in the ideas of our generation',[68] the group invited subscriptions for a school. What they had in mind was a public day school on the lines of those promoted by Maria Grey and they looked to their city 'to be true to itself . . . and to prove that where the interests of its own daughters are involved it will be no laggard nor wait until missionaries from other towns come to stimulate its liberality'.[69]

The school, which opened in adapted houses in January 1874, was at once successful. No question at all but that the demand for it existed. The sixty pupils rose to one hundred and fifty – all that could be taken – in the first two terms and many applicants were turned away. But those 'elements of *permanence and development*' which, the Association well understood, were essential to the future of their school, could not be achieved without endowment.[70]

They faced now the problem which had faced Miss Buss and we

saw how in that case it was overcome: the Endowed Schools Commissioners had looked around until they found some endowment for
her. Manchester was not so lucky. There was a large source of endowment in the city – the Hulme Trust, where income so far exceeded
what could be absorbed by the scholarships at Brasenose endowed by
William Hulme that in the 1870s there was some £7000 p.a. to spare.
When Fearon went to Manchester in 1873 to open discussions on a
Hulme Estates Scheme he had been directed to raise the question of
making substantial provision for girls. In 1873, though, no high school
existed. By 1875 when it did exist, indeed when its Committee was
appealing to Mancunians 'to provide for Manchester's daughters
what has been provided without stint for Manchester's sons',[71] the
crucial changeover had taken place.

There were many claims on the Hulme Estates money. The trustees
wanted to endow a hall of residence as well as professorships at Owen's
College. They hoped to establish a school for boys to rank below the
Grammar School, and one for girls also. As for the views of the Charity
Commissioners, it was not that they in any sense excluded the claim
of the High School to share in this endowment but that they did
nothing at all to advance it. Can one imagine their predecessors, with
Miss Buss's school under their noses, taking the line that some of the
Platt funds might very well go to a girls' school in North London but
not saying which? Can one imagine them drafting a Scheme to
endow the North London with £500 yearly on a temporary basis,
until such time as the Brewers might set up a girls' school of their
own? This is more or less what happened in Manchester. The Charity
Commissioners advised the trustees that they should aid girls in one
of two ways: by starting their own school or by subsidising 'some
existing girls' school';[72] by which phrase they did not necessarily
mean the High School since, later, they spoke of aid to the High
School or any other school in Manchester which educated girls to the
appropriate standard.[73] The High School Committee urged that
endowment given to them subject to possible withdrawal 'could only
be a very doubtful benefit',[74] and in the end the point was taken.
Even at that stage a legal snag arose from the fact that since the
Scheme had been published the High School Trust had been trans-
formed into a Company and could not come under the Endowed
Schools Acts. This problem, too, was surmounted in the end. But can
one imagine that William Latham would have let Miss Buss get into
such a difficulty?

Manchester High School, after a struggle, did get endowment from the Hulme Estates comparable with the Camden endowment from the Brewers. But all in all the Scheme was ungenerous to girls. As the *Women's Suffrage Journal* pointed out, their income of £500–£1000 p.a. was much less than the £1000–£1500 p.a. given to the Hulme school for boys; only two hundred girls were envisaged as against a school for three hundred boys; the girls' school curriculum was less ambitious and no scholarships for elementary schoolchildren were allowed for in the case of girls. That the boys did so much better, despite the fact that they were already served by Manchester Grammar School, struck the *Journal* as yet another instance of the way that 'men, as usual, seize the lion's share for themselves'.[75] The Hulme Scheme provided an illustration of 'the seemingly unconquerable indisposition to do justice to girls in the matter of . . . endowments'. Jacob Bright called upon the Charity Commissioners to urge the importance of doing more, while the High School pleaded the claims of girls to 'at least equal pecuniary support from the Trust funds; the more urgently because the claims of the other sex have long received large recognition'.[76] It was not only the feminists who thought this. Salford Town Council submitted a proposal that the boys' and girls' endowments should be equal. The Manchester School Board took the view that they should have equivalent accommodation, while a memorial from Owen's College and another signed by a group of citizens argued the need for more schools for girls.

In no case where provision was made to endow a school under Section 12 was opinion better organised or the need more established than in Manchester. It should, in theory, have been a case to demonstrate Section 12 to perfection. What it really showed was the weakness of the feminists once they had lost their friends in London.

Five years is a short time in the public service. In ten, perhaps, or twenty, the tremendous momentum which the Endowed Schools Commissioners derived from the Taunton Commission might have spent itself. As it was, they demonstrate a brief, late flowering of that missionary spirit which was not uncommon in public servants of an earlier generation but rare by 1870, and on its way out as the modern style of civil servant emerged. Lyttelton, Hobhouse and Roby in particular were 'zealots' in the sense in which the term has been applied to the greater names of Chadwick and Kay-Shuttleworth.[77] What they had, and shared with their Assistants, was a commitment to modernise the grammar schools, expressed in a rigorous application of their powers and including, beyond what might have been foreseen by those who appointed them, a strong determination to secure everything they could for girls.

Here it would be hard to improve on the comment of women at the time that the Endowed Schools Commissioners had considered their claims 'in a way they have never been considered before'.[78] The end of the Commission did not see the end of that. Lyttelton, shortly before his death, signed the memorial which Maria Grey's Union sent to the Charity Commissioners protesting that women were no longer put on governing bodies. Hobhouse was a good friend to Somerville College; Roby to Girton and to Manchester High School. As for the Assistant Commissioners, Fitch battled on for women to the end. The septuagenarian Emily Davies took up her pen in 1903 to set *The Times* right on a matter so integral to the life's work of this great educationist and so thoroughly ignored in his obituary: 'a trusted leader' of the movement to admit women to London University; active in the similar field at Cambridge; a member of the council of Bedford College and of Cheltenham Ladies' College and of the governing body of Girton, to which he was especially devoted – his last public service a meeting there less than a month before his death.

The images of Fitch crowd in one each other: he is writing or lecturing on women's education; he is speaking to Women University Teachers or telling Women Post Office Workers that they are pioneers in a great movement; he is making the little excursions of old age from his home in Bayswater down to Brook Green to watch the progress of the building which is going to be St Paul's School for Girls. 'After all, intellect is of no sex', he had written forty years before and Section 12 of the Endowed School Act is an episode for him in a long commitment. No one else comes near this, though Fearon in the nineties, 'these days of light for the education of girls', takes pleasure in recalling at a Camden speech day the 'dark days' of the 1860s and his first encounter with Miss Buss; and Latham, the 'occasional' Assistant Commissioner, never seeks release from the attachment born in him during the fight to endow her schools. They become his passion. For nearly twenty years, up to his death, he is chairman of the governors, and when he dies, in 1914, on the first day of the summer holidays, there is a hasty reassembling of North London girls to sing at his funeral. That is the last link between 'the cause' and bureaucrats of the Taunton era.

Appendix 1 *Schemes approved by 31 December 1874 which provided for the secondary education of girls*

Year	Place and endowment	Annual gross income £*	Provision for girls	Remarks	PRO Ed. 27
1871	Bradford Grammar School Yorkshire	800	£200 p.a. (£250 on cesser of pension to usher) to be applied to girls' education under supplementary scheme	This Scheme established first grade boys' school. Bradford Girls' Grammar School was established by Scheme of 1875	5721 5722
	GRAY'S THURROCK† Palmer's School Essex	900	Endowment shared equally between boys' third grade day and boarding school and girls' school 'of like character'. Both in new buildings		1147
	KEIGHLEY Drake and Tonson's Charities Yorkshire	336	Girls' day school to be established in grammar school buildings. Fees £4-£8 p.a.	Amalgamation of two charities. Endowment equally divisible between girls' school and Trade School in Mechanics Institute which is to cater for grammar school boys	5957
1872	Baddow, Great Jeffrey's Endowed School Essex	190	Extension of benefit of endowment to girls if funds admit	Boys' day school, third grade	1158
	Bath King Edward VI Grammar School and Black Alms Charity Somerset	900	Future extension of endowment to girls	Boys' boarding and day school, second grade. £280 p.a. to Trustees of Black Alms	4049

* The figures in this column are taken mainly from appendix A to the Endowed Schools Commissioners' Report of 1874 (PP, 1875) and are meant to give a rough idea of the importance of the endowment.
† Capital letters indicate a scheme which provided a *school* for girls.

	Beaminster Endowed School Dorset	200	Establishment of girls' school when funds admit. Meanwhile, £20 p.a. for girls' exhibitions	Scheme also subsidised elementary education and supported boys' third grade school. Superseded by scheme of 1881 which made no provision whatever for girls	824 826
	BURTON-ON-TRENT Allsopp's Charity and others Staffordshire	1000	Allsopp's Girls' School Fees £2–£5 p.a. Ages 8–17	Amalgamation of four charities. Boys' Grammar School, second grade, and Allsopp's Boys' School also on scheme	4217
	Giggleswick Grammar School Yorkshire	1200	£100 p.a. for girls' education. Girls admissible to third grade day school	Scheme for boys' day and boarding school, first grade, and boys' third grade day school in Settle	5834
	Mirfield Endowed School Yorkshire	220	Power to admit girls to the school	Boys' third grade day school	5997
	NEWCASTLE-UNDER-LYME Orme's School and others Staffordshire	2086	Orme Girls' School (day) Fees £3–£5 p.a. Ages 8–17	Amalgamation of four charities. Boys' first grade and boys' middle school also provided	4255
	Shaftesbury Lush's Charity Dorset	300	£40 p.a. for girls' exhibitions. When certain payments cease, trustees to apply for scheme for girls' school	Scheme provides boys' third grade day and boarding school	875
	Sherborne Foster and Digby's Charities Dorset	159	Half of Foster's Charity (about £45 p.a.) assigned to girls. Supplementary Scheme to be made eventually	Amalgamation of several charities, partly under § 30. 1880–3 girls' share of Foster's diverted to support boys' third grade school established under scheme. (See also scheme for Kings School, Sherborne, 1871	886 887
1873	AMBLESIDE Kelsick's Charity Westmorland	180	Girls' day and boarding school Fees £3–£6 p.a. Ages up to 17	Boys' elementary school with upper department also to be provided	5124

Year	Place and endowment	Annual gross income £*	Provision for girls	Remarks	PRO Ed. 27
1873	Audley Grammar School Staffordshire	350	Power to benefit girls by exhibitions or otherwise	Boys' third grade day school provided	4194
	Barnet Queen Elizabeth's Grammar School Hertfordshire	650	£100 p.a. for girls' education	Boys' second grade day and boarding school provided. Endowment much increased by funds from Jesus Hospital under Section 30, Endowed Schools Act, 1869	1685
	Batley Grammar School Yorkshire	210	Power to extend benefits to girls	Boys' second grade school	5653
	BEDFORD Harpur's Charity Bedfordshire	14,000	Girls' high school, first grade / Girls' modern school, second grade	Four schools established for boys and girls (two high schools, two modern). Provision for elementary education and for almshouses	8 A / 9
	Bideford Grammar School and the Bridge Trust Devon	174	£20 p.a. for girls' exhibitions	Boys' day school, third grade, provided	633
	BINGLEY Grammar School Yorkshire	550	£100 p.a. for girls' education: school to be established by Mechanics Institute	Boys' day and boarding school, second grade, provided	5697
	BOW Prisca Coborn's Charity Middlesex	950	Girls' day school Fees £3–£6 p.a. Ages 7–16	Third grade boys' school also provided (ages 7–15). £200–£300 p.a. for exhibitions mainly for children from elementary schools	3247

School				
Brentwood Grammar School Essex	1450	Power to establish girls' commercial school	1060	First grade boys' day and boarding school; second grade boys' commercial school, provided
Burnley Grammar School Lancashire	276	Power to benefit girls when funds admit	2053	Boys' day school, second grade, provided
CAMBRIDGE Perse School Cambridgeshire	745	When the interests of scholars have determined, governors to assign to girls £150 p.a.	149	Boys' first grade school established. For girls, the prospect was more definite than it looked. The Scheme in fact constituted girls' school managers and laid down details as to fees, ages, curriculum, so that no further Scheme was needed when they came to start the school in 1881
Gillingham Feoffee Charity Dorset	283	Power to benefit girls whenever the state of the funds admit	866	Boys' third grade day and boarding school provided
GREENWICH Roan's Charity Kent	2000	Girls' day school Fees £3-£6 p.a. Ages 7-16	3023	Third grade boys' school also provided (ages 7-15). £500 p.a. for exhibitions in the schools, £300 p.a. for exhibitions from the schools. (Exhibitions allotted between boys and girls according to number of scholars)
HOXTON Aske's Hospital Middlesex	8000	Third grade girls' school at Hoxton Second grade girls' school at Hatcham	2971	Similar boys' schools established. £1200 p.a. for exhibitions in the schools. £600 p.a. for exhibitions from the schools, divided proportionately to number of scholars. £1500 p.a. for alms
ILMINSTER Endowed School Somerset	990	Girls' high school, day and boarding Town school for girls	4129	Town school for boys also provided

Year	Place and endowment	Annual gross income £*	Provision for girls	Remarks	PRO Ed. 27
1873	LEICESTER Wyggeston's Hospital Leicestershire	2500	Girls' day school Fees £4–£8 p.a. Ages 8–17	Similar boys' school provided PRO ref. no. relates to Ed. Dept. file; papers which record making of Scheme are missing	2419
	London Grocers' Company Schools	1000	Power to convert to girls the middle class boys' school established by this scheme		3054
	Newchapel Hulme's Charity Staffordshire	138	Power to admit girls to school	Boys' third grade day school provided No records in PRO Ed. 27	—
	Sowerby Bairstow's Charity Yorkshire	135	'Girls may be admitted to the school'	Boys' third grade day school provided	6184
	STAMFORD Endowed Schools Lincolnshire	2348	Browne's Day School for girls Fees £3–£8 p.a. Ages 8–17	Radcliffe High School for Boys. Browne's School for Boys (ages 8–16) also established	2612
	THORNTON Grammar School Yorkshire	120	Third grade school(s) for boys and girls		5737
	UFFCULME Ayshford's School Devon	45	Girls' day and boarding school Fees £6–£10 p.a. Ages 8–17	Buildings of defunct boys' grammar school available	814
	WALLINGFORD Biggs' Charity Berkshire	260	Girls' day school Fees £2–£5 p.a. Ages 7–16	Comparable boys' school established. £26 p.a. reserved for doles	93
	Walsall Grammar School Staffordshire	960	Third grade girls' school 'as soon as the funds admit of it'	Boys' high school and boys' third grade school established	4323

WEST HAM Bonnell's Charity Essex	324	Girls' day school Fees £2–£5 p.a. Ages 7–15	40 exhibitions to the school for poor girls from elementary schools	1223
WESTMINSTER Greycoat Hospital	3500	Day school in Westminster for 300 girls; boarding school for 100 girls Fees £2–£4 p.a. Ages 7–15	At least 100 exhibitions in day school and 60 exhibitions in boarding school, of which two-thirds for poor girls from Westminster elementary schools, one-third for orphans	3284 3285 3289
WESTMINSTER St Martin-in-the-Fields	550	Girls' day school Fees £2–£5 p.a. Ages 7–16	Scheme provided for exhibitions tenable at Greycoat Boarding School	3322
1874 GREAT CROSBY Harrison's Trust Lancashire	1800	Girls' day school to be established in boys' old buildings Fees £5–£10 p.a. Ages 8–17	Boys' second grade day school provided	2086
Holbeach Grammar School Lincolnshire	300	When pension to retiring headmaster falls in, £60 p.a. to girls for exhibitions	Boys' second grade day and boarding school provided	2538
KINGSTON-ON-THAMES Grammar School etc. Surrey	247 (plus 342 under Scheme of 1871)	Tiffin's Day School for Girls Fees £3–£5 p.a. Ages 7–16	Boys' day school, second grade, and Tiffin's Boy's School, third grade (ages 7–15) provided	4611
Lutterworth Sherrier's Charity and others Leicestershire	403	£50 p.a. for girls' education by exhibition or otherwise	Boys' day and boarding school, third grade, and elementary schools provided	2460
March Consolidated Charities Cambridgeshire	1069	Girls' day school to be established 'as soon as practicable after 3 years from the date of this Scheme or earlier if funds will permit'	Boys' day and boarding school	173

Year	Place and endowment	Annual gross income £*	Provision for girls	Remarks	PRO Ed. 27
1874	Newport Grammar School Essex	300	Girls' day school when funds permit	Boys' day and boarding school, third grade, established	1186
	Rastrick Mary Law's Charity Yorkshire	100	Girls may be admitted	Boys' third grade day school provided	5750
	Repton and Etwall Port's Charity Derbyshire	2000	£100 p.a. for girls' education 'if the income of the Trust is sufficient for the purpose'	£900 p.a. reserved for Etwall Hospital. Boys' first grade day and boarding school. Provision for elementary education in Repton and Etwall	550
	Sedbergh Grammar School Yorkshire	1000	£200 p.a. for girls' education on cesser of pension to retiring headmaster. Girls admissible to third grade day school	Boys' first grade day and boarding school and third grade day school	6114
	TAUNTON Huish Charity Somerset	800	Girls' day school Fees £3–£6 p.a. Ages 7–15	£350 p.a. for alms £200 p.a. for university exhibitions (The endowment was mixed and only a minor part was available for secondary education) Boys' school similar to girls'	4167
	Thame Grammar School Oxfordshire	709	Trustees may establish girls' school 'if the state of the funds admits'	£200 p.a. for alms Boys' day and boarding school, second grade	3910
	TOTNES Grammar School and Municipal Charities Devon	337	Borough school, day and boarding for girls, second grade	Boys' day and boarding school, second grade PRO ref. relates to Ed. Dept file; papers which record making of Scheme are missing	803
	Yalding Cleave's School Kent	126	Girls may be admitted to the school	Boys' day school, third grade	2005

Appendix 2 *Schemes submitted to the Education Department by 31 December 1874 (but approved after that date) which provided for the secondary education of girls*

Place and endowment	Annual gross income £*	Provision for girls	Remarks	PRO Ed. 27
Aldenham Platt's Charity Hertfordshire	4500	£20,000 stock and £600 a year for North London Collegiate School and Camden School for Girls (see below, St Pancras)	Scheme approved May 1875. Provides for boys' first grade day and boarding school. Erection and partial support of elementary schools in Aldenham. £13,333 to endow schools at Watford. £200 p.a. for alms	1637
Borden Barrow's Charity Kent	1996	(Surplus to be used for girls' education) £50 p.a. for girls' exhibitions (until a school for girls is established)	Scheme approved Aug. 1875. Boys' second grade day and boarding school to be established. Brackets indicate provision deleted by Education Department	1792
BRADFORD† Girls' Endowed School Yorkshire	200 eventually 250	Girls' high school endowed with payment from funds of Bradford Grammar School (see appendix 1 above)	Scheme approved August 1875	5711
BRISTOL Queen Elizabeth's and Red Maids Gloucestershire	8106 and 4378	Red Maids Boarding School for 80 girls; leaving age 15. Whitson's Day School for Girls; leaving age 15. One other similar day school for girls	Scheme approved May 1875. On this foundation were also Queen Elizabeth's Boarding School for Boys, Queen Elizabeth's Day School for Boys, and Carr's Day School for Boys; all third grade	1289 1291

* The figures in this column are taken mainly from Appendix B to the Endowed Schools Commissioners' Report of 1874 (PP, 1875) and are meant to give a rough idea of the importance of the endowment.
† Capital letters indicate a Scheme which provided a *school* for girls.

Place and endowment	Annual gross income £*	Provision for girls	Remarks	PRO Ed. 27
BRISTOL, Colston's Hospital and Diocesan Trade School	6059	Girls' day school Fees £2–£4 p.a. Leaving age 15	Scheme approved Feb. 1875. Provides for boys' third grade boarding school and trade school	1274
CAMBERWELL, Dulwich College Surrey	15,600	Girls' high school Girls' middle school	Scheme provides for Dulwich College (first grade day and boarding) and for Wilson's Grammar School. There are assignments totalling £65,000 for schools in other London parishes as well as provision for the chapel, almshouses and picture gallery at Dulwich There were long and difficult negotiations and the Scheme as finally approved in 1882 made no provision for a high school for girls though the girls' middle school remained. (James Allen's Girls' School q.v.)	2830 2831 2835 2837 2839 (Action after 1874 is on 2840, 2841, 2842, 2863, 2865, 2869)
EXETER, (1) St John's Hospital etc.	2660	Maynard Girls' School Fees £6–£15 p.a. Ages 10–19	Schemes approved April 1876 and May 1875 after amendment by Education Department. No change in provision for girls. Other provision was for boys' first grade day and boarding school, third grade boys' school and elementary schools	695
(2) Episcopal School Devon	612	Girl's middle school		697
Grantham Grammar School etc. Lincolnshire	1000	Power to apply any surplus income for benefit of girls	Scheme as approved June 1876, provides one second grade day and boarding school for boys instead of first and second grade schools as in Scheme submitted Feb. 1874. No change in girls' provision	2597

LONDON Datchelor's	—	Authorises building of girls' middle school in Camberwell	Scheme approved May 1875 (Scheme of 1871 made by Charity Commissioners under Charitable Trusts Acts had divided endowments between alms and education)	2903
LONDON St Paul's School	12,000	High school for 400 or more girls	Scheme approved Mar. 1876. Main object first grade school for boys. Amending Schemes 1879 and 1900. Girls' school opened 1904	3104
LONDON Lady Eleanor Holles's Charity	1500	Girls' day school Fees £2.10s–£6 p.a. Ages 8–16	Scheme approved June 1875 £650 p.a. for existing elementary school	3037
LOUGHBOROUGH Endowed Schools Leicestershire	1328	Girls' school Fees £4–£8 p.a. Leaving age unspecified	Scheme submitted to Education Department 31 Dec. 1874 Approved Oct. 1875. Provides for first grade day and boarding school for boys, and for payment to elementary schools	2440
MANSFIELD Queen Elizabeth's Grammar School Nottinghamshire	926	£100 p.a. for girls' exhibitions or classes	Scheme approved June 1875. Provides boys' second grade day (or day and boarding) school. Envisages girls' school later. Like the Perse Scheme this one laid down all that was requisite for the girls' school and no further scheme was needed to start the school in 1883	3792
Oakham and Uppingham Archdeacon Johnson's Charity Rutland	4280	£200 p.a. for higher education of girls (on lapse of pension to headmaster)	Scheme approved May 1875. Assigns 3/7 endowment to alms, 2/7 for second grade day and boarding school at Oakham, 2/7 for first grade day and boarding school at Uppingham	3928
Pocklington Grammar School Yorkshire, East Riding	1300	£200 p.a. for higher education of girls, to commence within 3 years from date of Scheme	Scheme approved May, 1875, for first grade day and boarding school for boys. Girls' provision amended by Education Department to allow payment to be deferred to 'such later date as the Charity Commissioners shall direct'	5534 5535

Place and endowment	Annual gross income £*	Provision for girls	Remarks	PRO Ed. 27
READING Kendrick's Charity Berkshire	200	Girls' day school Fees £3–£5 p.a. Ages 7–16	Scheme approved June 1875. Provides for similar boys' school	85
Rivington Grammar School etc. Lancashire	570 300	£200 p.a. for higher education of girls	Scheme approved May 1875. Provides for second grade boys' day and boarding school	2264
ST HELEN'S Cowley Charity Lancashire	974	Girls' Day School Fees £4–£8 p.a. Ages 8–17	Scheme approved May 1875. Provides similar boys' school	2282
ST PANCRAS North London Collegiate, and Camden School for Girls Middlesex	—	Endowment of these schools with £20,000 stock and £600 p.a. from Platt's Charity at Aldenham (see Aldenham Scheme above)	Scheme approved May 1875	3191
Stourbridge Grammar School and others Worcestershire	851	Governors may establish girls' school if funds available	Scheme approved May 1875	5430 5431
WAKEFIELD Grammar School and many others Yorkshire	2930	Girls' day school Fees £6–£10 p.a. Ages 8–18	Scheme approved May 1875. Provides first grade day and boarding school for boys and trade school for boys	6224
WARWICK The King's School and many others Warwickshire	2455	Girls' day school Fees £2–£4 p.a. Leaving age 16	Scheme approved Aug. 1875. Provides first grade day and boarding school for boys and third grade day school for boys	5097
WESTMINSTER Holborn Estate Charity	about 4000	St Clement Danes Girls' School Fees £4–£6 p.a. Ages 8–18	Scheme approved Oct. 1875. Also provided boys' school (leaving age 17)	3316

Appendix 3 *Schools for girls established by Schemes made 1869–1903*

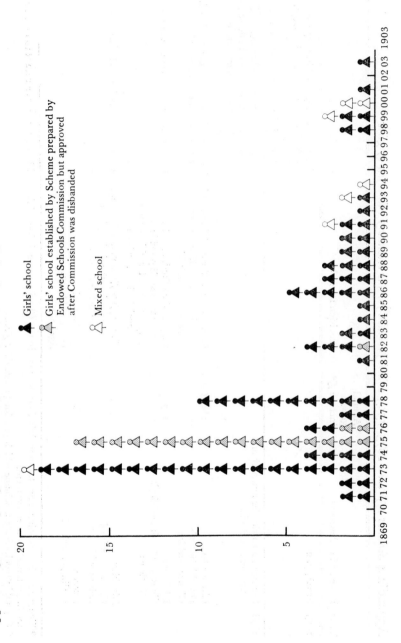

● Girls' school

◆ Girls' school established by Scheme prepared by
  Endowed Schools Commission but approved
  after Commission was disbanded

△ Mixed school

Appendix 4 *Schemes approved 1875–1903 which provided for the secondary education of girls*

Year	Place and endowment	Annual gross income £*	Provision for girls	Remarks	PRO Ed. 27
1875	See App. 2			All Schemes approved in 1875 were submitted to the Education Dept. by the Endowed Schools Commissioners before 31 Dec. 1874	
1876	See App. 2 entries for EXETER† and LONDON, St Paul's			These Schemes were submitted to the Education Dept by the Endowed Schools Commissioners before 31 Dec. 1874	
	Cirencester Powell's Schools Gloucestershire	about 1000	Cl. 61 provides for establishment of girls' school 'If and whenever the funds admit it'	Third grade boys' school established. Substantial aid to elementary schools	1344
	Highgate Sir Roger Cholmondeley's Middlesex	2254	Cl. 59: when funds sufficient governors shall provide middle or upper school for girls, or middle school for boys, or both	First grade boys' schools established	3501
	Hinckley Grammar School Leicestershire	505	Cl. 56: £50–£100 p.a. to be spent on exhibitions, scholarships or other prizes for girls	Third grade boys' school established	2389
	LONDON Burlington School	624	Girls' school Fees £2–£6 p.a. Ages 7–16		3069 3072

* The figures in this column are taken mainly from Returns in the Charity Commissioners' Annual Reports and are meant to give a rough idea of the importance of the endowment.
† Capital letters indicate a Scheme which provided a *school* for girls.

School	Endowment	Clause	Scheme	No.
Penwortham Grammar School Lancashire	1012	Cl. 57: when income sufficient governors to apply for scheme for girls: meanwhile, £50 for girls' exhibitions	Third grade boys' school established. / Substantial aid to elementary schools	2229 / 2230
THETFORD School and Hospital Foundation Norfolk	about 400 for schools	Girls' school Fees £2–£5 p.a. Ages 7–15	Scheme provides for preacher and almspeople and for small third grade school for boys and girls	3637
Tideswell Grammar School Derbyshire	about 300	Cl. 58: when funds admit governors may establish girls' department, school or exhibitions	Third grade boys' school established	601
Wellingborough Grammar School Northamptonshire	537	Cl. 61: governors may provide for admission of girls to benefits of foundation	Second and third grade boys' schools established	3708
1877 Bentham Collingwood and Baynes Foundation Yorkshire, West Riding	about 490 (of which £20 for doles)	Cl. 60: If governors think fit, girls may be admitted to the school	Second grade boys' schools established	5677 / 5679
Berkhamsted Grammar School Hertfordshire	1550	Cl. 61: So soon as income sufficient governors shall apply £250 p.a. to education of girls	First grade boys' school established	1657
Brigg Grammar School Lincolnshire	585	Cl. 57: When first of two pensions lapses, £50 p.a. for girls' education / When second pension lapses further £50 p.a.	Second grade boys' school	2633
NEWCASTLE-ON-TYNE Allan's Endowed Schools Northumberland	713	Girls' school Fees £3–£5 p.a. Ages 7–16	Scheme established third grade boys' school similar to girls' school	3753
Northleach Westwood's Grammar School Gloucestershire	687	Cl. 62: When a pension lapses, governors shall apply for scheme to establish girls' school	Third grade boys' school	1426

Year	Place and endowment	Annual gross income £*	Provision for girls	Remarks	PRO Ed. 27
1877	TIVERTON Middle Schools Devon	400	Girls' school Fees £3–£7 p.a. Ages 7–16	This Scheme established third grade schools for boys and girls. Scheme of 1876 had established a first grade boys' school (Blundell's)	788
	Upholland Grammar School Lancashire	74	Cl. 53: Girls may be admitted, if governors think fit	Third grade boys' school established (girls were pupils at this grammar school before the Scheme was made)	2298
1878	BIRMINGHAM King Edward VI Warwickshire	14,600	High school for girls. Four middle schools for girls (Aston, Bath Row, Camp Hill, Summer Hill)	Scheme also established high school for boys and three middle schools for boys	4891 4893 4899 4910
	CANTERBURY Simon Langton Kent		Girls' school Fees £4–£8 p.a. Ages 7–16	Scheme also established third grade boys' school	1818 1819
	COGGESHALL Sir Robert Mitcham's Essex	500	Girls' school Fees £3–£6 p.a. Ages 7–16	Scheme established similar boys' school. Girls' school provision deleted in amending Scheme, 1890	1172
	Clee Humberstone's Foundation Lincolnshire	789 (of which 200 is non-educational)	Cl. 49: Not later than 3 years from opening of boys' school, £100 p.a. to be applied to girls' education	Third grade boys' school established. (By a simultaneous scheme, subsidy to church, to alms and to elementary school)	2647
	Hastings Grammar School Sussex	474	Cl. 59: as soon as endowment and income of foundation are sufficient, governors shall apply for Scheme extending benefits to girls	Second grade boys' school established	4669

School				
Kirkby Stephen Grammar School Westmorland	78	Cl. 53: If governors think fit, girls may be admitted	Third grade boys' school established	5208
London, Hammersmith Latymer Foundation	1030	Cl. 64: When funds admit, governors shall apply for Scheme for girls' school	Scheme provides for elementary boys' school and third grade boys' school (Latymer Upper)	3091
LONDON, Islington Dame Alice Owen's	8000 (including income devoted to alms)	Girls' school Fees £3–£6 p.a. Leaving age 15	Scheme established similar boys' school	3117 3119
Longwood (Huddersfield) Grammar School Yorkshire, West Riding	126	Cl. 54: girls may be admitted, if governors think fit	Third grade boys' school established	5920
LOUTH Grammar School Lincolnshire	1570	Girls' school Fees £6–£12 p.a. Ages 8–17	First grade boys' school established	2699 2702
Newport Adam's Grammar School Salop	1841	Cl. 30: Girls' school shall be established as soon as funds permit	Second grade boys' school established. Apprentice fees, payment to vicar and to almspeople continues	3977
Rochester Sir J. Williamson's Mathematical School Kent	1487	Cl. 59: After 5 years from date of Scheme governors to invest £100 p.a. towards girls' school	Third grade boys' school established. 1935 Scheme of 1886 (q.v.) establishes girls' school	
WELLS Blue Schools Somerset	535	Girls' school Fees £2–£5 p.a. Leaving age 16	Similar boys' school established	4181
Yardley Charity Estates Worcestershire	900	Residue of income to be invested and when it amounts to £2000 governors shall apply for Scheme establishing boys' and girls' second grade schools	Scheme established two boys' elementary schools	4955

Year	Place and endowment	Annual gross income £*	Provision for girls	Remarks	PRO Ed. 27
1879	Dorchester Grammar School Dorset	312	Cl. 56: if governors think funds sufficient, can apply for Scheme to extend benefit of foundation to girls	Scheme established second grade boys' school	857
	Macclesfield Grammar School Cheshire	2058	Cl. 90: from date not later than 3 years from date of Scheme governors shall apply £100 p.a. to education of girls	Scheme established grammar school and modern school for boys	266 269
1880	Bury St Edmunds The Guildhall Feoffment Suffolk	580	Cl. 30: as certain pensions fall in governors shall accumulate capital fund for girls' middle school	Scheme established boys' middle school. Substantial aid to boys' and girls' elementary schools	4426
	Kirkham Grammar School Lancashire	889	Cl. 59: £200 p.a. shall be applied to higher education of girls (but application may be postponed for 3 years from date of Scheme or longer if Charity Commissioners approve)	Second grade boys' school established	2109
1881	Croydon Whitgift Foundation Surrey	4580	Cl. 88: when income sufficient, benefits of Foundation to be extended to girls	Scheme established first and second grade boys' schools	4517 4532b 4535 4544
	IPSWICH Endowed Schools Suffolk	1667	Girls school Fees £3–£6 p.a. Ages 7–16	Scheme established similar school for boys and also first grade boys' school	4379
	Manchester Hulme Trust Estates	about 6800	£500–£1000 p.a. for girls' school	Scheme also provided hall of residence and professorships at Owen's College; Hulme exhibitions at Brasenose; boys' middle school	2181 2182 2183 2184 2185

1882	CAMBERWELL James Allen's School Surrey	—	Girls' school Fees £3–£8 p.a. Ages 8–17	The school was established on endowment from Dulwich College (see App. 2 above)	—
	GLOUCESTER United Endowed Schools	3324	Upper school for girls (to be started when funds admit) Lower school for girls Fees £2–£5 p.a. Ages 8–16	Scheme also established Sir T. Rich's Boys' School (third grade) and the Crypt Grammar School for Boys (second grade)	1382 1396 1408
	Nottingham High School	3000	Cl. 59: £200 p.a. shall be applicable for the higher education of girls	Scheme established first grade boys' school	3843
	WATFORD Endowed Schools Hertfordshire	630	Girls' school (leaving age 16)	Similar boys' school established	1750
1883	LINCOLN Christs Hospital	500	Girls' school Fees £4–£10 p.a. Ages 8–17	The Scheme redistributed the Christ's Hospital endowment of over £2000 p.a. to provide for a girls' school, the support of 20 boarders at the boys' middle school and the substantial endowment of exhibitions there	2676 2686 2688
	LONDON, Poplar George Green's Schools	990	Girls' school Fees £4–£8 p.a. Ages 6–16	Similar boys' school established	3170
	Scorton Leonard Robinson's Charity Yorkshire, North Riding	260	Cl. 55: foundation may be applied for benefit of girls instead of boys	Third grade boys' school established (in place of mixed elementary school with upper department established by Scheme of 1875)	5626
	Welton Christ's Hospital Lincolnshire		Exhibitions for girls from Welton elementary schools		2724

Year	Place and endowment	Annual gross income £*	Provision for girls	Remarks	PRO Ed. 27
1884	London, Bethnal Green Parmiter's	1245	Girls' school to be established as soon as funds will allow	Third grade boys' school established. File for making this scheme missing from PRO Ed. 27	2796
	London, Stepney Bancrofts	—	Cl. 50: Any surplus income to be invested for girls	Boys' school established. Nothing in PRO Ed. 27	—
	MANCHESTER High School	1000	Girls' school	Follows Scheme of 1881 (q.v.) for Hulme Trust Estates	2171
	Walthamstow Sir George Monoux Essex	210	Cl. 53: As soon as funds sufficient, governors shall apply for Scheme extending benefits to girls	Third grade boys' school established	1215
1885	Ashby-de-la-Zouch Grammar School Leicestershire	about 1000	Cl. 12: governors to apply £200 p.a. to advance education of girls	A grammar school and an English school for boys were established on this foundation	2358
	Leicester Alderman Newton's	832	£100–£150 p.a. for girls' exhibitions	Scheme established boys' elementary school	2412 2413 2414
	PENDLETON High School Manchester	—	Girls' school	Subsidy from Hulme Estates. No records in PRO Ed. 27	—
1886	LONDON, Hackney Skinners' School	1500	Girls' school. Fees £4–£10 p.a. Ages 8–17	Scheme made on initiative of Skinners who, by Schemes of 1880, established two boys' schools at Tonbridge, Kent	3060
	MAIDSTONE Grammar School Kent		Girls' school. Fees £4–£10 p.a. Ages 7–17	Endowed with £6500 from Rochester Bridge Charity	1899

Year	School	Endowment	Type / Fees	Notes	No.
	ROCHESTER Sir J. Williamson's Mathematical School Kent		Girls' school Fees £4–£10 p.a. Ages 7–17	This Scheme follows Scheme of 1878 (q.v.)	1922
	SALISBURY Godolphin School Wiltshire	463	Girls' school Fees £12–£20 p.a.	An eighteenth-century endowment for orphan gentlewomen; one of the few endowed secondary schools for girls existing when the Taunton Commission reported	5282
	SKIPTON Petyt's Charity and Girls' Middle School Yorkshire, West Riding	583	Girls' school Ages 8–17	The subsidy for girls' education authorised in the Giggleswick Scheme of 1872 (see app. 3–i) was now assigned to Skipton	6171
	Tadcaster Dawsons' Charity Yorkshire, West Riding	116 (for education)	The educational part of this mixed endowment was to accumulate till sufficient to establish a girls' school	Scheme apportioned income between annuities to widows and etc. and education	6194
	Wotton-under-Edge Katharine, Lady Berkeley's Grammar School Gloucestershire	about 800	Cl. 55: £50 p.a. shall be applicable to education of girls	Second grade boys' school established	1468
1887	BERKHAMSTED Grammar School	100 (to be increased as soon as funds allow to £250)	Girls' school	Scheme follows boys' school Scheme of 1877 (q.v.)	1665
	LONDON, Lewisham Grammar School for Girls	383	Girls' school Fees £4–£8 p.a. Ages 9–16		3131 3134 3135 3141a

Year	Place and endowment	Annual gross income £*	Provision for girls	Remarks	PRO Ed. 27
1887	OLDHAM The Hulme Grammar Schools Lancashire	1500	Girls' school Fees £4–£10 p.a. Ages 8–17	Scheme, which also established boys' school, followed Scheme of 1881 for Hulme Trust Estates (q.v.) which provided for suspense fund to be used for schools at Oldham and Bury	2214
1888	BARNET Queen Elizabeth's Grammar School Hertfordshire		Girls' school	Scheme follows Scheme of 1873 (q.v. app. 1)	1688
	DEWSBURY Wheelwright Grammar Schools Yorkshire, West Riding	about 770	Girls' school Fees £8–£12 p.a. Ages 8–17	Scheme established similar boys' school	6074 6082 6083 6086
	HITCHIN Grammar School Hertfordshire		Girls' school Fees £6–£12 p.a. Ages 8–17	Scheme established similar boys' school	1710
1889	ASHBY-DE-LA-ZOUCH Grammar School Leicestershire	200	Girls' school	Scheme follows Scheme of 1885 (q.v.)	2363
	TADCASTER Dawson's Charity Yorkshire, West Riding	116	Girls' school Fees £2–£5 p.a. Ages 7–16	Scheme follows Scheme of 1886 (q.v.)	6200
1890	Handsworth Grammar School Staffordshire	924	Cl. 59: residue to be invested and accumulated for education of girls	Third grade boys' school established	4869

Date	Place / School	Number	Description	Notes	Refs
	LONDON Christ's Hospital	60,000	Girls' school		4717, 4721, 4722, 4725, 4726, 4727, 4730, 4772
	London St Olave's Grammar School	8000	Cl. 59: for 3 years from date of Scheme governors must set apart £500 p.a. for girls: after that £1000 p.a.	Second grade boys' school established substantial assignment to boys' elementary school	2750 2760 2765
	TAUNTON Bishop Fox's Somerset		Girls' school Fees £3–£6 p.a. Ages 7–16		4159
1891	FRAMLINGHAM Mills' Grammar School Suffolk	about 300	Girls' school Fees £2–£5 p.a. Ages 8–16		4372
	Lanteglos-by-Camelford Sir James Smith's School Cornwall	37	Cl. 10: governors empowered to admit girls		364
	LONDON Central Foundation Schools of London	about 4000	Girls' school Ages 7–17	Scheme combined funds from Dulwich College, the Corporation for Middle Class Education in the Metropolis, et al., to establish 2 boys' schools and 1 girls' school	
	MANSFIELD Brunt's Charity Nottinghamshire	750	Technical school for boys and girls in two departments Fees 6d.–1/- per week Ages: entry – must have passed Standard IV Leaving age 16		3784

Year	Place and endowment	Annual gross income £*	Provision for girls	Remarks	PRO Ed. 27
1891	Woodbridge Seckford Hospital etc. Suffolk	4660	Cl. 64: As soon as income sufficient further Scheme shall be made to extend to girls benefits of foundation	A Scheme of 1880, which established a boys' grammar school, was here amended to reconstitute the school in two branches: general and scientific (agricultural) and assignment to elementary education	4400
1892	NORTH MANCHESTER High School for Girls Lancashire		Girls' school	Endowment from the Hulme Estates Charity No records in PRO Ed. 27	—
1893	Carlisle Charity School and Technical Instruction Fund Cumberland	156	Cl. 23: Scheme provides for application of part of endowment in aid of school or schools for boys and girls	No records in PRO Ed. 27	—
	LONDON, Deptford Addey and Stanhope	893	School for boys and girls in separate departments Fee 3d. a week Entry: standard vi		2956a 2956b
	Normanton Grammar School Yorkshire, West Riding	400 after 1897	If and when funds suffice, girls' school to be established	This Scheme, which established a boys' second grade school, but made only contingent provision for girls, appears erroneously in Schedule B submitted to the Bryce Commission, instead of Schedule E. No girls' school established by 1902	6003 6005

Year	School	No.	Provision for girls	Establishment	Ref.
	WALSALL Queen Mary's Schools Staffordshire	200–250	Girls' school Fees £8 p.a. Ages 10–17	Eventual provision of a girls' school had been contemplated in the Scheme of 1873 (see app. 1) which had also established two boys' schools. These two were now merged	4326
1894	Bakewell Lady Manners School Derbyshire	70	Cl. 28: the school shall be for boys and, if the governors think fit, for girls	Second grade boys' school established	483
	SLAITHWAITE The Slaithwaite School Foundation Yorkshire, West Riding		Mixed school	Scheme provides that 'on the fulfilment of certain conditions' a school for boys and girls may be established. (PP 1895 XLIX Royal Commission on Secondary Education, Summary and Index to Minutes of Evidence, Schedule B, p. 203). No records in PRO Ed. 27)	—
1895	Knaresborough Grammar School Yorkshire, West Riding	387	School for boys and, if the governors think fit, for girls	Second grade day and boarding school for boys established	5968
	Monks Kirby Grammar School Warwickshire	150	Residue for technical institution of boys and girls	Boys' elementary school established	5034
	Newcastle-upon-Tyne Grammar School Northumberland	1100	Residue to be invested towards maintaining girls' school		(Ed. 35/2022)
1896	Donnington Cowley's Endowed Schools Lincolnshire	1195	Cl. 61: governors shall arrange for girls to attend classes in suitable subjects	Commercial and agricultural school for boys established	2526

Year	Place and endowment	Annual gross income £*	Provision for girls	Remarks	PRO Ed. 27
1896	Lancaster Royal Grammar School Lancashire	870	Cl. 72: if and so soon as the income allows a girls' school shall be established	Boys' grammar school established	2118
1897	—	—	—	—	—
1898	Durham Johnston Technical Schools	100	Day school for boys and girls may be established in or near Technical School		982
	KIRKHAM Grammar School Lancashire		Girls' school Fees £5–£10 p.a. Ages 8–17	Scheme follows Scheme of 1880 (q.v.)	2114
	Leeds Grammar School Yorkshire, West Riding	about 4500	Cl. 64: sets aside £12,000 to endow girls' school	First grade boys' school established	5976 5979 5981 5982
	Leyland Balshaw's School Lancashire	392	Cl. 32: school for boys 'and if . . . the governors think fit . . . for girls also'	Second grade day and boarding school for boys	2127
	WIGTON Grammar School Cumberland	about 70	Girls' school Fees £6–£12 p.a. Ages 8–18	A bequest of 1893 made it possible to rehouse Wigton Boys' Grammar school and provide £3000, plus the old grammar school buildings, for a girls' school	462
1899	BURY Grammar School Lancashire	1125 plus further income from Hulme Trust	Girls' school Fees £9–£15 p.a. Ages 8–18	Similar boys' school established. £18,000 from Hulme Trust for school buildings	2065

Year	School				
	LONDON St Saviour's and St Olave's	over 2000	Girls' school Fees £3–£6 p.a. Ages 8–17	Scheme combined foundations of St Saviour's and St Olave's with St John, Horselydown, to establish one second grade school for boys, and one for girls	2772 2786 2791
	NEW ALRESFORD Perins Grammar School Hampshire	71	Mixed school Fees £4–£8 p.a. Ages 8–17	Hampshire County Council, at whose instance Scheme made, willing to make substantial grants for scientific apparatus and to maintain efficient teaching staff	1529
	Stockton-on-Tees Blue Coat School Durham	449	Cl. 29(2): 'When funds permit a girls' school . . . shall be established'	Second grade boys' school established	1038 1040
1900	FOCKERBY-IN-ADLINGFLEET Grammar School Yorkshire, West Riding	94	Mixed school Fees £3–£8 p.a. Ages 8–16		5824
	LEIGH Grammar School Lancashire	495	Mixed school Ages 8–17		2125 (also Ed. 35/1308)
1901	LEEDS Girls' Grammar School Yorkshire, West Riding	12,000 capital plus accumulation of income thereon from date of 1898 Scheme	Girls' school Fees £12–£20 p.a. Ages 8–19	Follows Scheme of 1898 (q.v.)	(Ed. 35/2982)
1902	—	—	—	—	—
1903	LONDON Godolphin and Latymer	about 1700	Girls' school Fees £4–£8 p.a. Ages 7–18	Follows Latymer Scheme of 1878 (q.v.). Combines subsidy from Latymer with subsidy from endowment of Godolphin Boys' School, now defunct	3094 (also Ed. 35/1677 1678)

Notes

INTRODUCTION: THE ENDOWED SCHOOLS ACT

1 Eric Midwinter, 'Non-events in the history of education', *Trends in Education* (July 1968), p. 20.
2 Quoted by B. M. Allen, *Sir Robert Morant* (London, 1934), pp. 125–6.
3 Parliamentary Papers (hereafter PP), 1873, VIII, Select Committee on Endowed Schools Act (1869), Evidence, Q. 1414.
4 Gillian Sutherland, *Policy-making in Elementary Education 1870–1895* (Oxford, 1973), examines closely the dynamics of change in such central areas as compulsory school attendance, free education and the grant system. In none did any significant initiative come from civil servants.
5 Gillian Sutherland (ed.), *Studies in the Growth of Nineteenth-century Government* (London, 1972), p. 8.
6 Letter, 7 Sept. 1873, quoted by L. T. Hobhouse and J. L. Hammond, *Lord Hobhouse: A Memoir* (London, 1905), p. 46.
7 *Journal of the Women's Education Union*, II, 16 (15 Apr. 1874).
8 Alice Zimmern, *The Renaissance of Girls' Education in England* (London, 1898), p. 83.
9 Notably, through Section 17 of the Endowed Schools Act 1869, which forbade exclusion from governing bodies for religious reasons, and Section 18, according to which schoolmasters need not be in holy orders. Where the religious character of a school had been expressly established by the founder, Section 19 waived these provisions.
10 The Act was expressly framed to give effect to the changes recommended by the Taunton Commission; these included the abolition of free education except as the reward of merit, the admission of pupils on examination and their annual examination thereafter.
11 *Cy près* (law), as near as possible to a testator's intentions. In disregard of *cy près*, Section 30 of the Endowed Schools Act allowed for the diversion to education of obsolete endowments, such as had been bequeathed for marriage portions, ransoms and apprenticeship fees. Apart from this, Section 9 conferred a general power 'to make new trusts directions and provisions'.
12 Hansard, *Parliamentary Debates* (hereafter *Parliamentary Debates*), 194:1382 (15 Mar. 1869).
13 Quoted by Hobhouse and Hammond, p. 46.

14 *Times*, 23 July 1874.
15 *Parliamentary Debates*, 194:1415 (15 Mar. 1869).
16 *Ibid.*, 194:1411 (15 Mar. 1869).
17 *Ibid.*, 194:1402 (15 Mar. 1869).

I THE SHAPING OF SECTION 12

1 'Female education', *Edinburgh Review*, Jan. 1810, pp. 299–300.
2 Quoted by J. Kamm, *How different from us* (London, 1958), p. 52.
3 Lady Stanley of Alderley, 'Personal recollections of women's education', *Nineteenth Century*, vol. 6 (Aug. 1879).
4 'Female industry', *Edinburgh Review*, 109, (Apr. 1859), p. 298. For a different contemporary view of the problem, see W. R. Greg, 'Why are women redundant?', *National Review*, Apr. 1862; for a modern view, see J. A. and Olive Banks, *Feminism and Family Planning in Victorian England* (Liverpool, 1965), ch. 3.
5 For accounts of this group, see Helen Blackburn, *Women's Suffrage* (London, 1902); Barbara Stephen, *Emily Davies and Girton College* (London, 1927); and Ray Strachey, *The Cause* (London, 1928).
6 Thomas Love Peacock, *Gryll Grange* (London, 1861), p. 59.
7 *Transactions of the National Association for the Promotion of Social Science* (hereafter *Transactions*), 186.
8 *English Woman's Journal*, 2 (Oct. 1858), p. 124.
9 *Ibid.*
10 Hastings, 'The industrial employment of women', *Transactions*, 1857, p. 535.
11 Boucherett, 'On the education of girls with reference to their future position', *ibid.*, 1860, p. 434.
12 Bodichon, 'Middle-class schools for girls', *ibid.*, 1860, pp. 432–3.
13 Boucherett, *ibid.*, 1862, p. 357.
14 Robinson, 'Suggestions for the improvement of middle-class education', *ibid.*, 1864, pp. 367–79.
15 Girton College Archives, *Family Chronicle*, p. 259.
16 *Ibid.*, LOC. 250, 'Report of a discussion on the proposed admission of girls to the University Local Examinations held at a special meeting of the National Association for the Promotion of Social Science on Friday, April 29, 1864.'
17 *Ibid.*, LOC. 255, 'The proposed admission of girls to the University Local Examinations'. Emily Davies was delighted with this pamphlet 'in which our question is, I think, very judiciously treated. We have ordered a large supply for distribution and it has occurred to me that it might be a good plan to send them round at Cambridge.' *Ibid.*, LOC. 171.
18 See note 14 above.
19 Davies, 'On secondary instruction as relating to girls', *Transactions*, 1864, pp. 394–404.
20 PRO, 30/29/18/12, no. 11, Granville Papers.

21 Girton College Archives, SIC. 2, 11 Oct. 1864.
22 *Ibid.*, SIC. 3, 4, 6.
23 *Ibid.*, SIC. 10, letter of 22 Feb. 1865 to Emily Davies from her brother.
24 PP 1867–8 xxviii, Report of Schools Inquiry Commission, ix, pp. 278–9.
25 Girton College Archives, LOC. 151, Arnold to Emily Davies, 14 Oct. 1864.
26 Stephen, *Emily Davies*, pp. 85–6.
27 E. C. Sandford (ed.), *Memoirs of Archbishop Temple by Seven Friends* (London, 1906), p. 142.
28 Note his championship of girls in the Select Committee on the Endowed Schools Bill, PP 1868–9, viii.
29 *Dictionary of National Biography.*
30 Girton College Archives, SIC. 11, Roby to Emily Davies, 18 Mar. 1865.
31 *Ibid.*, SIC. 12, Roby to Davies, 21 Mar. 1865.
32 *Ibid.*, SIC. 15, Roby to Davies, 25 Apr. 1865.
33 *Ibid.*, SIC. 16, Roby to Davies, 28 Apr. 1865.
34 *Ibid.*, SIC. 17, draft letter to Roby, 8 Nov. 1865.
35 *Ibid.*, SIC. 18, Roby to Davies, 16 Nov. 1865.
36 Schools Inquiry Commission, v, Evidence, Q. 11490.
37 *Ibid.*, Q. 16229.
38 *Ibid.*, Q. 9129.
39 *Ibid.*, Q. 13150.
40 *Ibid.*, Q. 13481.
41 *Ibid.*, Q. 12894.
42 Undated letter, quoted by Stephen, *Emily Davies*, p. 138.
43 *Quarterly Review*, vol. 126 (1869), p. 450.
44 Schools Inquiry Commission vii, p. 69.
45 *Ibid.*, viii, p. 482.
46 *Ibid.*, vii, p. 68.
47 Davies, 'On secondary instruction as relating to girls', *Transactions*, 1864, p. 395.
48 Undated letter to Barbara Bodichon, quoted by Stephen, *Emily Davies*, p. 138.
49 Schools Inquiry Commission, vii, p. 383.
50 'Girls grammar schools', *Contemporary Review* (1869), pp. 333–54.
51 Schools Inquiry Commission, ix, 288.
52 'The education of women', *Victoria Magazine* (1864), p. 441.
53 Schools Inquiry Commission, ix, p. 301.
54 The *Stroud Journal*, 20 Dec. 1873, prints extracts from an impressive battery of obituaries in national and provincial newspapers.
55 For this and the discussion that followed, see Report, 4th meeting, North of England Council for Promoting the Higher Education of Women, 1869.
56 *Parliamentary Debates*, 196:1752–65 (14 June 1869).
57 *Englishwoman's Review* (July 1869), p. 284.
58 *Parliamentary Debates*, 197:1876 (15 July 1869).

2 THE MEN WHO REJECTED THE DEAD HAND

1 'Educational endowments', *Fraser's Magazine*, LXXIX (1869), pp. 1–15.
2 Address by Lord Lyttelton on education, *Transactions*, 1868, pp. 38–74.
3 *Journal of the Society of Arts* (16 July 1869), p. 683.
4 *Parliamentary Debates*, 197:1870–2 (15 July 1869).
5 Gladstone Papers, Brit. Mus. Add. MSS. 44240, fos. 97, 98.
6 *Ibid.*, fo. 5.
7 PP, 1873 VIII, Select Committee on Endowed Schools Act (1869), Evidence, Q. 1231.
8 Lyttelton Papers, Worcester Co. Records, bulk accession 5806, ref. 705:104, parcel 9, no. 140.
9 Quoted by Hobhouse and Hammond, *Lord Hobhouse*, p. 2.
10 *Times*, 26 Apr. 1876.
11 Edward Lyttelton, *Alfred Lyttelton* (privately printed, 1916), p. 8.
12 Gladstone Papers, Brit. Mus. Add. MSS. 44240, fo. 5.
13 *Ibid.*, fos. 97, 98.
14 John Bailey (ed.), *Diary of Lady Frederick Cavendish* (2 vols., London, 1927), vol. 1, p. 136n.
15 James Winter, *Robert Lowe* (Toronto, 1976), pp. 163–4.
16 *Journal of the Women's Education Union*, IV, 41 (15 May 1876), 70.
17 Schools Inquiry Commission, I, appendix I, Lord Lyttelton on the conscience clause.
18 PP, 1873, VIII, Committee, Evidence, Q. 1263.
19 Lyttelton, 'Address on education', *Transactions*, 1868, p. 55.
20 His letters to the universities form appendix 4 of the Endowed Schools Commissioners' report to the Education Department, PP, 1872, XXIV. He was unsuccessful.
21 *Journal of the Society of Arts* (16 July 1869), p. 686.
22 Quoted by Hobhouse and Hammond, *Lord Hobhouse*, pp. 31–2.
23 'On the authority accorded to founders of endowments', a paper read to the Jurisprudence Dept of the Social Science Association in May 1869; published in Hobhouse, *The Dead Hand* (London, 1880).
24 'The Endowed Schools Commission: Shall it be continued?' Unsigned pamphlet, 1873, D.11.2, Dept of Education and Science Library.
25 Schools Inquiry Commission, IV, Evidence, QQ. 6365–6529.
26 Quoted by Hobhouse and Hammond, *Lord Hobhouse*, p. 48.
27 *Times*, 5 Jan. 1915, Roby's obituary.
28 PP, 1873, VIII, Select Committee, Evidence, Q. 1240.
29 For the quality of examiners in the Education Department at this time, see Sutherland, *Policy-making in Elementary Education 1870–1895*.
30 Ripon Papers, Brit. Mus. Add. MSS. 43536, fos. 216–19.
31 See note 1 above.
32 Quoted by Betty Askwith, *The Lytteltons* (London, 1975), p. 155.
33 Lyttelton, 'Address', *Transactions*, 1868, p. 70.
34 *Englishwoman's Review* (July 1869), p. 284.
35 PP, 1872, XXIV, Report of Endowed Schools Commissioners, para. IX.

H

36 Quoted by Hobhouse and Hammond, *Lord Hobhouse*, p. 49.
37 Paper F. It is printed in full in appendix 2 to the Report of the Endowed Schools Commissioners, PP, 1872, XXIV.
38 These Instructions are printed in appendix 1 to the Report of the Endowed Schools Commissioners, PP, 1872, XXIV.
39 PP, 1873, VIII, Select Committee, Evidence, QQ. 11, 12.
40 Schools Inquiry Commission, IX, map before fly leaf.
41 PP. 1873, VIII, Select Committee, Evidence, QQ. 1525, 1526. There appears to be no copy extant of Robinson's complete scheme for the West Riding but Fearon is reported by the *Leeds Mercury* in Dec. 1870 as explaining to people in Dewsbury that the Riding was divided for the purposes of his inquiries into seven districts: Sedbergh and Giggles-wick, Leeds and Ripon, Halifax and Huddersfield, Sheffield, Don-caster, Dewsbury and Wakefield. (The report omits Bradford, pre-sumably by accident.) A similar statement, for Feb. 1871, is reported on the Batley file in the Public Record Office (hereafter PRO) Ed. 27/5653.
42 See the minute headed *Bradford Centre* and the table headed *Bradford Circle*, PRO, Ed. 27/5722.
43 Files in PRO, Ed. 27: Haworth (5873, 5878), Drighlington (5815), Guiseley (6032), Ilkley (5935) and Thornton (5737).
44 PRO, Ed. 27: Otley (6016), Keighley (5957) and Bingley (5697).
45 PRO, Ed. 27/5722, suggestions submitted by governors, 30 July 1870.
46 *Ibid.*, 'Notes by H.G.R.'
47 PRO, Ed. 27/5721, Commissioners to governors, 12 Nov. 1870.
48 PRO, Ed. 27/5721, governors' account of their deputation to Endowed Schools Commission, 12 Oct. 1870.
49 PRO, Ed. 27/5721, governors' memorial.
50 PRO, Ed. 27/5722, *Bradford Observer*, report of inquiry held 10 Jan. 1871.
51 PRO, Ed. 27/5721, Commissioners to governors, 12 Nov. 1870.
52 PRO, Ed. 27/5834, Instructions to Fearon, 28 Apr. 1870.
53 *Ibid.*
54 PRO, Ed. 27/6114, Fearon's report of conference with governors on 14 July 1870.
55 PRO, Ed. 35/3034. Date of 'cesser of the said pension' is given as 10 Feb. 1900. An amending Scheme to use £200 p.a. of the money for girls was made in 1902.
56 PRO, Ed. 27/5900, Instructions to Fearon, 10 May 1870.
57 PRO, Ed. 27/6038 (Ripon).
58 PRO, Ed. 27/5976, governors to Commissioners, 5 Mar. 1870.
59 *Ibid.*, Instructions to Fearon, 20 Jan. 1871.
60 PRO, Ed. 27/5854 (Halifax, Heath Grammar School).
61 PRO, Ed. 27/5887, outlines of proposed scheme, 6 Dec. 1870.
62 *Ibid.*, Fearon to Commissioners, 21 Nov. 1871.
63 PRO, Ed. 27/6074, Fearon's memorandum of conference with governors on 11 Aug. 1871.

64 PRO, Ed. 27/5750 (Rastrick), 5997 (Mirfield) and 6184 (Sowerby).
65 PRO, Ed. 27/5819, trustees' memorial, 19 Nov. 1872.
66 PRO, Ed. 27/6139 (Sheffield), 6094 (Rotherham), 5796 (Doncaster), 6224 (Wakefield) and 5653 (Batley).
67 PP, 1873, VIII, Select Committee, Evidence, Q. 1592.
68 Report, *Bradford Observer*, 30 Sept. 1875.

3 THE MONEY PROBLEM

1 Quoted by Annie E. Ridley, *Frances Mary Buss* (London, 1896), p. 114.
2 Quoted by Roby, to Select Committee, PP, 1873, VIII, Evidence, Q. 262.
3 *Times*, 30 Mar. 1872.
4 Quoted by Ridley, *Frances Mary Buss*, p. 129.
5 North London Collegiate School Archives, T.F.2, letter, 25 July 1872.
6 Quoted by Ridley, *Frances Mary Buss*, p. 109.
7 *Ibid.*, p. 152.
8 PP, 1873, VIII, Select Committee, Evidence, Q. 1240.
9 PRO, Ed. 27/1637, Lyttelton to Latham, 16 May 1872.
10 North London Collegiate School Archives, letter, 2 Aug. 1872, in governors' minutes.
11 PRO, Ed. 27/1637, Latham's Report, Aug. 1872.
12 *Ibid.*, Latham's Report, 13 Apr. 1873.
13 North London Collegiate School Archives, T.F.2, letter, 20 Mar. 1874.
14 PRO, Ed. 27/1637, letter, 8 Nov. 1873.
15 North London Collegiate School Archives, T.F.2, Latham to Miss Buss, 20 Mar. 1874.
16 *Ibid.*, 30 Mar. 1874.
17 *Ibid.*, 7 Aug. 1874.
18 *North London Collegiate School Jubilee Magazine*, 1900, p. 138.
19 PP, 1872, XXIV, Report of Endowed Schools Commissioners, para. XXXIX.
20 Schemes made by the Endowed Schools Commissioners to establish girls' schools, or make some form of provision for girls, are summarised in appendix 1 (if they received the Royal Assent during the Commissioners' term of office) and appendix 2 (if they became law after 31 Dec. 1874).
21 PRO, Ed. 27/1147, Roby to Cumin, Education Department, 13 June 1870.
22 Report, 4th meeting, North of England Council, 1869, p. 12.
23 PP, 1872, XXIV, Report of Endowed Schools Commissioners, Instructions to Assistant Commissioners, para. XXIV.
24 PRO, Ed. 27/4217, Commissioners to Stanton, 6 June 1870.
25 PRO, Ed. 27/6194, Robinson to Fearon *re* Tadcaster, date 1879 but consistent with earlier practice.
26 PRO, Ed. 27/1637, Latham to Commissioners, Aug. 1872.
27 Schools Inquiry Commission, I, p. 570.

28 *Ibid.*, v, Evidence, Q. 9133, Dr Hodgson.
29 PRO, Ed. 27/5819, 4 May 1871.
30 PRO, Ed. 27/173, 14 July 1872.
31 PRO, Ed. 27/8A, memorial to Commissioners, 13 Jan. 1871.
32 PRO, Ed. 27/6074, trustees' objections, 12 Oct. 1871.
33 PRO, Ed. 27/5815, Fearon to Robinson, 9 May 1870.
34 PRO, Ed. 27/3322, memorial of 2 Apr. 1872.
35 *Parliamentary Debates*, 196:1754 (14 June 1869).
36 PP, 1872, xxiv, Report of Endowed Schools Commissioners, Instructions, para. xxiv.
37 PRO, Ed. 27/5737, minute, undated, probably 1870.
38 PRO, Ed. 27/5777, July 1871.
39 PRO, Ed. 27/2053, memorial, 5 Sept. 1872.
40 Report, 4th meeting, North of England Council, 1869, pp. 12–13.
41 Report, 5th meeting, North of England Council, 1870, p. 12.
42 PRO, Ed. 27/4323, Report, Feb. 1871.
43 PP, 1872, xxiv, Report of Endowed Schools Commissioners, para. xxviii.
44 PRO, Ed. 27/4181, letter, 2 Aug. 1871.
45 PRO, Ed. 27/2725, Welton, Report of Inspection, 5 Dec. 1888.
46 PP, 1872, xxiv, Report of Endowed Schools Commissioners, pp. 23–4.
47 *Times*, 8 June 1872.
48 *Journal of the Women's Education Union*, iv, 41 (15 May 1876), p. 70.
49 Ridley, *Frances Mary Buss*, p. 102.
50 *Journal* (May 1876), p. 70.
51 Archives of Girls' Public Day School Trust (hereafter GPDST), 'Autograph letters to Mrs Grey – relating to Women's Education Movement 1871-6', no. 10.
52 See his obituary by Emily Davies, *Girton Review*, Lent Term 1915.
53 PRO, Ed. 27/5124, Commissioners to memorialists at Ambleside, 13 Jan. 1870.

4 OPPONENTS

1 Quoted by Hobhouse and Hammond, *Lord Hobhouse*, p. 42.
2 'The Endowed Schools Commission: shall it be continued?' D.11.2, Dept of Education and Science Library.
3 PP, 1873, viii, Select Committee, Evidence, Q. 4180.
4 *Ibid.*, Q. 2043.
5 *Ibid.*, Q. 186.
6 Fully discussed by F. E. Balls, 'The origins of the Endowed Schools Act 1869 and its operation in England 1869–1895' Unpublished Ph.D. thesis, University of Cambridge, 1964.
7 *Sherborne Journal*, 2 June 1870.
8 Schools Inquiry Commission, ix, p. 152.
9 *Dorset County Chronicle*, 29 Sept. 1870.
10 *Cambridge Independent Review*, 10 Aug. 1872.

11 Schools Inquiry Commission, XII, p. 477.
12 PRO, Ed. 27/8A, 3 May 1870.
13 Schools Inquiry Commission, VIII, p. 698.
14 PRO, Ed. 27/8A, letter from Mr John Bycroft, summer 1870.
15 PRO, Ed. 27/4611, letter, 17 Apr. 1872.
16 PRO, Ed. 27/85, letter, 5 Oct. 1874, and annotations on Draft Scheme.
17 *Westmorland Gazette*, letter from William Donaldson, Apr. 1873.
18 Report, *St Helen's Standard*, 18 Apr. 1874.
19 PRO, Ed. 27/2282, title of pamphlet marked 59 on file.
20 Report, *North Staffordshire Advertiser*, 22 July 1871.
21 PRO, Ed. 27/1223, 1 Jan. 1872.
22 Report, *Greenwich and Deptford Chronicle*, 24 Feb. 1872.
23 PRO, Ed. 27/173, 30 Oct. 1873.
24 *Parliamentary Debates*, 105:1557 (24 Apr. 1871).
25 PRO, Ed. 27/3284, 1 Feb. 1871.
26 *Parliamentary Debates*, 107:895 (30 June 1871).
27 *Ibid.*, 107:876 (30 June 1871).
28 Hammond and Hobhouse, *Lord Hobhouse*, p. 42.
29 PRO, Ed. 27/3284, 2 Mar. 1872.
30 *Parliamentary Debates*, 105:1555 (24 Apr. 1871).
31 'Charity Schools', *Westminster Review* (1873), p. 458.
32 PRO, Ed. 27/3289, Roby to trustees, 2 Mar. 1872.
33 PRO, Ed. 27/3285, trustees to Education Department, 14 Feb. 1871.
34 PRO, Ed. 27/3284, Greycoat Draft Scheme, Feb. 1871.
35 PRO, Ed. 27/6074, trustees' objections to Scheme published August 1872.
36 Extract from *Bristol Times and Mirror* in *Exeter and Plymouth Gazette*, 2 May 1871.
37 Temple to Mayor of Exeter, 5 Feb. 1872, printed as appendix 6, Endowed Schools Commissioners' Report, PP, 1872, XXIV.
38 Report, *Western Times*, 26 Feb. 1872.
39 PRO, Ed. 27/1289, Explanations to accompany Schedule in re – Bristol Charities, 19 Dec. 1870; Schedule Shewing the Proposed Reorganisation of the Bristol Endowed Schools.
40 *Western Daily Press*, 7 June 1870. The *Press* was the least hostile of the Bristol papers.
41 *Bristol Times and Mirror*, 17 May 1870.
42 PRO, Ed. 27/1289, trustees' letter, 13 Nov. 1871.
43 *Ibid.*, Fitch's note of deputation, 15 June 1871.
44 *Ibid.*, memorandum of conference with trustees at Bristol, 10 Oct. 1873.
45 PRO, Ed. 27/1296, Stanton's Report, 27 Feb. 1885.
46 *Bristol Times and Mirror*, 2 Apr. 1873.
47 PRO, Ed. 27/5722, governors' suggestions, 30 July 1870. My italics.
48 *Mansfield Reporter*, 28 Nov. 1873. My italics.
49 PRO, Ed. 27/1792, trustees' objections, 1 Sept. 1874. My italics.
50 PRO, Ed. 27/866, trustees' letter, July 1871.
51 PRO, Ed. 27/3792, trustees' letter, 10 Apr. 1873.

52 PRO, Ed. 27/5431, Stanton to Lyttelton, July 1872.
53 *Ibid.*, summary of objections, 31 Mar. 1873.
54 PRO, Ed. 27/5534, memorial, 28 Aug. 1873.
55 *Ibid.*, trustees' letter, 24 Nov. 1873.
56 PRO, Ed. 27/1657, governors' comments, 1 July 1874.
57 *Ibid.*, 28 July 1874.
58 *Ibid.*, 21 Aug. 1874.
59 PP, 1875, xxviii Report, Endowed Schools Commissioners, p. 7.

5 SUPPORTERS

1 PRO, Ed. 27/93, prefatory Address to Draft Scheme submitted by Mr Tyso, Mar. 1871.
2 PRO, Ed. 27/1289, 15 Mar. 1870.
3 *Parliamentary Debates*, 207:874 (30 June 1871).
4 *Ibid.*, 215:1891 (13 May 1873).
5 *Ibid.*, 220:1633 (14 July 1874).
6 Quoted by G. R. Parkin, *Edward Thring* (London, 1898) p. 179.
7 For Roundell as an academic radical, see C. Harvie, *The Lights of Liberalism* (London, 1976).
8 PRO, Ed. 27/2830, 30 Nov. 1872.
9 PRO, Ed. 27/5834, Resolution of special governors' meeting, 10 Aug. 1870.
10 PRO, Ed. 27/93, Mar. 1871.
11 PRO, Ed. 27/4217, Stanton to Commissioners, Jan. 1871.
12 PRO, Ed. 27/2612, 16 Apr. 1872.
13 PRO, Ed. 27/8A, letter, July 1870.
14 PRO, Ed. 27/149, Report of Charities Committee to Borough Council, summer 1872.
15 *Birmingham Morning News*, 19 Jan. 1871.
16 PRO, Ed. 27/2005, form AC1, 13 Dec. 1872.
17 PRO, Ed. 27/2440, Fitch to Commissioners, 16 July 1872.
18 PRO, Ed. 27/1426, Report, 27 Apr. 1874. This unusual man had upset local farmers by chairing a meeting addressed by Joseph Arch.
19 *Pulman's Weekly News*, 4 Mar. 1873.
20 PRO, Ed. 27/5431, resolutions, 4 Dec. 1871.
21 *Ibid.*, letter, 7 May 1874.
22 Report, *Mansfield and North Nottinghamshire Advertiser*, 21 Mar. 1873.
23 PRO, Ed. 27/3792, letter, 14 Feb. 1874.
24 PRO, Ed. 27/5887, letter, 23 Nov. 1872.
25 *Ibid.*, cutting from *Bradford Observer*; letter signed 'Publicity and Right', 23 Nov. 1871.
26 *Halifax Courier*, 4 Nov. 1871.
27 *Chelmsford Chronicle*, 21 Jan. 1870, report of public inquiry.
28 PRO, Ed. 27/1657, cutting from *The Hertfordshire Standard*, Dec. 1869.
29 *Ibid.*, letter, 1 July 1872.
30 Kingsley, *Transactions*, 1869, p. 344.

31 Hastings, *ibid.*, 1872, p. 59.
32 Hastings, *ibid.*, 1872, p. 278.
33 Elizabeth Wolstenholme, 'The education of girls: its present and its future', in Josephine Butler (ed.), *Woman's Work and Woman's Culture* (London, 1869).
34 PRO, Ed. 27/5124, 11 Jan. 1870.
35 *Ibid.*, 11 Jan. 1870.
36 *Ibid.*, 13 Jan. 1870.
37 *Ibid.*, 27 June 1872, to William Donaldson.
38 *Ibid.*, letter to *Westmorland Gazette*, May 1873.
39 Report, 4th meeting, North of England Council, June 1869, p. 7.
40 Report, 5th meeting, North of England Council, June 1870, pp. 7–8.
41 PRO, Ed. 27/5722, 2 Apr. 1870.
42 Leeds Ladies' Educational Association Report, 1871.
43 Quoted by Manchester Association for Promoting the Education of Women, Report, December 1871, p. 9; writer not named – probably Roby.
44 Report, 5th meeting, North of England Council, June 1870, p. 12.
45 *Ibid.*, p. 15.
46 *Women's Suffrage Journal* (1 Nov. 1875), p. 141.
47 *Journal of the Women's Education Union*, II, 15, (15 Mar. 1874).
48 Quoted by H. Blackburn, *Women's Suffrage*, p. 145.
49 Report, 6th meeting, North of England Council, June 1871, p. 25.
50 ' "Endowment or Free Trade" by the Rt. Hon. Robert Lowe M.P.', London, 1868 (Dept of Education and Science Library).
51 *Times*, 1 Jan. 1872.
52 *Ibid.*, 30 Mar. 1872.
53 *Ibid.*, 23 May 1872.
54 *Ibid.*, 13 June 1872.
55 *Ibid.*, 8 June 1872.
56 *Journal of the Women's Education Union*, I, 10 (15 Oct. 1873), p. 166.
57 Mary Gurney, 'What are the special requirements for the improvement of the education of girls?', *Transactions*, 1871, p. 368.
58 Second annual report of National Union for Improving the Education of Women, p. 14.
59 *Journal of the Women's Educational Union* II, 15 (15 Mar. 1874), p. 44.

6 WHAT WAS ACHIEVED

1 *Journal of the Women's Education Union* I, 5 (15 May 1873), p. 89.
2 PP, 1872, XXIV, Report of Endowed Schools Commissioners, para. VII.
3 These Schemes, which were still in the pipeline on the Endowed Schools Commissioners' demise, are summarised in appendix 2 above.
4 See tables in appendices 1 and 2 above.
5 PP, 1875, XXVIII, Report of Endowed Schools Commissioners, appendices A and B.
6 PP, 1873, VIII, Select Committee, Evidence, Q. 1751.

7 *Ibid.*, Q. 186.

8 *Ibid.*, QQ. 4180, 4335.

9 *Journal of the Women's Education Union* I, 10 (15 Oct. 1873), p. 171.

10 'Personal recollections of women's education', *Nineteenth Century*, vol. 6 (Aug. 1879).

11 *Journal of the Women's Education Union*, III, 34 (15 Oct. 1875), p. 157.

12 John Bailey (ed.), *Diary of Lady Frederick Cavendish* (2 vols., London, 1927), vol. II, p. 192.

13 This aspect is explored in greater detail in S. M. Fletcher, 'The part played by civil servants in promoting girls' secondary education 1869–1902', unpublished Ph.D. thesis, London University, 1976, ch. v.

14 See appendix 3 above.

15 PP, 1873, VIII Select Committee, Evidence, Q. 4316.

16 *Times*, 1 Nov. 1872.

17 PRO, Ed. 27/2835, memorial, 29 Jan. 1873.

18 Archives of GPDST, letter, 14 Nov. 1872.

19 Unfortunately, the upper school was later expunged from the Scheme by the Education Dept.

20 Girton College Archives, SIC. 29, draft letter, Mar. 1870.

21 *Ibid.*, SIC. 31, draft letter, Mar. 1870.

22 Schools Inquiry Commission, I, pp. 553.

23 Girton College Archives, SIC. 31, draft letter, Mar. 1870.

24 *Ibid.*, SIC. 29, draft letter to Roby, Mar. 1870.

25 *Ibid.*, SIC. 30, 17 Mar. 1870.

26 PP, 1872, XXIV Report of Endowed Schools Commissioners, appendix v, letter to Duke of Devonshire, Chairman of Royal Commission on Scientific Instruction.

27 Schools Inquiry Commission, I, p. 551.

28 PRO, Ed. 27/5957, Report on Draft Scheme, 30 July 1870.

29 Schools Inquiry Commission, IX, p. 290.

30 PRO, Ed. 27/5722, memorandum, 2 Apr. 1870.

31 PRO, Ed. 27/814, letter, 28 May 1873.

32 Girton College Archives, SIC. 30, 17 Mar. 1870.

33 *Ibid.*, SIC. 31, draft, Mar. 1870.

34 PRO, Ed. 27/1289, Scheme approved May 1875.

35 PRO, Ed. 27/4255, Stanton's Report, 11 Jan. 1871.

36 Manchester Association for Promoting the Education of Women, Report, Dec. 1872, p. 7.

37 *Ibid.*

38 Kingsley, 'Address', *Transactions*, 1869, p. 361.

39 Girton College Archives, SIC. 29, 30.

40 Schools Inquiry Commission, IX, p. 281.

41 Manchester Association, Report, Dec. 1872, p. 9.

42 PRO, Ed. 27/6171 (Skipton), 9 Jan. 1885.

43 Head Mistresses' Association, minutes, 22 Dec. 1874.

44 Girton College Archives, SIC. 29, draft letter, Mar. 1870.

45 PRO, Ed. 27/3284, 14 Feb. 1872.

46 Archives of GPDST, council minutes, 27 Nov. 1872.
47 *Women's Suffrage Journal* (Sept. 1871), pp. 94–6.
48 Report, 9th meeting, North of England Council, June 1874, p. 9.
49 Annie E. Ridley, *Frances Mary Buss* (London, 1896), p. 11.
50 PP, 1873, VIII, Select Committee, Evidence, Q. 1375.
51 PRO, Ed. 27/3284, Commissioners to trustees, 1 Feb. 1871.
52 PRO, Ed. 27/3289, Commissioners to trustees, 2 Mar. 1872.
53 PP, 1873, VIII, Select Committee, Evidence, Q. 1375.
54 PRO, Ed. 27/1289, summary of objections, 1 Apr. 1872.
55 PRO, Ed. 27/695, Fitch's minute, 31 July 1874.
56 PRO, Ed. 27/5431, Stanton to Lyttelton, 9 July 1872.
57 PRO, Ed. 27/824, note of Fitch's meeting with trustees on 22 Apr. 1870.
58 PRO, Ed. 27/4049, 3 May 1871.
59 No opposition at Bedford, Bonnell's (West Ham), Haberdashers' Aske's, Lady Eleanor Holles, Wakefield, Wallingford, Warwick.
60 PRO, Ed. 27/4891, Hammond's report of meeting with trustees, 3 Dec. 1870.
61 PRO, Ed. 27/3284, Aug. 1870. At Lady Eleanor Holles and Bonnell's the proportion was 3 : 12 at Kendrick's (Reading) and Roan's (Greenwich) it was 2 : 16.
62 *Parliamentary Debates*, 205:1553 (24 Apr. 1871).
63 PRO, Ed. 27/4129, 4 Nov. 1870.
64 PRO, Ed. 27/5957, 30 July 1870.
65 PRO, Ed. 27/4049, 28 Dec. 1870.
66 PRO, Ed. 27/2440, 31 Dec. 1874.

7 THE CHANGEOVER OF 1874

1 *Parliamentary Debates*, 221:529 (20 July 1874).
2 *Ibid.*, 221:1124 (3 Aug. 1874).
3 PP, 1886, IX, Select Committee, Evidence, Q. 1046.
4 Report, 6th meeting North of England Council, June 1871, p. 26.
5 Letter of 1904, quoted by Hobhouse and Hammond, *Lord Hobhouse*, p. 45.
6 Letter, 14 July 1874, *ibid.*, p. 46.
7 *Parliamentary Debates*, 215:1882 (13 May 1873), in reference to the views Hobhouse expressed in July 1869 at a joint meeting of the Society of Arts and the Social Science Association; see p. 35 above.
8 *Keighley News*, 5 Apr. 1873.
9 'Perverting the benefactions of the past', *Exeter and Plymouth Gazette*, 2 May 1871.
10 *Parliamentary Debates*, 221:1136 (3 Aug. 1874).
11 *Ibid.*, 205:1564 (24 Apr. 1871).
12 PP, 1872, XXIV, Report of Endowed Schools Commissioners, p. 39.
13 *Parliamentary Debates*, 217:1316–17 (31 July 1873).
14 *Ibid.*, 205:1564 (24 Apr. 1871).

15 Hobhouse and Hammond, *Lord Hobhouse*, p. 49.
16 PP, 1872, xxiv, Report of Endowed Schools Commissioners.
17 Schools Inquiry Commission, i, p. 504.
18 *Lincoln Journal*, 29 Oct. 1872.
19 *Ibid.*
20 *Cambridge Chronicle*, 21 Feb. 1874, letter signed C.S.M.
21 *Parliamentary Debates*, 214:292 (11 Feb. 1873).
22 'Lady Frederick Cavendish's diary', vol. xii, p. 408 (Devonshire MSS., Chatsworth).
23 PP, 1873, viii, Select Committee, Evidence, Q. 1263.
24 *Ibid.*, Q. 985.
25 *Ibid.*, Q. 1129.
26 *Ibid.*, Q. 969.
27 *Times*, 5 Jan. 1915, Roby's obituary.
28 Schools founded after the Toleration Act i.e. at a time when it could reasonably be supposed that the testator had a choice of denominations, were brought within the scope of Section 19 if it was required that governors, master or pupils should belong to a particular church. The Anglicans also stood to gain by provisions in the new Act which exempted elementary school endowments of up to £100 p.a. from the Endowed Schools Acts and which made it possible for clergy to continue as governors *ex officio*.
29 *Parliamentary Debates*, 217:1316 (31 July 1873).
30 *Ibid.*, 221:1124 (3 Aug. 1874).
31 North London Collegiate School Archives, 20 Mar. 1874.
32 PRO, Ed. 27/1289, Lyttelton, 23 Feb. 1874.
33 *Parliamentary Debates*, 217:1315 (31 July 1873).
34 Goodwood Papers, W. Sussex Co. Record Office, 866:2108, 20 June 1874.
35 *Ibid.*, 866:2112, 26 June 1874.
36 PRO, Ed. 10/105, 'Memorandum as to End. S. Commission'. Cumin was at this time an Assistant Secretary; he became Secretary of the Education Department in 1884.
37 Duke of Richmond to Lyttelton, quoted by Betty Askwith, *The Lytteltons* (London, 1975), p. 185.
38 *Parliamentary Debates*, 221:450 (28 July 1874).
39 *Ibid.*, 221:440 (28 July 1874).
40 *Ibid.*, 221:450 (28 July 1874).
41 *Ibid.*, 221:498 (28 July 1874).
42 *Ibid.*, 221:503, Mr Melly (28 July 1874).
43 *Ibid.*, 221:366 (28 July 1874).
44 *Ibid.*, 221:345 (28 July 1874).
45 Disraeli Papers, Hughendon Manor, B/XXI/5/38, Sandon to Disraeli, 18 July 1874.
46 'Lady Frederick Cavendish's diary', vol. xii, p. 330 (Devonshire MSS.).
47 *Parliamentary Debates*, 221:1115 (3 Aug. 1874).
48 For Lyttelton's speech, *ibid.*, 221:1124–37 (3 Aug. 1874).

49 PRO, Ed. 27/3928, 24 Aug. 1874.
50 *Journal of the Women's Education Union*, II, 16 (15 Apr. 1874), p. 49.
51 *Ibid.*, II, 20 (15 Aug. 1874), p. 114.
52 *Times*, 26 Apr. 1876.
53 Lyttelton Papers, Worcester Co. Records, 705:104, parcel 9, no. 58, Denison to Lyttelton, 27 Apr. 1873.
54 PP, 1873, VIII, Select Committee, Q. 1263.
55 *The Guardian*, 26 Apr. 1876.
56 Letter to *The Standard* from Dr Andrew Clark, quoted in *The Guardian*, 26 Apr. 1876.
57 *Times*, 22 and 24 Apr. 1876.
58 *Journal of the Women's Education Union*, IV, 41 (15 May 1876), pp. 69–70.
59 *Ibid.* No biography of Lyttelton exists. Betty Askwith, *The Lytteltons*, includes interesting material on his family life from the Hagley Papers. Peter Stansky's article 'Lyttelton and Thring', *Victorian Studies* (March 1962) looks at him on the Endowed Schools Commission but is superficial and rather misleading.
60 See his evidence to the Select Committee on the Endowed Schools Acts, 1886.
61 Hobhouse and Hammond, *Lord Hobhouse*, letter, 7 Sept. 1873, p. 46.

8 THE LONG HAUL

1 PRO, Ed. 27/2440, letter to Archdeacon Fearon on Loughborough file.
2 PP, 1895, XXVI, Report of Charity Commissioners.
3 PP, 1895, XLIII, Report of Royal Commission on Secondary Education, vol. I, p. 75.
4 PRO, Ed. 27/1346, Wilfred Cripps to Stanton.
5 PP, 1886, IX, Select Committee on Endowed Schools Acts, Evidence, Q. 1659.
6 For making of Scheme, see PRO, ED. 27/4955; for subsequent action, see PRO, Ed. 27/4959.
7 PRO, Ed. 27/2760, Murray's memorandum, 20 Dec. 1883.
8 PP, 1886, IX, Select Committee, Evidence, QQ. 4392, 4464.
9 PRO, Ed. 27/2760, 'Notes on the Proposed Scheme of the Charity Commissioners . . . by the Vestry Clerk of the Parish of St. John, Horselydown'.
10 PRO, Ed. 27/2765, governors' circular sent by Education Department to Charity Commissioners on 12 Feb. 1889.
11 Clause 59 of the Highgate Scheme made in 1876 provided that, when funds sufficed, a middle school for girls or boys, or both, should be established. In 1888–9 Hornsey Vestry pressed the Charity Commissioners, without success, to apply this clause. In 1897 the Commissioners spent some time balancing the rival claims of clause 59 and the governors' plans to extend the school. Clause 59 lost out (see especially, report of conference with governors on 13 Feb. 1897, PRO, Ed. 27/3515).

12 PRO, Ed. 27/2109, Scheme, 31 July 1880.

13 PRO, Ed. 27/1935, Scheme, 27 Nov. 1878.

14 PRO, Ed. 27/4869, Scheme, 1 May 1890.

15 The Commissioners' action on Blandford 1870–88 may be followed on PRO, Ed. 27/838.

16 PRO, Ed. 27/838, Sir George Young's draft letter, 7 Dec. 1883.

17 *Ibid.*, 28 Jan. 1884.

18 *Ibid.*, 19 Apr. 1883.

19 PP, 1886, IX, Select Committee, Mayor's evidence, QQ. 4941–5019.

20 *Ibid.*, rector's evidence, QQ. 5020–5112.

21 PRO, Ed. 27/838, Assistant Commissioner's report of meeting 7 Apr. 1888.

22 PP, 1886, IX, Select Committee, Q. 1150.

23 *Gloucester Mercury*, 21 Apr. 1877.

24 PRO, Ed. 27/2686, 24 Jan. 1882.

25 PRO, Ed. 27/6082, 12 June 1883.

26 An excellent account of the problems posed by reorganisation is given by C. M. E. Seaman, *Christ's Hospital: The Last Years in London* (London, 1977).

27 *Daily Telegraph*, 1 May 1873.

28 PRO, Ed. 27/4717, pt II, Report submitted 3 Mar. 1875.

29 *Ibid.*, governors' letter, 24 Apr. 1877.

30 PRO, Ed. 27/4726, governors' objections, 5 Sept. 1885.

31 PRO, Ed. 27/4326, Report, 7 Jan. 1892.

32 *The Schools of Medieval England* (London, 1915), pp. 88–9.

33 PRO, Ed. 27/483, 4 Aug. 1891, *et seq.*

34 Charity Commissioners Minute Book, 18 Nov. 1892.

35 PRO, Ed. 27/6139, Leach to Young, 8 Mar. 1885.

36 PRO, Ed. 27/4330, 12 Mar. 1894.

37 PRO, Ed. 27/4326, Report, Dec. 1888.

38 PRO, Ed. 27/2445, Report, 1890.

39 PRO, Ed. 35/1533, note of conference, 8 Nov. 1901.

40 PRO, Ed. 27/271, Report, 28 Jan. 1893.

41 From the point in 1888 when Leach, on inspection, proposed to the governors that they were now well able to fulfil their obligations under the Scheme of 1873 and provide a girls' school he faced obstruction in varying degrees from governors, town-council and chamber of commerce. In 1891 he held a public inquiry. After the Scheme went through in 1893 he struggled to prevent the girls' school being crammed on a congested site where it would have no room to develop.

42 What follows is based on PRO, Ed. 27/3784, Leach's Report of 13 Apr. 1889.

43 *Times*, 8 July 1930, letter from Dr W. M. Childs.

44 John Morley, review of *Essays on Reform* in the *Fortnightly Review* (1 Apr. 1867), p. 492, and quoted by C. Harvie, *The Lights of Liberalism*, p. 12. Dr Harvie's study examines Young's role in this group.

45 PRO, Ed. 27/6171, memorial to Education Department, Jan. 1885.

46 *Ibid.*, Charity Commissioners to Education Department, 9 Mar. 1885.

47 *Ibid.*, Young to Cumin, Education Department, 20 May 1885.

48 PRO, Ed. 27/5981, 14 Mar. 1884.

49 *Ibid.*, Report of meeting with trustees, 14 Mar. 1884.

50 PRO, Ed. 27/5981, note of Mr Beckett Denison's interview with Sir George Young, 12 Apr. 1886.

51 *Ibid.*, 15 Nov. 1887.

52 *Ibid.*, Young to Stanton, 13 June 1888.

53 *Ibid.*, Stanton to Young, 14 June 1888.

54 PRO, Ed. 27/5982, objections sent to Education Department before deputation of 15 May 1895.

55 PRO, Ed. 27/5984, trustees' letter forwarded from Education Department to Charity Commissioners, 8 Apr. 1897.

9   THE CHARITY COMMISSION SPIRIT

1 PRO, Ed. 10/105, 'Memorandum as to End. S. Commission'.

2 Schemes which established girls' schools are summarised in appendices 1 and 2 above (if the Endowed Schools Commissioners were responsible for them) and in appendix 4 above (if the Charity Commissioners were responsible). Figures for the total number of grammar schools established have been arrived at, in the case of the Endowed Schools Commission, on the basis of data included in appendices A and B to their final Report to the Committee of Council on Education (PP, 1875, xxviii); and, for the Charity Commission, on the basis of data included in their return to the Bryce Commission (PP, 1895, xlix, Royal Commission, vol. ix, appendix A (1) Roby Return) and in subsequent Annual Reports.

3 For time-scale, see appendix 3 above.

4 PP, 1886, ix, Select Committee on Endowed Schools Acts, Evidence, QQ. 120, 621.

5 *Journal of the Women's Education Union*, iv, 37 (15 Jan. 1876), 2.

6 *Walsall Free Press*, 9 May 1891, report of Town Council meeting.

7 PP, 1886, ix, Select Committee, Q. 1150.

8 *Ibid.*, Q. 1594.

9 PRO, Ed. 27/2359, Stanton's Report, 21 Jan. 1876.

10 PRO, Ed. 27/5889, letter from Mr John Oakes, numbered 240 on file.

11 *Journal of the Women's Education Union*, iv, 40 (15 Apr. 1876), pp. 53–4.

12 *Ibid.*, p. 55.

13 PRO, Ed. 27/4893, Report, 21 Apr. 1871.

14 *Journal of the Women's Education Union*, iv, 43 (15 July 1876), 107–9.

15 Charity Commission, General Minute Book, 9 June 1876.

16 PP, 1895, xliv, Report of Royal Commission, vol. ii, Evidence, Q. 159.

17 *Journal of the Women's Education Union*, iv, 40 (15 Apr. 1876), 53–4.

18 North London Collegiate School Archives, Latham to Miss Buss, 25 July 1876.

19 PRO, Ed. 27/1410, GPDS Co. to Commissioners, 7 Oct. 1891;

Commissioners to GPDS Co., 2 Nov. 1891 and GPDS Co.'s reply, 3 Nov. 1891.

20 PRO, Ed. 27/1695, 15 Apr. 1891.
21 *Ibid.*, 14 Feb. 1893.
22 *Ibid.*, 8 Feb. 1893.
23 *Ibid.*, 23 Nov. 1894.
24 *Ibid.*, 2 Jan. 1895.
25 *Ibid.*, 12 Jan. 1895.
26 PP, 1886, IX, Select Committee, Q. 6242.
27 PP, 1895, XLIX, Report of Royal Commission on Secondary Education, vol. IV, Evidence, QQ. 16, 542-3.
28 *Ibid.*, vol. IX, appendix A.
29 A table showing in detail the outcome of the various clauses designed to benefit girls forms appendix IX of S. M. Fletcher, 'The part played by civil servants in promoting girls' secondary education 1869-1902', unpublished Ph.D. thesis, London University, 1976.
30 PP, 1889, XXVIII, Report of Charity Commissioners.
31 PRO, Ed. 27/4326, Leach's Report, Dec. 1888.
32 PRO, Ed. 35/1468, 25 Oct. 1900.
33 Minutes of governors of Berkhamsted Grammar School, 12 July and 1 Oct. 1878, 1 Apr. 1879, 3 and 6 Oct. 1882, 3 and 20 Oct. 1884.
34 PRO, Ed. 27/1665, Lefroy's Report, 20 Feb. 1885.
35 PRO, Ed. 27/3848, Report, 24 Nov. 1893.
36 *Ibid.*, 12 Feb. 1895.
37 Nottingham High School, governors minutes, 3 Apr. 1895, 1 May 1895.
38 PRO, Ed. 27/3848, letter of resignation, 17 June 1896, forwarded to Commissioners 12 Dec. 1896.
39 See ch. 3 above.
40 PRO, Ed. 27/1750, Dr Brett to Commissioners, 26 Oct. 1879.
41 *Watford Observer*, 9 Apr. 1881.
42 The Local Taxation (Customs and Excise) Act 1890 imposed an additional duty on wines and spirits which it was intended should form a fund to compensate publicans dispossessed through the reduction of licences. When the temperance interest opposed such compensation the money was passed on to the newly formed County Councils to be used either in aid of the rates or in aid of technical education.
43 PP, 1895, XLVIII, Royal Commission, vol. VI, p. 98.
44 PP, 1894, XXVIII, Report of Charity Commissioners, para. 34.
45 PRO, Ed. 27/2056, Report of Inquiry, Oct. 1897.
46 PRO, Ed. 27/1161, letter from Technical Instruction Committee, 14 Feb. 1899.
47 PRO, Ed. 27/2467, 2471.
48 PRO, Ed. 27/483.
49 PP, 1900, XVIII, Report of Charity Commissioners, para. 38.
50 PRO, Ed. 27/2634. The Charity Commissioners expressed their concurrence with these views of Lindsey County Council in a letter of 17 Apr. 1899 to the trustees of Brigg Grammar School who had asked

for permission to postpone payment of the assignment due to girls
because the school was suffering from the effects of the agricultural
depression.

51 PRO, Ed. 27/2706. Lindsey's views are quoted by the Assistant Commissioner, Eddis, in his report of Mar. 1899 on the Louth case.
52 PRO, Ed. 27/2706, Eddis's report of Mar. 1899.
53 *Ibid.*, 13 July 1899.
54 *Ibid.*, 12 Sept. 1899.
55 *Ibid.*, 20 Apr. 1900.
56 *Ibid.*, interview note, 21 June 1900.
57 *Ibid.*, 15 Apr. 1901.

10 THE WOMEN'S MOVEMENT IN THE LATER YEARS

1 Ray Strachey, *The Cause* (London, 1928), p. 246.
2 PP, 1878–9, xx, Report of Charity Commissioners, p. 10.
3 PRO, Ed. 27/2808, Report, 12 June 1894.
4 PRO, Ed. 27/2366, Report, Jan. 1890.
5 PRO, Ed. 27/2418, Report, 28 Oct. 1889.
6 PRO, Ed. 27/3144, Report, 6 Mar. 1894.
7 PRO, Ed. 27/700, Report, 20 Oct. 1888.
8 PRO, Ed. 27/4943, Report, 23 May 1893.
9 PRO, Ed. 27/4615, Report, 20 Nov. 1889.
10 PRO, Ed. 27/4258, Report, July 1881.
11 PRO, Ed. 27/2283, Report, 16 Apr. 1889.
12 PRO, Ed. 27/3758, Report, 23 Dec. 1890.
13 PRO, Ed. 27/4219, Report, Mar. 1882.
14 PRO, Ed. 27/3784, Report, 13 Apr. 1889.
15 PRO, Ed. 27/2445, Report, 20 Mar. 1890.
16 PRO, Ed. 27/4326, Commissioners to Education Department, 8 Nov.
1892.
17 *Ibid.*, 16 Feb. 1894.
18 PRO, Ed. 27/3784, Report, 13 Mar. 1889.
19 PRO, Ed. 27/2809, Report, 17 June 1894.
20 PRO, Ed. 27/2903, Report, 5 Apr. 1894.
21 PRO, Ed. 27/799, Report, 11 May 1888.
22 PRO, Ed. 27/2367, Report, 6 Dec. 1899.
23 PRO, Ed. 27/5108, Report on visit, 29 July 1882.
24 PRO, Ed. 27/4381, Report on visit, 20 July 1892.
25 PRO, Ed. 27/3117, Report, 14 Aug. 1899.
26 PRO, Ed. 27/2445, Report, 20 Mar. 1890.
27 PRO, Ed. 27/95, Report, July 1891.
28 PRO, Ed. 27/799, Eddis' Report, 11 May 1900.
29 PRO, Ed. 27/6228, Murray's Report, 8 Jan. 1886.
30 PRO, Ed. 27/1229, Lefroy's Report, 30 Oct. 1883.
31 PRO, Ed. 27/3117. In his report of 14 Aug. 1899 Mitcheson thus

describes the clientele of Dame Alice Owen's which, before Taunton, had catered for the artisans of Islington.

32 This tendency is fully discussed in F. E. Balls, 'The origins of the Endowed Schools Act 1869 and its operation in England from 1869 to 1895', unpublished Ph.D. thesis, University of Cambridge, 1964, esp. pp. 457ff.

33 PRO, Ed. 27/700, Lefroy's Report, 20 Oct. 1888.

34 PRO, Ed. 27/1922, memorandum, Feb. 1898.

35 PRO, Ed. 27/1408, Bruce's report on visit of 5 Nov. 1889.

36 PRO, Ed. 27/4219, letter to a governor, 26 July 1881.

37 *Journal of the Women's Education Union*, II, 15 (15 Mar. 1874).

38 *Times*, 30 Nov. 1874.

39 *Journal of the Women's Education Union*, II, 20 (15 Aug. 1874), p. 114.

40 Third Annual Report of the Women's Education Union, 1873–4.

41 *Journal of the Women's Education Union*, II, 20 (15 Aug. 1874), p. 114.

42 *Ibid.*, III, 25 (15 Jan. 1875), pp. 1–3.

43 *Ibid.*, III, 34 (15 Oct. 1875), p. 146.

44 *Ibid.*, VIII, 87 (15 Mar. 1880), p. 33.

45 *Ibid.*, V, 50 (15 Feb. 1877), pp. 21–2.

46 *Ibid.*, VII, 75 (15 Mar. 1879), p. 36.

47 *Ibid.*, VIII, 90 (15 June 1880).

48 Minutes of Association of Head Mistresses of Endowed and Proprietary Schools, 22 Dec. 1874.

49 *Ibid.*, 7 Apr. 1896.

50 *Ibid.*, 7 Mar. 1891.

51 Letter to *The Times*, 23 May 1872.

52 Speech, 12 June 1877, quoted by H. Blackburn, *Women's Suffrage*, pp. 144–5.

53 *Westmorland Gazette*, letter, May 1873.

54 PRO, Ed. 27/5127, Durnford's Report, July 1880.

55 *Ibid.*, letter, 13 July 1880.

56 *Ibid.*, letter, 14 July 1881.

57 *Ibid.*, letter, 30 July 1881.

58 *Ibid.*, letter, 30 July 1881.

59 *Ibid.*, 29 Nov. 1881.

60 *Ibid.*, Durnford's Report, 7 Dec. 1881.

61 PRO, Ed. 27/5148, Report of Leach's visit, June 1895.

62 PRO, Ed. 27/5127, Durnford's Report, 7 Dec. 1881.

63 Report of Leeds Ladies' Educational Association, 1871.

64 Their memorial of 16 July 1877 to the Committee for the Execution of Charitable Uses, PRO, Ed. 27/5979, is the basis of the account which follows.

65 PRO, Ed. 27/5127, letter, 20 July 1877.

66 Sara Burstall, *Manchester High School for Girls* (Manchester, 1911), p. 3.

67 The letter is quoted on p. 9 of the Association's Report for Dec. 1871. The writer is not named but it may well have been Roby.

68 Report of the Manchester Association, Dec. 1871, p. 10.

69 *Ibid.*, Dec. 1872, p. 12.
70 *Ibid.*, Dec. 1872, p. 7.
71 *Ibid.*, Jan. 1875, p. 9.
72 PRO, Ed. 27/2182, 'Proposals for a Scheme', 19 Mar. 1875.
73 *Ibid.*, 'Draft for consideration', Apr. 1877.
74 *Ibid.*, memorial, May 1877.
75 Quoted by the *Englishwoman's Review*, 15 Sept. 1879, p. 412.
76 PRO, Ed. 27/2185, memorial, 18 Aug. 1879.
77 Henry Parris, *Constitutional Bureaucracy* (London, 1969), ch. v. Belief in a cause and single-minded devotion to its realisation are, he suggests, the true mark of the zealot. Chadwick, Kay Shuttleworth, Rowland Hill, Leonard Horner, Charles Trevelyan, G. R. Porter and George Nicholls are among his examples.
78 *Journal of the Women's Education Union*, II, 16 (15 Apr. 1874) 49.

Select Bibliography

MANUSCRIPT SOURCES

OFFICIAL PAPERS

As explained in the Preface, the main body of manuscript material consists of individual endowment files in the Ed. 27 class at the Public Record Office relating to Schemes that made provision for girls. Reference numbers to the relevant files are given in the notes and in the tables which form appendices 1, 2 and 4.

PRIVATE PAPERS

Berkhamsted School, governors' minutes 1870–85.
British Museum, Gladstone Papers, Add. MSS. 44086–835; Ripon Papers, Add. MSS. 43510–664.
Chatsworth, Devonshire MSS., 'Lady Frederick Cavendish's Diary'.
Girls' Public Day School Trust, council minutes of Girls' Public Day School Company 1872–1902; correspondence of Maria Grey.
Girton College Archives.
Hughenden Manor, High Wycombe, Bucks., Disraeli Papers.
North London Collegiate School Archives.
Nottingham High School, Governors' Minute Book No. 3.
Public Record Office, Granville Papers.
Secondary Heads Association, minutes of Association of Head Mistresses of Endowed & Proprietary Schools, 1874–1900.
West Sussex County Record Office, Chichester, Goodwood Papers.
Worcester County Record Office, Worcester, Lyttelton Papers (part of this accession was sold in December 1978).

PRINTED SOURCES

PARLIAMENTARY PAPERS

Hansard, *Parliamentary Debates*, third and fourth series
Reports of Commissioners and Committees
    Charity Commissioners Annual Reports, 1870–1903.
    PP 1867–8 xxviii (i–xvii), Schools Inquiry Commission (**Taunton**).

PP 1872 xxiv, Endowed Schools Commissioners to Committee of Council on Education.
PP 1873 viii, Select Committee on Endowed Schools Act (1869).
PP 1875 xxviii, Endowed Schools Commissioners to Committee of Council on Education.
PP 1884 ix, 1885 viii, Select Committee on Charitable Trusts Acts.
PP 1886 ix, 1887 ix, Select Committee on Endowed Schools Acts.
PP 1894 xi Select Committee on the Charity Commission.
PP 1895 xliii–xlix Royal Commission on Secondary Education (Bryce).
PP 1895 lxxiv, Departmental Committee to inquire into the constitution of the Charity Commission.
Endowed Schools Acts
  32 & 33 Vict. Chap. 56, Endowed Schools Act, 1869.
  36 & 37 Vict. Chap. 87, Endowed Schools Act, 1873.
  37 & 38 Vict. Chap. 87, Endowed Schools Act, 1874.
Estimates, Class iv PP, 1870, xlviii.

CONTEMPORARY JOURNALS, REPORTS AND TRANSACTIONS

English Woman's Journal 1858–65.
Englishwoman's Review 1866–95.
Journal of the Women's Education Union 1873–81.
Leeds Ladies' Educational Association, Reports 1871–80 (Leeds City Archives).
Manchester Association for Promoting the Education of Women, Reports 1871–77 (Manchester Central Library).
Manchester High School Committee, Reports 1872–83 (Manchester Central Library).
National Association for the Promotion of Social Science, *Transactions*:
  1859 Jessie Boucherett, 'The industrial employment of women'.
  1860 Barbara Bodichon, 'Middle-class schools for girls'.
        Jessie Boucherett, 'On the education of girls with reference to their future position'.
  1864 Dorothea Beale, 'University examinations for women'.
        Emily Davies, 'On secondary instruction as relating to girls'.
        J. G. Fitch, 'The proposed Royal Commission of Inquiry into middle-class education'.
        J. P. Norris, 'On the proposed examination of girls of the professional and middle Classes'.
        H. G. Robinson, 'Suggestions for the improvement of middle-class education'.
        William Thomson, Archbishop of York, 'Address on education'.
  1865 Dorothea Beale, 'The Ladies College at Cheltenham'.
        Thomas Chambers, mp, 'Address on education'.
        F. D. Maurice, 'What better provision ought to be made for the education of girls of the upper and middle classes?'
        Elizabeth Wolstenholme, 'What better provision ought to be

made for the education of girls of the upper and middle classes?'

1866 J. Kay-Shuttleworth, 'What central and local bodies are best qualified to take charge of and administer existing endowments for the education of girls of the upper and middle classes?'

1867 Isabella Tod, 'Advanced education for girls of the upper and middle classes'.

1868 Emily Davies, 'Some account of a proposed new college for women'.

Lord Lyttelton, 'Address on education'.

Arthur Hobhouse, 'Is it desirable to amend the present law which gives the personal property and earnings of the wife to her husband?'

Whately Cooke Taylor, 'On indirect sources of advanced female education'.

1869 Dorothea Beale, 'On the formation of an educational loan society'.

Mary Carpenter, 'On female education'.

Charles Kingsley, 'Address on education'.

1871 Maria Grey, 'What are the special requirements for the improvement of the education of girls?'

1872 G. W. Hastings, 'Address on education'.

Emily Shirreff, 'What public provision ought to be made for the secondary education of girls?'

1875 F. Merrifield, 'Is a fair proportion of the endowments of the country applicable to female education?'

National Union for Improving the Education of Women of all Classes, Reports 1871–4 (Fawcett Library and Department of Education and Science Library).

North of England Council for Promoting the Higher Education of Women, Reports 1867–74 (Newnham College, Cambridge).

Women's Suffrage Journal, 1870–90.

OTHER PRIMARY SOURCES

'Ancient Charities and Endowed Schools', unsigned pamphlet, 1865 (Fawcett Library).

Bailey, J. (ed.), *Diary of Lady Frederick Cavendish*, 2 vols., London, 1927.

Blackburn, H., *Women's Suffrage*, London, 1902.

Bremner, C. S., *The Education of Girls and Women in Great Britain*, London, 1897.

Burstall, S. A., *English High Schools for Girls*, London, 1907.

Manchester High School for Girls, Manchester, 1911.

Butler, J., *The Education and Employment of Women*, London, 1868.

Butler, J. (ed.), *Woman's Work and Woman's Culture*. London, 1869.

'The Endowed Schools Commission: shall it be continued?', unsigned pamphlet, 1873 (Department of Education and Science Library).

Fearon, D. R., 'Girls' grammar schools', *Contemporary Review*, 1865.

Fitch, J. C., 'The education of women', *Victoria Magazine*, 1864.

'Educational endowments', *Fraser's Magazine*, 1869.

'Women and the Universities', *Contemporary Review*, 1890.

Frances Mary Buss Schools Jubilee Record, London, 1900.

Gurney, M., 'Are we to have education for our middle-class girls?' National Union Pamphlet II, London, n.d. (Fawcett Library).

Hobhouse, A., 'On the limitations which should be placed on dispositions of property to public uses', *Journal of the Society of Arts*, 16 July 1869.
The Dead Hand: Addresses on the Subject of Endowments and Settlements of Property, London, 1880.

Hobhouse, L. T. and Hammond, J. L., *Lord Hobhouse: A Memoir*, London, 1905.

Lady Stanley of Alderley, 'Personal recollections of women's education', *Nineteenth Century*, vol. 6, Aug. 1879.

Lowe, R., 'Endowment or Free Trade?' pamphlet 15, London, 1868 (Dept of Education and Science Library).

Martineau, H., 'Female industry', *Edinburgh Review*, vol. 109, Apr. 1859.

Maurice, F. D., 'Queen's College, London. Its objects and method', lecture 29 Mar. 1848 (Brit. Mus.).

Maurice, F. (ed.), *Life of Frederick Denison Maurice*, London, 1884.

Ridley, A. E., *Frances Mary Buss*, London, 1896.

Shirreff, E., 'The work of the National Union', National Union Pamphlet III, London, 1873 (Fawcett Library).

Smith, S., 'Female education', *Edinburgh Review*, Jan. 1810.

'Suggestions on the Application of Endowments to the Education of Girls', unsigned pamphlet, 1870 (Fawcett Library).

Zimmern, A., *The Renaissance of Girls' Education in England*, London, 1898.

SECONDARY SOURCES

Archer, R., *Secondary Education in the Nineteenth Century*, Cambridge, 1921.

Askwith, B., *The Lytteltons*, London, 1975.

Balls, F. E., 'The origins of the Endowed Schools Act 1869 and its operation in England from 1869 to 1895', unpublished Ph.D. thesis, University of Cambridge, 1964.
'The Endowed Schools Act, 1869 and the development of English Grammar Schools in the nineteenth century', *Durham Research Review*, v, 20 (1968), pp. 202–27.

Bishop, A. S., *The Rise of a Central Authority for English Education*, Cambridge, 1971.

Eaglesham, E. J., *From School Board to Local Authority*, London, 1956.

Girls' Public Day School Trust, *Centenary Review 1872–1972*, London, 1972.

Gosden, P. H. J. H., *The Development of Educational Administration in England and Wales*, Oxford, 1966.

Hamer, D. A., *Liberal Politics in the Age of Gladstone and Rosebery*, Oxford, 1972.

Harvie, C., *The Lights of Liberalism*, London, 1976.

Kamm, J., *Hope Deferred: Girls' Education in English History*, London, 1965. *Indicative Past*, London, 1971.

Kilham, J., *Tennyson and The Princess*, Liverpool, 1958.

Lawson, J. and Silver, H., *A Social History of Education in England*, London, 1973.

Lilley, A. H., *Sir Joshua Fitch*, London, 1906.

McWilliams-Tullberg, R., *Women at Cambridge*, London, 1975.

North London Collegiate School, *Centenary Essays*, Oxford, 1950.

Parris, H., *Constitutional Bureaucracy*, London, 1969.

Price, M. and Glenday, N., *Reluctant Revolutionaries: a Century of Headmistresses 1874–1974*, London, 1974.

Roach, J., *Public Examinations in England 1850–1900*, Cambridge, 1971.

Rover, C., *Women's Suffrage and Party Politics in Britain 1866–1914*, London, 1967.

Seaman, C. M. E., *Christ's Hospital: The Last Years in London*, London, 1977.

Simon, B., *Studies in the History of Education 1780–1870*, London, 1960.

Steadman, F. C., *In the days of Miss Beale*, London, 1931.

Stephen, B., *Emily Davies and Girton College*, London, 1927.

Strachey, R., *The Cause*, London, 1928.

Sutherland, G., *Policy-Making in Elementary Education 1870–1895*, Oxford, 1973.
    Government and Society in Nineteenth-century Britain: Commentaries on British Parliamentary Papers: Education, Dublin, 1977.

Sutherland, G. (ed.), *Studies in the Growth of Nineteenth-century Government*, London, 1972.

Vincent, J., *The Formation of the Liberal Party*, London, 1966.

Index

endowments, reorganisation of 17–18,
36–7, 65, 66, 133; distribution of
43–4, 52; non-educational, conversion
of 65, 66, 81, 98, 135–6, 184–7;
inadequacy of 45, 48–9, 60–1, 67,
97; effect of agricultural depression
on 153, 158, 167; and free education
('robbing the poor') 70–82, 95,
136–7; and girls' education 6, 16,
21–2, 25, 27–9, 39, 44–5, 52, 53, 55ff,
62, 63, 65–9, 70–85, 100–2, 178–80,
182; see also Companies, City;
schools, girls' secondary, endowed
under Endowed Schools Acts;
schools, grammar, reorganised under
Endowed Schools Acts; Schools,
Hospital, reorganised under
Endowed Schools Acts; schools,
mixed
English Woman's Journal 12, 14, 15
Englishwoman's Review 39, 40
examinations, for girls, Cambridge Local
17, 27, 37; in new girls' schools
110–11

Fearon, D. R., Assistant Commissioner,
Taunton 24, 25, 38, 54; Assistant
Commissioner, Endowed Schools
23, 38, 42, 44, 45, 48–9, 50, 62, 64,
73, 92, 109, 132, 138, 153; Secretary,
Charity Commission 136, 143;
Charity Commissioner 133;
evidence to Select Committee (1886)
152; concern for girls' education 24,
25, 191
Fitch, Joshua, inspector of schools 16,
17, 18; Assistant Commissioner,
Taunton 20, 23, 24, 25, 39, 43, 44,
49, 64, 71, 109, 111; Assistant
Commissioner, Endowed Schools
38, 39, 42, 62, 67, 79, 83, 86,
116, 117, 133, 135, 138; and the
dead hand 30, 39; supports Miss
Buss 54, 55, and Girton College
68; on North of England Council
61, 65, 96, 97; opinion of
endowments 102; feminist
commitment 17, 24, 143, 191
Forster, W. E. 7, 8, 20, 28, 37, 38, 52,
60–1, 80, 161

Garrett, Elizabeth 14, 99, 109
Girls' Public Day School Company 14,
68, 87, 100, 102, 113, 131, 147, 152,
158, 162, 171, 177, 179, 188
Girton College, Cambridge 68, 99, 139,
171, 176, 191

Gladstone, W. E. 6, 26, 31, 32, 87,
119, 122, 130
Gloucester Mercury 140
governing bodies, and Endowed Schools
Act 2, 3, 8, 10, 26, 31; women on
97, 112, 114–18, 154–6, 179; see also
(for particular governing bodies)
schools, grammar, reorganised under
Endowed Schools Acts; and (for
individual governors) Kay-
Shuttleworth; Nash; Rothera;
Roundell; Tyso
government, Conservative (1874–80) 57,
58, 125ff
government, Liberal (1868–74) 6–7, 57;
see also Gladstone
Granville, Lord 19, 37
Greek in schools see education, classical
Green, T. H. 27
Grey, Maria: support for North London
Collegiate School 53, 54; founds
Women's Education Union 68,
101, and Girls' Public Day School
Company 68, 87, 102, 171; views
on endowment for girls 101, 119,
178, first grade girls' schools 106,
headmistress's authority 113, and
women governors 115, 155–6, 191;
gratitude to Endowed Schools
Commissioners 104, 105, 129;
tribute to Lyttelton 130–1; views on
suffrage 181–2
Grocers' Company 59

Haberdashers' Company 59
Halifax Courier 91
Hammond, J. L. 23, 38, 42, 88, 89, 92,
143, 155
Harcourt, Sir William, M.P. 127
Hardy, Gathorne, M.P. 124, 127
Hart Dyke, Sir William, Vice-President
Committee of Council for Education
148
Hastings, George Woodyatt, Secretary
Social Science Association 16, 94
Head Mistresses' Association 112, 178,
180–2
headmistresses of endowed schools: powers
110, 112; qualifications 112, 176;
salaries 113–14; ambition and
vitality 174, 176–8
Henderson, Dr, Headmaster, Leeds 185,
186
Hertfordshire Standard 92
Hobhouse, Arthur: Charity Commissioner
4, 40; opinion on passing of Endowed
Schools Act 7, 119–20; expectation